The
Embattled
Parent

The Embattled Parent

GLORIA LENTZ

ARLINGTON HOUSE / PUBLISHERS

Westport, Connecticut

TO
William Nicholson Lentz, Anna Dabov Fenton,
Dorothy E. Holt, and Tom Cooney

Library of Congress Cataloging in Publication Data

Lentz, Gloria, 1933—
    The embattled parent.

    1. Parent and child—United States.
2.   Parenthood—Psychological aspects.
3.   Conflict of generations.
4.   United States—Moral conditions   I.   Title.
HQ755.85.L46   1980   306.8'7   79-27276
ISBN 0-87000-440-9

Manufactured in the United States of America

Contents

The
Embattled
Parent

1.

Everyone Is Talking About It

There was a time that most adults can reflect on, when more children than not brought a mixture of pleasure and pride to their parents. But conditions have so reversed themselves, I find I cannot stand in the checkout line of a store for any length of time without overhearing parents commiserating publicly about today's children.

As a journalist, I have scarcely been able to interview a soul, be it on any totally unrelated subject, without the interviewee almost spontaneously and without apparent provocation embarking on a problem he is having with his own teen-ager, a neighbor's or a relative's child. It has become an obsession of many to air the incredible change in today's youth. Perhaps it is a catharsis of sorts.

A chance meeting with an acquaintance I had not seen in some time is typical of the verbal outpouring of today's harried parent. She told me of her venture into a new sect of her religion that was helping her to cope with her 17-year-old son. "He got a girl pregnant," she confided, "was arrested twice for stealing, and has been picked up for smoking marijuana. If he put a gun to his head tomorrow, I'd say it's God's will. I don't know if I'd even feel anything for him," she said in a voice heavy with the pain and exhaustion of what she and her family have endured.

Knowing their situations are far from unique, parents speak with hurt etched on their faces; but nevertheless, unashamedly they bare their souls to almost anyone who will listen. Many have long since passed the initial stumbling block of feeling guilt or shame for their children's behavior. They know, almost instinctively, that they have tried their darndest, but still things are not right for their children.

So widespread is the urge to communicate about the problems with their children, that many parent groups are forming across the country that permit parents to talk to each other about their children's puzzling behavior and to lend support to the parents who have suffered the crushing aftermath of their children's activities.

At one such meeting of parents who have been shredded by children on drugs, some of the following comments were elicited: "Thank God, five years of hell are over," said a mother about her young son, who had been on drugs and was killed in an auto accident. And another, whose daughter had been drinking and taking drugs since she was 11 years old, said, "That came from her values, her choices—not from anything I did."

So critical and almost impossible is rearing decent children today that many of the children of the '60s are opting out of parenting. An article by AP newsfeatures writer John Barbour asks, among other questions, if these young people are just selfish or just scared. It drew responses from both camps.

On the "selfish" side was one young woman who said she was aware that a lot of people look upon childless young marrieds as members of "a pleasure-seeking, hedonistic society" that only cares about the "here and now." "We have enjoyed a standard of living now that we know would be cut into," said another young woman. "Perhaps we're a bit selfish. But our time is such that we go wherever we want. I feel like going off to play tennis, I just leave. You can't do that with a child."

On the "scared" side of the seesaw was a childless woman whom Barbour described as fast approaching the fertility deadline. "In the fifties," she said, "when my parents raised me, if you put out your best effort, you probably had a 60 to 70 percent chance that your child would turn out fine, have no problems with drugs, sex in high school or anything else. I'm not sure that's true anymore."

The schools around her, she pointed out, were having horrendous problems with students. "You have less control over their friends. There is less that a parent can do, and you're worried that even if you put your best foot forward and you've done the most you can, it may not be enough. That scares me a lot."

The fear articulated by this young woman is reality for today's parents. In many major areas parents only play cameo roles. In other areas they are exempted entirely from major decision-making in the lives of their children. For some, it is by choice. Other times it is by law that parents are denied a part in their child's choice. And in other cases, by the time the child has reached his teens, he is sometimes beyond redemption.

The late famed anthropologist, Dr. Margaret Mead, put her finger directly on the pulse of what is wrong with this society when she said, "When we examine how any society works, it becomes clear that it is precisely the basic taboos—the deeply and intensely felt prohibitions against 'unthinkable' behavior—that keep the social system in balance."

Today that balance has been greatly disturbed, if not totally eroded. While parents still subscribe to certain behavior as unthinkable, their children have no such inhibitions. Unfortunately, there are those who applaud the children for their "liberated" stand and support them as "surrogate parents" at every important turn of their young lives. It has placed parents on the battlefield with their own children.

As one young father said to me, "It seems today like you're against everything as a parent. You're against the movies, against the TV, against the schools—against, against, against. It's a terrible image you have as a parent."

There is no common denominator to spot the child who has partaken of this wild and new world that he is so ill-suited to cope with, for in most instances, this world knows no economic, social, ethnic or religious barrier. "Even the best of 'em," said the superintendent of a large suburban high school, "even the best of 'em—[the one] that I can say: That's a good kid; he will have been involved somehow or another in a scene, experimenting, or a part of it on a modified scale," he said of the changing social and moral upheaval among the young.

Many have made public and private note that today's youth presents a frightening picture. Newspaper columnist Dr. Saul Kapel said, "If the America of tomorrow will be determined by how we raise our children today, the future looks bleak. There are indications all around us that something is very wrong with the way millions of youngsters are being reared."

"Go to any school and you'll be shocked. The disrespect, the lack of discipline," noted actor George Savalas. "It's unbelievable. Maybe my ideas are corny," he continued, "but it's about time we returned to those old-fashioned principles and values, like love, respect, honor and justice—values that are nurtured in the home by the family."

Unfortunately, countless families that have nurtured and fashioned principles for their children are among those who find their love spurned and their values rebuffed.

So apparent is the change in today's children that even the notorious Dr. Benjamin Spock has capitulated and publicly confessed, saying that the "brattiness" of America's children belongs in part to the so-called "experts"—"the child psychiatrists, psychologists, teachers, social workers and pediatricians, like myself," he said. "Parents have been persuaded that [these are] the only people who know how children should be managed. This is a cruel deprivation that we professionals have imposed on mothers and fathers." Alas, Dr. Spock, your confession, along with those of others who spawned the sexual revolution and the drug culture, comes too late for many children and their parents. It does little to diminish the stranglehold the experts you named above—and others that you failed to name—still hold on our children. They continue to push parents into relatively obscure positions.

Are the sexual revolution and the drug culture myths? Ask any parents and they will do a soliloquy on the issues. Jim Mallon, then president of the student body at the University of Wisconsin, only confirmed what parents already knew when he replied to the question: What does today's average college student think about? Mallon answered, "Sex, drugs and rock 'n' roll. In that order."

So heavy is the toll that various segments of society have exacted from parents through their children that unfortunately there grows a love/hate relationship between child and parent that is another phenomenon of our times. Who would expect to read in print that a mother thanks God because her son was killed in an automobile accident? And yet, when one has suffered through a child on drugs, it is understandable.

What kind of a society are we living in when so many children are running away from home and so many parents are throwing their children out of their homes in record-breaking numbers?

When at last the comic strips and stand-up comics recognize some of the dilemmas parents are faced with, you can be sure it is a fait accompli. But parents who face the reality of these problems find little humor even in a comic of the stature of Johnny Carson. It was Carson who said on his late-night talk show, during one of his famous monologues, that today's kids are now able to get birth-control pills in their school colors and the eighth-graders run a day-care center for the babies of the ninth graders.

The anguish of this ongoing battle is in watching the children trash their lives as they shed any semblance of decency and the rules that their parents have lovingly set down for them.

Parents, and mothers in particular I have found, are hard-pressed to throw in the towel. Somewhere amidst the cobwebs in the attics of their minds, they remember the sweet baby they carried in their arms, finding the first tooth, the first day of school, reading bedtime stories. Because the children of today know of this soft spot, they capitalize on it. Many have extracted tremendous ransoms from their parents on every plane.

Making concession after concession, parents bargain with their children and even capitulate in areas that cause them great pain. I have found that they are hoping against great odds that it is only "a phase," or their children will "grow up" or "change." But in many instances the die has been cast. We see before us hordes of morally crippled and selfish children, exacting a pound of flesh from anyone who will give it to them in order to fulfill their latest desire.

While many parents appear to be liberal toward their children's trespasses, it is my observation that they have already suffered too much heartache. To merely survive, they give in to the system of things. Standing your ground as a parent today, many have told me, brings the possibility and fear of total annihilation of their offspring. It is too painful for many parents to contemplate, so they surrender and suffer their battles internally.

No matter how outrageous their demands, no matter how large their appetites, if their parents will not pay the toll, many of today's children, often minors, can always turn to their favorite "relative" for a handout—good old Uncle Sam. With his help, by digging into the pockets of the parents, a host of services and agencies have stepped in between the child and the parent, stamping the parent—officially, in many important areas—null and void.

An ardent soldier in the battle to harmoniously reunite parent and child, Mary McCarthy of Worcester, Mass., said, "No greater disservice can be given a child than to destroy his sense of trust and confidence in his parents. All his future relationships will show the effect of this shattered confidence and lost security."

If the parents of the '60s thought it was bad, parents of the '70s found it worse in many respects. In the '80s one need not be a prophet to predict that effective parenting will be even less effectual unless something is done.

Today the courts and various institutions and organizations are supporting the child all along the crucial years of his young life. They make a formidable army of surrogate parents that lend support to the destructive aspects of our society from which our children have drunk so deeply. They show up by way of the TV screen, in the classroom, in literature (if it can really be classified as such), in the medical profession, in legislative rulings, courts, private institutions, various government agencies, ad infinitum. All of these elements have been busily chipping, chipping away at all the ground rules that parents have traditionally put down for their progeny. When the child becomes a teen-ager, the job done by others all too often emerges in full, albeit mutated, bloom. It resembles not one whit the seed that the parents thought they planted.

At last the die has been indelibly cast, and the surrogate parents can gloat that their premises have been accepted by the young, while yours as a parent have been disregarded.

When putting this book together, I set out to try to discover why our children—who have more money spent on them educationally than in any other civilized country of comparable size; with parents whose goal was to "give them everything I didn't have"—have turned out in such numbers to be tumbling backward into a dark abyss that is academically and morally void.

2.

A "Fantastick" Actor/Producer/Father Looks at Entertainment

The four-story building at 181 Sullivan Street in Greenwich Village, New York, is the home of what has been billed as the longest running show ever—"The Fantasticks."

Visible from the street in one of the long first floor windows of the Sullivan Street Playhouse is a canvas chair with the name Lore Noto lettered on its back. Noto is the producer of this show, which has been running nonstop for twenty years. He also plays one of the leading roles. Lore Noto: actor, well-recognized figure in the theatre world, and severe critic of what is taking place on the stages and screens of the entertainment media.

In between the matinee and the evening performance, Noto, my husband Bill and I walk around the corner to Rocco's restaurant where we will talk over dinner. Noto, in spite of the recognition he gets wherever he goes, is unpretentious, as I have so often found serious actors of the theatre to be. Out of costume, he wears a dress shirt open at the neck and old, uncreased trousers.

Lore Noto blows away like bubbles from a child's ring every argument that a deprived childhood makes for a troubled adult. Raised from an early age in the Brooklyn Home for Children, and forced upon leaving to work in his father's poolroom, he has become a man of stature, with deep moral convictions. He is also a father and feels an obligation to the youth of our country to speak out on the turn that the entertainment business has taken.

Noto hits his first sour note on the music sound of today and the $3 billion-a-year record industry. "I call it simple trash and junk. I think it's highly dangerous. I think it's hedonistic. I think it's wrong.

I think," he says with lowered tones, "the kids today are very, very unfortunate. I think they have not met the promise of what we would have expected from our children and of the parents before us—of what their children's children would become. I blame it entirely on the culture. First of all, I think the music is debased."

Married and the father of two sons and a daughter, he continues: "What I'm saying to you is that as a parent raising children in a world that you don't approve of—and I really don't approve of it, you know. I'm an artist. I'm sensitive. I am highly aware of many levels of art and culture. Music is part of it. I don't like the debasement," he repeats.

The Reverend Jesse Jackson would agree with Lore Noto. "One of the ways of appraising a civilization, of determining its spiritual tone and moral values, is to listen to its music," wrote Reverend Jackson in his syndicated column.

Dr. Joyce Brothers, who has come into the public eye via her many guest appearances on TV and through her syndicated column, has told parents not to worry about today's lyrics. The kids, she claims, are more interested in the beat.

I could not disagree more. How do I know that kids are interested in the lyrics? Just as the rest of society knows, whether or not they have children. We are all familiar with how dedicated a teen-ager is to listening to certain explicit lyrics by the very volume that is turned up when those certain words are sung. So they don't miss a syllable, they walk down the streets, drive their cars, travel on public transportation, lie on the beaches, with their portable radios blaring out the latest trash. With no regard for the rest of the populace, the volume becomes an irritant.

"We are all shaped by the contacts we make with our society," said Noto. "Now look, I'm an artist and I'm all for expression, but I'll be damned if I go for the glorification of it. In other words, I am pretty much in the Hays syndrome—you know, Will Hays in Hollywood—in morality; because I have seen from my own experiences the effects it has on others."

"The audiences are so susceptible," said the lead guitarist of one rock group. "Their minds are empty of original ideas and they're being brainwashed," he said of today's music.

Back in 1975 a spokesman for a population group said that Paul Anka's song, "(You're) Having My Baby," encouraged hundreds and hundreds of thousands of young girls to consider childbearing outside marriage.

"Dr. John," a deejay at KHJ in Los Angeles, said he thought the lyrics to "Disco Lady" were "highly offensive," but the station never received a dissenting call. Why should they? The audiences that are glued to these stations see nothing wrong with such lyrics. They have been absorbing them for too long. But even Peter Starr of Columbia Records, which distributed "Disco Lady," admitted the meaning of the lyrics was obvious. "You can't help but get the obvious suggestions of the song," he said. "And when you say things like that, people listen. Getting the hooks in, that's the name of the game," he said with brash candor.

Noto, when asked why performers would put out such offensive materials, said, "I think these people are doing it for the money and for the fame and the spectacle. Just the other day," he continued, "I read about some family in the theatre—a terribly 'cute' remark—a girl sleeping with the guy and the father comes along and says, 'Oh, that's my son-in-love,' and she refers to him as 'the father-in-love.' It's a very clever thing," he says, but it further pollutes society.

Noto is extremely unhappy that newspapers will review some of the "debasing" movies and Broadway shows and call them "exciting," "wonderful" and even "thrilling." That the newspapers will print stories about performers and their sexual proclivities or drug habits is also painful to him. It all has an influence on our children, he says.

Personally, Noto says, he is making "a very strong protest" by avoiding movies, theatre, television, any form of the arts that is indulging in the areas that add to the "brainwashing" of society. "I remember going to the theatre and I remember enjoying it. But by heaven, I'm not going to be paying money to be uncomfortable, to be insulted, to be offended, to have my mind polluted. I just refuse to do it. I'm a strong boycotter of this concept of culture," he said.

In the movies, it probably all started to fall apart with *I Am Curious Yellow*. Those promoting it said it was what the public wanted—the long lines at the movie houses attested to it. It took comedian/actor Jerry Lewis to point out in 1970 that while 2 million Americans did see that movie, 200 million did not go to see it. Hardly a majority.

However, more of the same would follow. In the ensuing years, almost without exception, family newspapers began advertising the X-rated movies. They come with such titles as *Memories of a Madam*, *Seduction of Amy* or *Highway Hookers*.

Gail Palmer, a 23-year-old X-rated-movie director who told Merv Griffin she was a Catholic but didn't go to church anymore, said the X-rated films were "very entertaining" and "sexually stimulating." Discussing the profit aspect of the business, she said that a film that cost $156,000 to make was expected to gross a million dollars in the first year.

Way back in 1972 Jack Valenti, president of the Motion Picture

Association of America, said, ". . . the excessive nudity and sex are passing." Since then, and as recently as 1979, many newspapers were saying the same thing in their feature stories while they advertised and reviewed the opposite in their movie sections.

What has happened is a growing tolerance by moviegoers, causing the G-rated (family) movie to fall into the category of the endangered species. "Most companies are afraid of the G rating," remarked Samuel Z. Arkoff, president of American International Pictures. "They're afraid that teen-agers will be turned off when they see a G . . ."

It distresses Noto that no matter how tasteless things get in the entertainment field, audiences continue to show up and pay for this type of fare. "What was the expression?" he says, grasping for it in his memory bank. "If you don't give people what they like, they like what they get."

What happened to Pratt Institute in New York might well be termed poetic justice. Pratt had flung open its facilities to movie producers who said they were filming an educational movie. It turned out to be a hard-core pornographic film. With the drug and sexual attitudes that prevail on today's campuses, I think the producers, in the style of the old Hollywood days, simply wanted to film on location.

I bait Noto with the commonly held belief that kids today want to view sex and violence. "They always did," he says, "but why should we give it to them just because they want [it]?"

Through the world of entertainment, Noto said, today's youth are "being hammered at, they're being subverted, they're being exploited, they're being manipulated. There is ultimately within every human being that need to stop and assess and evaluate and criticize and judge. And that will be the only hope. What does that mean to the parents? We have to continually remind them that that is what their responsibility is."

So far that has not been the case, and our youth are still enjoying aspects of entertainment that good parents abhor. Joe Baltake, movie reviewer for the *Philadelphia Daily News*, writing about the movies, *Up in Smoke* and *Animal House*, made the observation that vulgarity seems to be enough for today's audiences. Baltake said at the showing he attended of *Up in Smoke* the "youngish audience was beside itself with pleasure, laughing at every cheap, pathetic toilet joke—sometimes laughing when nothing at all was even happening on screen." Since *Up in Smoke* was about marijuana, he attributed the audience reaction either to "bad taste [or, perhaps, too much marijuana?]."

In the interest of research, I had planned to see the movie teen-agers were flocking to: *Saturday Night Fever*. When I read that the four-letter euphemism for intercourse that begins with the sixth letter of the alphabet and ends with the eleventh was used a hundred times, I changed my mind. Like Lore Noto, my sensibilities couldn't stand it.

Occasionally I am pleasantly surprised by the moviemakers. *Julia* was such a movie.

Not only have movies changed, but so have Broadway and Off-Broadway gone into transformation. The themes of recent hits have woven into them rape, murder, corruption, homosexuality, drugs.

One of the longest running Off-Broadway shows in Philadelphia's history is *Let My People Come*. According to one reviewer, the show "is more of a therapeutic workshop for the sexually confused than mere entertainment." It contains total nudity, four-letter words and sexual titles you will not see in most newspapers (although they will advertise the show). It is subtitled "a sexual musical" and has such degrading song titles as "Fellatio 101," "I'm Gay" and "Dirty Words."

Noto brings this show up in conversation. "You know Earl Wilson was quoted as having said that when his son wrote the dirtiest show—whatever it was called—*Let My People Blank*" he says, obviously disgusted with the title. Stumbling verbally the loqua-cious Noto says, "I, I can't call it anything but *Let My People Arrive*.

"Now here's a mother and father proud of their children—who is Earl Wilson, and what is Earl Wilson? Earl Wilson has been showing undressed dames, with as minimal dress as the paper will allow, in his column all these years, you know. Now he was supposed to have said to somebody, 'I hope we get away with this—*Let My People*———. Now, you know, some of the things they did—if you know anything about this work . . ."

Noto's rich and resonant voice falters again, unwilling to give the work any value by even discussing it. I tell him I am aware of the content. "I have seen the program," he continues. "I've never gone to it. It's about fellatio and the joys of it and it's what we would have called thirty or forty years ago degenerate. Today you've got people who don't know what degenerate is—they don't know what it is. It's all changing because as each one of these little drops of cultural pollution falls it becomes a powerful storm.

"What has happened is they go a little further, a little further—how much can they get away with?" he asks of the entertainment media. "They get away with as much as they can until it becomes absolutely beyond control. Now where is the control? The parents?

What can the parents do? They don't know how to cope with it themselves."

Our culture, he says, is one that reeks with words like "Get," "Take," "Gimme." What is lost is spiritual values. Absent from our culture are such terms, that take others into consideration, such as: We serve others. We're happy to be of service. Do unto others as you would have others do unto you.

All the garbage that has spilled onto the Broadway stages, the movie houses, into recordings, he said, has absolutely had a damaging effect on the youth, "because we have been shaped by those forces and influences and stimuli," and that in turn has "shaped them and their judgment."

Returning to the fare that is offered our youth in the way of entertainment, Noto says with deep emotion, "I feel sorry for the kids." The joys of parenting today are "minimal."

He was angry that reviewers and newspapers did not discourage the musical, *Hair,* and other productions that followed that were not fit for a civilized society. "Now what happened to their standards?" he asks of the newspaper world. "Who are the people who have allowed that kind of degeneration to set in?"

Noto said he subscribes intuitively to George Bernard Shaw's notion that what is brought to the stage, people will be doing in life. "In other words, there's a great responsibility," because the artist has power in influencing. "We ape what we see. We ape our culture."

The movie, *The Warriors,* is a case in point. The film, which deals with gang warfare, has caused Paramount Pictures to authorize approximately two hundred theatres around the country to add security personnel at their expense. This action followed when an 18-year-old youth died of stab wounds after a fight in a theatre lobby where the movie was shown and a 19-year-old was shot in the head in a separate incident.

"Maybe we're just naive, but we just didn't think there would be this kind of reaction to the film," said Gordon Weaver, Paramount's senior vice president in charge of marketing. But did Paramount pull the film? No. Instead they hyped the interest of many kids by ordering security personnel at theatres that were showing it.

I ask Noto, as a father, if he would forbid his children access to some of the entertainment available today. "Put it another way," he says. "I would always forbid them. Yes. But that doesn't mean they will do it."

Of records he does not approve of, he said, "I tell my kids: What are you buying that garbage for? Taking my money that I worked hard for, and you're spending it on things like that." He says he can justify such purchases as an artist in that he should know what is happening. But, he says, "I won't do it because I don't want to give them any economic support of any kind."

I ask his opinion of the experts who say that if parents set a good example, children will follow. "They're liars. Damned liars and experts in that order," he says hotly.

Just how dedicated to rock groups are our children? They turn out by the hundreds of thousands at rock concerts, with air so heavily laden with marijuana one can get high by just breathing.

In 1977, seeking even more bizarre methods of entertainment, our youth were taken in by punk rock. The groups chose equally punky names: The Sex Pistols, The Damned, The Vibrators, Clash. Their members went by such bizarre names as Johnny Rotten, Rat Scabies, Dee Generate. They lived up to their stage names as they chose such inspiring and uplifting titles for their songs as "No Love," "No Feelings," "No Fun," "There Is No Future" and "Boredom."

Dressed in outrageous, nightmarish fashion, the young audiences could watch them stab Santa Claus, spit at each other, or throw up blood, for which they paid Minnesota Mining and Manufacturing Company $45 per gallon.

One performer—who slashed himself on stage with a whiskey bottle and then vomited on stage—commented after his appearance at Birmingham University: "I threw up to my heart's content. It's simple and basic." Sure. So is defecation.

Talking about his distaste for rock music, Lore Noto, like so many other parents I talked with, confesses something about one of his children. "I have a son who does the concert bills for rock-and-roll concerts. He's in a field that I think is a very dangerous one and a very wrong one. And he gets into the bizarre. He grows the beard and whatever, and all I can say is, 'You look disgusting. Why do you destroy your features? You know I don't like you that way.' And so he'll shave . . . we play games."

What has brought about this trend for sexual explicitness, drug use being called beneficial in song, the whole turnaround in entertainment? "I put it down to the wrong kind of people getting into positions of control and power," said Noto. "I mean control of the culture. When I say wrong kinds of people, I mean people who will do anything for a buck, who will justify any action for the money."

There was a time, he said, when pride and responsibility in how one made his money was important. "If you ran a whorehouse, you were less esteemed. Today you're glamorized. Anything goes today."

Meanwhile, "The Fantasticks," which my husband and I see as

the guests of Lore Noto, is like a beacon in the dark. It is a timeless piece about young lovers, their fathers, their growing pains and the effect the outside world has on them. It is a show for the entire family.

Probably the most popular musical piece to come out of "The Fantasticks" is "Try to Remember." I find I am particularly taken with the words to the song, "Plant a Radish." This clever song compares what happens when you plant a vegetable seed to the planting of the seed that helps to create a child. Vegetable seeds are called "dependable" and "befriendable," but with children, goes the song, until the seed is nearly grown, you don't know what you've sown.

Today Lore Noto believes the entertainment fare our children are exposed to has something to do with it all.

3.

Let Them Watch TV

So you are reluctant to let your children go to the movies, the theatre, and you've already thrown out all their raunchy records and tapes. Let them watch TV.

Of course if no parent is home after school, or in the evening, or children stay up later than their working parents, or kids are watching TV on their own sets, that still leaves a lot of unsupervised television viewing.

Today there is so much violence and sex in both programming and ads, often a family is well into watching a program before the objectionable parts crop up. It takes a strong parent to get up, turn to another channel, or turn the set off completely. All too often, by the time you realize what the theme of a story is, the entire family has become engrossed in watching. Parents tell me they reason that the objectionable portion has passed and they are anxious to see the story's outcome. Therefore the TV set is usually left on.

Almost like subliminal advertising (which has been outlawed), where a suggestion flashed momentarily is imposed on the subconscious, the sex and violence and promiscuity begin to pile up in the young mind. When enough of these episodes and messages get through, they become more acceptable to our youth.

How far has TV gone since the days when Faye Emerson was the talk of the town in her plunging necklines and Elvis Presley, with his gyrating pelvis, was shown only from the waist up on the home screen when he appeared on Ed Sullivan's show?

Lucille Ball, guesting on the Mike Douglas Show, said when she was pregnant with Desi, Jr., on the "I Love Lucy" TV series, they were not permitted to use the word "pregnant." "Now they show you how to do it," she said with obvious disgust.

Referring to the TV show, "All in the Family," she said she had come out against the program because she found the ethnic labels "frightening" and felt it would influence a whole generation, who would begin using those labels again.

Well, Lucy, I for one can back you up on just how accurate your fears were. We, like millions of other Americans, tuned in to see what all the hubbub was about. Our son, Billy, who loves to mimic, learned from that program in the short span of time we watched it, to use ethnic slurs and labels he had never before been exposed to or heard spoken in our home.

If Archie Bunker got laughs, he puzzled, why weren't we laughing when he copied him? At our son's school, I realized from listening to conversations that a lot of kids learned to use Bunkerisms.

In other areas of entertainment, as Lucille Ball said, the American TV audiences were becoming more and more "tolerant" of what they would sit still for in the name of entertainment. There is no question in my mind that while you may not settle for an X-rated movie, other areas, once taboo, are now becoming tolerable if not totally acceptable.

Since our children are now past the stage of watching cartoons, I was at once startled and my day brightened when I read a letter from a youngster—a Jenny Erb of Harleysville, Pa.—in a television newspaper supplement. "I think it's really stupid that you put swearing on kids' cartoons like 'Tom and Jerry,'" she wrote. "What are you trying to teach us kids?" Good girl, Jenny! If you can be that vocal and discriminating for the rest of your life, your parents and all of society will benefit.

In television, the tastelessness, the sexual innuendoes, the violence should have limits, but they don't.

In the fall of 1978, television viewers were exposed to 1,054 profanities during 864.5 hours of prime-time viewing according to the National Federation of Decency, a citizens' monitoring group.

In a recent issue of the *Journal of Communication*, researchers who conducted a study entitled "Physical Contact and Sexual Behavior on Prime-Time TV" reported that from 1975 to 1977 "flirtatious behavior" had quadrupled; "seductive behavior" more than tripled from one per hour in 1975 to more than three per hour in 1977; "sexual innuendoes" increased from one per hour to almost seven per hour; and "sexual intercourse," which was not recorded in 1975, was implied fifteen times in 1977.

In the area of complaints about TV are the products that are sold with sexual overtones. "That sort of stimulus in advertising only is effective or only gets attention when it shocks," said an advertising spokesman. "It has a certain adolescent taboo built into it. It only works when you're not supposed to talk that way." And so, we can justifiably ask, when that stops shocking—what is next?

Back in 1972 the National Association of Broadcasters' Code Authority banned the advertising of contraceptives on participating stations (about 60 percent of TV stations subscribe to the NAB code). But the code was revised to allow the advertising of sanitary napkins, douches and other personal and sanitary products.

The "Television Vigilante," is the name given to Bob Cramer, an editorial writer for the *Atlantic City Press*. Cramer, who began Admonitor, a group that involves itself with advertising, said that without question the ads most heavily objected to on TV are the feminine hygiene ads.

It took picketing of Sears, Roebuck and Company stores throughout the nation before their sponsorship of "Charlie's Angels" and "Three's Company" was dropped. "We are disgusted with the low level of television programming and we intend to make our voices heard where it counts—in the advertiser's pocketbooks," said a spokesman for the National Federation of Decency. "Sears isn't going to get any of our money to pay for their trash," said an NFD leader.

By 1973 a major commission of the National Council of Churches called for research in test markets to determine if televised advertising of nonprescription contraceptives could help to reduce unwanted pregnancies and venereal disease. It is difficult to believe that churches would be pushing for such an ad, but it is merely another sign of our declining times.

While the National Association of Broadcasters' code board was considering a further relaxation concerning contraceptive ads, a three-month study came up with nothing conclusive, so it was shelved. But do not breathe a sigh of relief yet, parents. It may still come to pass, since Zero Population Growth was agitating as far back as 1975 to break the ban on the advertising of the condom contraceptive. In fact, stations in California and Ohio have already aired such ads.

Is there a do-as-I-do attitude that transfers itself from the TV image to our young people's minds, or does TV have no influence one way or the other on our children?

Dr. David Loye, a UCLA researcher, conducted a study of 260

married couples in the Los Angeles area that asserted that violent shows tend to breed aggression, while family-type programs with moral-intellectual premises tend to bring about more moderate behavior. "We are at a juncture in history," said Dr. Loye, "where technology has presented us with the opportunity either to dramatically advance or to degrade and possibly annihilate ourselves."

In 1978 two cases involving the possible effects of TV on our youth caught the nation's attention. One was that of Ronny Zamora. Ronny, 16, and his parents, sued all three major networks after Ronny was convicted of murdering his 83-year-old neighbor in Miami Beach, Fla. The Zamora suit claimed that television "showed the impressionable teen-ager . . . how to kill." The $25 million lawsuit was dismissed when a federal judge ruled that violence on TV was protected by the First Amendment.

In a subsequent case a judge dismissed an $11 million lawsuit against NBC that contended a prime-time drama showing a sexual assault of a young girl led a gang of youngsters to commit a similar attack. The judge said the plaintiff would have to prove that NBC intended for viewers to imitate the assault. The plaintiff's attorney contended NBC was "negligent and reckless" in putting on the show when the children might be watching.

The show in question was called, "Born Innocent." It included a scene in which a runaway girl had a plumber's helper thrust forcibly into her body while she was confined in a juvenile home. The 9-year-old girl in the NBC suit had been attacked in a similar manner by three young girls and a boy who thrust a bottle into her body. The girl's mother, Valeria Niemi, of San Francisco, said her daughter was assaulted four days after the film was aired on TV.

In Delran, N.J., a 13-year-old boy suffocated after putting a plastic bag over his head in what police believe was an attempt to simulate a warrior's mask on the show he was watching called "Battlestar Galactica."

How many of our teen-agers have watched car-chase scenes on TV? And what effect has it had on them? Columnist Cynthia Parsons feels there is a connection between highway fatalities and TV car-chase scenes.

By 1978 the swing, said the industry and image-makers of TV, would be toward "soft-core sex." The advertising firm of Batten, Barton, Durstine & Osborn predicted in a report that "jigglers"— defined as "shows which include a proliferation of shots of the gelatinous parts of the female anatomy"—would become a "bona fide staple."

If anyone remembers the steamy 1957 *And God Created Woman*, that was initially banned in several towns, watch for it popping up on the TV screen. It was recently rereleased with a PG rating for home TV screens.

I made it a point to watch the highly publicized "James at 15" that so many high school students in our daughter's school were talking about. The show, one of a series, marked James' 16th birthday. It was incredible, to say the least. The TV blurb in one newspaper read: "A distraught James worries that his sluggishness is more than just a case of the blahs when he checks into a free medical clinic to undergo tests for venereal disease."

In the showing, James is attracted to a Swedish exchange student and consummates his affair by going to bed with the girl in his home when his parents and family are away. James' uncle furnishes him with a hotel room, complete with a prostitute, as a birthday gift.

I will say the story covered a lot of the realities parents are faced with today . . . the VD clinic where a minor can go without parental knowledge or consent in most states; the now common practice of bringing the girl home to go to bed when both parents are absent from the house; and the uncle figure, who could very well have been dear old Uncle Sam in disguise, willing to offer sex to minor children.

I found it interesting that the National PTA's TV Action Center was directing its fight against sex-oriented television programs. "Parents obviously cannot be with their children every moment of the day, particularly working parents. Broadcasters should not thrust parents into the position of having to stand guard over the TV set," said National PTA president Grace Baisinger. A laudable stand, but just substituting the words public schools for broadcasters, and sex education for the TV set, would be enough to tell Mrs. Baisinger that the PTA should clean up its own backyard and curriculum before it reaches out to criticize other areas of society.

Action for Children's Television (ACT) has been fighting ads aimed at children. The Federal Trade Commission opened hearings in January of 1979 on how to protect the child against advertisements and still preserve the First Amendment rights of advertisers. The FTC has proposed a ban on all ads directed at children under 8, and ads for highly sugared foods aimed at children 8 to 12.

Bill Holland, managing editor and columnist for the *Burlington County Times* newspaper in New Jersey, hit the nail right on the head when he wrote: "It's as though the kids, while not old enough to understand the force being exerted upon them, nevertheless have sufficient control of the family purse strings to respond economically. Apparently the advertisers are going over the heads of the parents and carrying their messages to the real decisionmakers."

Several weeks later, at the FTC hearings that were being held in San Francisco, Holland's accuracy in diagnosing one of the ills of today's society was confirmed. Psychiatrist Michael Rothenberg of the University of Washington said commercials were causing parent-child conflicts, with children often begging for an item that a family could not afford. Rothenberg pointed out that some 25 million unsupervised children watch television each day while both parents work.

A survey by the Consumers Cooperative in Berkeley showed that 60 percent of 335 parents bought products their children demanded. Of those who gave in, 93 percent said the requests caused family tension. But give in they did.

We are all too familiar with the bratty kids in supermarkets, screaming, kicking, salivating all over the floor in a fit of temper until they get their parents to buy them everything from cereals with little nutritional value to plastic toys that aren't worth the price tag. Children are, to a large degree, catered to beyond belief by sacrificing parents. Parents are made to feel, in many instances, that they owe so much to their children today.

It brings to mind a commercial for a bank that I have seen on TV. As far as I can recall, it starts out showing a young father with his baby daughter. He is urged to save his money to insure she will go to college. On graduation from the ivy-covered halls of academia, the father, his hair now graying, is glad he saved more money so he can pay for his daughter's graduate school. What next? Is he expected to buy her the office equipment and set her up in business? The theme of the commercial: "Put a little love away." Love, of course, meaning sacrifice and money on the part of the parents, with the daughter seemingly sailing unperturbed and unconcerned through life on her father's financial coattails.

On my car radio one afternoon I heard an ad for a finance company, urging the father to come in to borrow money to buy his son a ten-speed bicycle for Christmas. "He's a good boy," reasons the voice of the "commercial" father. "He's worth the $180 for the bicycle." It doesn't matter that the father hasn't the means to buy that bicycle. His child must have it, no matter that his father has to borrow the money and pay it back at a high rate of interest.

What do we do about TV? Well, one enterprising young man is manufacturing foam rubber bricks that you can throw at your television set.

On the more serious side, Joanne and Ray Dobson, concerned

about the effects of television on their own children, have developed what may well be the answer for many homes. It is a small computer that enables the parent to select an entire week's TV viewing for their children in advance. Expected to be put on the market for $150, the screen will remain dark if a child tunes in a show that has been programmed out by his parents.

"The kids may scream and holler," said Dobson. "They may resent it." But, he continued, "It's the same as having a parent in the room watching TV with them."

I say it's better, considering some of the TV fare even parents get roped into watching by their bossy kids.

On the popular TV show, "Happy Days," Joanie is always being sent upstairs when her parents don't want her to hear a particular conversation. On one such occasion, exasperated, Joanie turned to her mother and said, "How am I ever going to become an adult?" "The same way I did," said her mother, "very slowly."

That's not happening with our kids today.

4.

A Priest, a Rabbi, a Minister Join Hands

After pointing out the young prostitutes along the way, my chatty New York taxicab driver stopped at my destination—475 Riverside Drive. I am headed for room 239, the home of Morality in Media, or MM as it is often called. MM is a maze of busy rooms with ringing telephones, people typing, people conferring, and literature stacked on tables neck high.

In the hallway leading to the maze is a line of large, framed cartoons hanging on the wall. They are the originals that appeared in the *New York Daily News.* Some bear the signature of Frank Springer, some of Dick Hodgins, but most are signed by Warren King. All are inscribed by their originators to Father Morton A. Hill, S.J., one of the three members of the clergy that are the backbone of MM.

I am later told by Father Hill, whom I have come to talk with, that the cartoon showing a hypodermic needle going into an arm with the word "Dope" above it, and another hypodermic needle penetrating the head with the word "Smut" above it, generated over 14,000 letters of praise in the way of letters-to-editor. The "smut" is what MM is all about.

"This whole thing has been built around Father Hill's personality and his energy and drive and his perseverance," said Evelyn Dukovic, a volunteer at MM for over five years. She also tells me that Father Hill has dragged himself out of bed for this interview. He is recovering from pneumonia. She seems a bit distressed that I will be meeting Father Hill in a suit that was bought for him for $2 at a mission. She mentions the vow of poverty Father Hill honors in the same breath. I am more pleased than she knows to find a man of the cloth so dedicated to his cause, and one who practices his priestly vows.

MM exists from contributions and Father Hill's campaigning for funds. The largest bequest ever made to MM came from the late Lewis Rosenstiel, founder of the Schenley Whiskies empire.

The door to the adjoining office opens and Father Hill's tall frame emerges, his hand extended in greeting. Father Hill, with hair cropped short, is wearing the Roman collar and the $2 suit. It looks well on him. He has blue, blue eyes and a voice reminiscent of that of actor Howard Duff.

Throughout the interview, whenever he refers to the American Civil Liberties Union, Father Hill drops the word American from the title. I get the distinct impression that it is a purposeful omission.

I sit across from Father Hill at his desk, in his office, and listen to the beginnings of Morality in Media.

In 1962 a group of mothers, meeting at St. Ignatius Church at Eighty-fourth and Park Avenue in New York City, were subjected to a package of material that one mother had confiscated from a group of 7-year-old boys. The pictures in the package dealt with sado-masochism. The parents sent for the Jesuit rector who in turn sent for Father Hill, asking him to scout the neighborhood to see what was available along these lines for children.

Today pornography is a $4 billion racket. It ranks third behind gambling and narcotics.

Father Hill admits that having been buried in the world of theology was being in an ivory tower of sorts. What he was to discover in the way of pornography was to bring him into the realities of what parent and child can be exposed to. It would, eventually, culminate in the forming of Morality in Media, an organization that operates without government funds and is dedicated to eradicating obscenity and pornography. It has now branched out to include what Father Hill calls the "Ideology of pornography" that lights up the homes of America via television.

What Father Hill found on his initial trek into the degrading atmosphere of obscenity and pornography was that materials abounded. A meeting was called involving some two hundred representatives of every major organization from hospitals to the major political parties. The meeting ended with every person contributing one dollar to send then President John F. Kennedy a "l-o-n-g" telegram articulating the flood of pornographic and obscene materials on the market. "We didn't get an answer," said

Father Hill. So much for a Catholic President who, it was feared, would bow to the wishes of the church.

The next step was to organize the mothers of St. Ignatius School. "Of course the first thing people do is blame the Supreme Court for things," said Father Hill. Ignorant in law and the mechanics of this world of obscenity and pornography, the 300 mothers involved began a nine-week campaign that involved each mother sending one hand-written postcard a week to the home of a Supreme Court justice. (Since his initiation, Father Hill spent a record-breaking three years of study to obtain a law degree.) The object of using a postcard as a protest, he said, was that it would be read, hopefully, by the people in the post office, the doorman, the superintendent, the maid, the wife, and each Supreme Court justice. They called their campaign "Operation Feather," with the principle behind it being that one feather could unbalance one hundred thousand pounds, equally balanced on both sides. What the mothers were hoping was to unbalance the Supreme Court and to have obscenity and pornography come crashing to destruction with their "feather." Not one word came back from one single member of the Supreme Court.

At this point Father Hill met Rabbi Dr. Julius G. Neumann, now Chairman of the Board of MM, and a minister, Rev. Robert E. Wiltenburg, a vice president of MM today. They formed an association called Operation Yorkville in the Upper Manhattan area, which existed under that title from 1962 to 1967. It was the forerunner of Morality in Media.

In 1967 Father Hill was appointed to the President's Commission on Obscenity and Pornography, a commission set up by Congress to determine how this traffic in pornography and obscenity could be stopped effectively and constitutionally. At the same time, in what Father Hill calls an "ecumenical invention," Operation Yorkville became Morality in Media, a name suggested by a Greek Orthodox priest at a meeting in a kosher restaurant. The following year MM was incorporated.

Meanwhile Father Hill shuttled back and forth from Washington to New York City. There were weeks and even months when he did not hear from the Washington Commission. But from the start he was concerned with the makeup of the majority on the President's Commission on Obscenity and Pornography. "The chairman of the Commission turned out to be the architect of the (American) Civil Liberties Union, William B. Lockhart, and the appointment of the staff was geared in that direction. The general council was also an executive of the Civil Liberties Union," said Father Hill.

Also on the Commission, he pointed out, were those "representing the vested interest involved in this thing. So it was obvious that it was going to be a slanted Commission with all those money interests involved," he said, citing Barbara Scott, "Jack Valenti's right hand," as an example. It was Scott who was representing the Motion Picture Association.

"In a way, the true story of this Commission has never been written, never been published, the way this thing was rigged," said Father Hill.

And how was it rigged? To begin with, there was the unbalancing of the Commission, which, at its conclusion, Father Hill said, broke down to six against and twelve weighted in favor of saying obscenity and pornography had no bad effect on the citizenry. The conclusion that the press played up, for the most part, he said, was the majority's opinion that "there are no bad effects."

"I was at the press conference in Washington when the Commission report was released and the coverage of the minority opinion was very, very scattered, very shallow. The big coverage went to those who wanted to give a green light to this traffic," he said.

Scant space was given and little public attention was focused on the fact that the majority's recommendations and conclusions were rejected by the Nixon White House and by the United States Senate by a vote of 50 to 5. "One of the 5, incidentally," Father Hill pointed out, "was Vice President Mondale."

But the real intrigue had set in once the battle lines were obviously drawn—when Father Hill and Dr. Winfrey C. Link, also a member of the Commission, saw that the "feather" was falling on the side of obscenity and pornography. In trying to fulfill their obligation to the public, they teamed up against great odds and opposition to dig deep into the studies that had been submitted to the Commission. What they uncovered would eventually become known as the Hill-Link Report, or the report of the minority.

In trying to conduct hearings into what they had been appointed to do, the minority were not only denied funds from the huge budget that had been allotted to the Commission, but, Father Hill said, in an attempt to ferret information out of the reports that were supposedly available to all members of the Commission, they met with opposition and were treated as interlopers.

Father Hill and Dr. Link, a minister, forged ahead anyway. "We paid for the hearings out of our own pockets, and they were very, very expensive." In nine different cities hearings were set up and transcripts of the same typed out. Each hearing, he estimated, cost at least $2,000. When the reports were typed up they came to roughly five hundred pounds of paper.

"You know, this was a lot of money for two clergymen," said

Father Hill. "We had to come up with this money. Well, Morality in Media agreed to pay for it."

At the hearings, experts in various fields were brought in to testify as to the adverse effects of obscenity and pornography. But the hearings were only a part of what would become the minority's report. Father Hill said they also wanted to incorporate the studies commissioned by the President's Commission. Father Hill went to Washington to obtain the reports—reports to which he was entitled as a member of the Commission. "And the majority would not give me anything that interfered with their thesis that obscenity was not harmful. So if any report came out negative, they wouldn't give it to me. I'd have to fight for it."

"Anything that was negative," he said, the majority bypassed, "because they wanted to conceal any evidence that interfered with their general thesis that obscenity was a good thing."

Not only did the majority bypass such reports, he said, "but they would keep that evidence from me. So I would have to fight like mad—stay a whole day to get one study."

It more than aroused Father Hill's suspicions. "Why," he wondered, "were they keeping it from me? And then, to our amazement, we discovered that so many of these studies indicated that pornography was dynamite! It was just blowing up the American family."

For one, there was the Martin Propper Study, conducted with 476 males who were in prison and were between the ages of 16 and 21. "This study indicated that of those who had high exposure to pornography, fifty-three percent had intercourse before they were eleven years of age; eighty-six percent had intercourse before they were fourteen, ninety-five percent had intercourse with seven or more partners. You see, the whole concept of promiscuity is built into pornography," said Father Hill.

"Another was the Berga Study. This is also very interesting because this was of the subconscious; this indicated a relationship between exposure and low marks—low grades. In other words, once a child gets involved with this, his concentration powers are weakened and he can't produce in school."

The most recent serious study along these lines was conducted by two UCLA psychologists, Seymour Fishback and Neal Malamuth. They conducted experiments in human behavior only to discover what so many good people initially knew by using mere common sense. "We have found," they said, "that portrayals of aggression in books, magazines and films can raise levels of sexual arousal. By the same token, materials that are sexually exciting can stimulate aggressive behavior."

The two psychologists went on to say that they were "concerned by the possible impact of pornography in which sex and violence are fused—as in sadomasochistic encounters. For one of the most troubling results of our research," they said, "suggests that men who view such materials tend to be more stimulated than others by the idea of rape and less sympathetic to the victim."

It is interesting to note here that from 1968 to 1978, forcible rapes have increased 99 percent.

Referring back to the reports of the Commission, Father Hill said, "My point here is that all of these things were kept from us."

So adamant was the Commission leadership in keeping these types of reports from the minority, that some were released to them only one day before the Commission's set deadline for submission of the minority report, said Father Hill.

As for media coverage on the minority report, Father Hill said, "We got practically none." Making headlines was the obverse—the report of the majority.

With the public being reassured that obscenity and pornography did not have a deleterious effect on society, Father Hill turned his efforts back to his baby, Morality in Media. And they have become quite a force.

Until several years ago, television was considered out of MM's scope. But then, Father Hill said, "We started to get more and more complaints about television material going into the home, material that exploits both sex and violence."

While commercial television, he said, is not pornography, the emphasis on sex and violence is closely related to it. "The ideology of pornography is there. And the ideology, as opposed to the actual depiction, is sex anywhere, anytime, any place, any person, any circumstances. That is the ideology being beamed into the American home through television."

Faced with a growing concern over the problem, MM mulled it over. It was a new area for them. When they finally entered the picture, they were once again naive. MM advocated that people write back, speak back, call back and talk back to the networks about offensive television material. MM printed in their newsletter the addresses of the presidents of the three major networks. "Well, we soon found out that that meant absolutely, positively, nothing. Zero!" said Father Hill.

MM's next step was to write to the affiliate stations. "And here we started to notice a very marked difference, because the affiliate is licensed and the network isn't licensed. And the affiliate has to worry about that license renewal; the network doesn't." That maneuver, he said, got some action. However it was still not enough.

By chance Father Hill was in the offices of a large beer company when one of the vice presidents in charge of advertising was reacting to a letter received from a lawyer who said he did not like what was going on in programming sponsored by this particular beer company. The lawyer threatened to tell his employees, friends and colleagues not to buy that particular brand of beer.

"Well, that executive was out of his mind!" Father Hill said. "He was screaming that he got this letter involving maybe twenty-five people—and they were selling their beer to millions. At that point I realized how sensitive these advertisers were to even one letter. So we started writing to advertisers as well as the affiliates."

In spite of it all, television for the most part became even more aggressive in the areas of violence and sex.

It was at that point that MM sponsored a May 23, 1978 blackout. "The American public took to this like a duck to water," said Father Hill. "They were just waiting for something like this." An estimated 6 million sets were blacked out that day as the American public joined MM in showing its disfavor for the type of programming being hammered out for home viewing.

At the offices of MM mail in favor of the blackout poured in, in bundles six hundred strong. Most came from organizations. The Mormon Church had recommended the blackout to all of its 3.5 million membership. The National Religious Broadcasters had sent out a half dozen spot announcements to each of 1,400 radio stations. Some of the stations were airing the spots up to thirty times a day.

Prior to the blackout, MM had conducted public hearings on television's effect on the American public. One of the hearings was held in Sioux City, Iowa. Father Hill told of a farmer who had traveled to the hearing to testify of the effects television had had on his family. He had a farm of 120 acres, was married, and had four sons. Shortly after he bought a TV set for his family, he noticed that communication between parents and children was cut off. The boys' marks in school dipped, and church activities slowed down. Even the running of the farm was degenerating.

So the farmer took an axe and chopped the TV set into silenced splinters. "The family happiness returned, the kids' marks went up, the farm started to be productive again, and their whole life was changed," said Father Hill. "He traveled two hundred miles to tell that story. It took two days out of his life. He was a noneducated man, but he was a smart man, and his whole heart was in telling that story."

On a more personal level, Father Hill recalled a "S.W.A.T." episode that involved criminals taking captive a doorman and superintendent of an apartment building, permitting the criminals to gain access to each and every apartment with the intent to rob them. "Well, the day after I saw this, I was walking up Park Avenue, and I used to know all the doormen along the route, because I passed them every day. I was talking to this friend of mine, a doorman, and he said, 'You know, after that program the other night, my wife wants me to retire. She knows it's just a matter of time before they're going to put a gun to my head, and I'll have to open up every apartment in this place. And if I don't do it, they're going to pull the trigger.' Now that man only lasted another month or two and he retired," Father Hill said. "He was just afraid that once that thing was aired, this type of crime would spread."

Today MM has grown from the original group of 300 mothers to a readership of 200,000 that encompasses every state.

MM's function, said Father Hill, is "to educate and alert parents and community leaders to the problem, the scale of, and the danger in the distribution of obscene materials. Secondly, to encourage these parents to express themselves in a unified, organized way.

"We don't believe in censorship, we don't believe in prior restraint. We believe in free expression, but in the free expression of *all* people. In other words free expression is not just the right of the producer, the publisher, the author, the man behind the microphone, but it also belongs to the viewers, the readers, the listeners, to the community. We believe that vocal, reasoned, unremitting, organized community expression can change media, can turn the tide and bring a media that is based on love and truth and taste— which we don't have."

One of the most violent reactions to TV, he said, is the fear of contraceptives being advertised.

Father Hill also says that the concept of the Family Hour for TV is "no good. Television is what we call massive mass media. And even at midnight you have families listening. Millions of children at midnight are watching. So you can't distinguish on time when you're dealing with massive mass media."

I give him the argument that children should be in bed by midnight, that if adults want sexual innuendoes or foul language or explicit sexual acts or violence, they should be permitted to have it.

He patiently says, "Obscenity is never permitted. Any place. Much less on television. It's inside the home. That's what the Seven Dirty Words Case did, to establish the fact that the standards have to be stricter than the standards in an adult movie theatre."

The case referred to by Father Hill involved one man who was incensed after hearing a radio broadcast of comic George Carlin's album, *Occupation: Fool.* He sent off a heated note to the Federal Communications Commission. This culminated in a court case that went all the way to the Supreme Court. In 1978, the Court ruled that seven of the words used by Carlin were indecent and forbidden on the airwaves.

Referring to the Court's decision, Father Hill said, "The federal law affects both radio and TV. You have the same thing with *Saturday Night Fever,*" he says of the movie. "Now, if we had lost this case, the Seven Dirty Words Case, *Saturday Night Fever* could be aired on TV. It can never be aired on TV, certainly not on home box office, because there's a contract they're not to bleep out anything. And if they air it on commercial TV they'd have to bleep out the four-letter word for intercourse a hundred times. It can't be done. The end does not justify the means." The same applies, he says, to educational channels.

If someone should dare to air one of the Seven Dirty Words, I ask, what will happen? I tell Father Hill that I have read reports in the press that some of those in the media are suggesting they will not abide by the court's decision.

"What they should do is to inform the FCC with a copy to us right away. We would help that person to make a proper complaint. It was one man who got this decision through in the Seven Dirty Words case. One man made one complaint, one letter. But it was done correctly," he points out.

Within a matter of weeks after I interviewed Father Hill, Channel 12, the educational channel out of Philadelphia, flexed its muscle. In a docudrama called "The People vs. Inez Garcia," one of the Supreme Court's "forbidden" words is used more than once. To date I have not read of any complaint registered with the FCC.

For those who will never be able to read what words are now forbidden on radio or television, I put them down here, so parents can be vigilant in enforcing the Court's ruling. They are: "shit, piss, fuck, cunt, cocksucker, mother-fucker, tits."

As to stopping pornography, Father Hill says the laws to halt it are already on the books, but they are not being enforced. "The mail problem is probably the biggest problem," he says. "There are a hundred and seventy corporations mailing this material. Many of these carry second, third, fourth class mailing permits, so the taxpayer is subsidizing the mailing of this stuff. It is in defiance of federal law, which is very clear and very strong. It's not being enforced," he said of the laws pertaining to pornography and interstate transportation.

"This is up to the Attorney General of the United States—to

inform U.S. attorneys to enforce that law. And they have been told not to enforce it instead of to enforce it by Edward Levy, who was the Attorney General before Griffin Bell. That has not changed with Griffin Bell. So that now you have practically no enforcement of federal law. The only one who could change that is the President, and Carter hasn't done it."

President Carter has been MM's target of the month, and letters have subsequently gone to the President. But again there is only silence from the Oval Office.

"Of course this whole thing is controlled by organized crime," said Father Hill. "So it's a series of networks: the pornography industry, organized crime, the all-powerful Civil Liberties Union, all working with one another."

Father Hill fights on. He has perhaps the most lethal weapon of all—it is called the National Obscenity Law Center, and is housed at MM's headquarters. It is headed by crack attorney Paul J. McGeady, known far and wide as an expert in obscenity and pornography law.

Father Hill has been instrumental in raising the initial $500,000 for the National Obscenity Law Center. The Center was not always located in New York City at MM. The original Center, which was the chief recommendation in the Hill-Link report, was funded by the government for slightly over two years. It was located in Thousand Oaks, Calif., at the California Lutheran College. It was, said Father Hill, highly successful as the most authoritative source of obscenity and pornography law in the country until the American Civil Liberties Union stepped in.

"The Civil Liberties Union decided they'd have to knock it out," said Father Hill. "Which they did. They went to the campus, said it shouldn't be on the campus, that it was interfering with academic freedom and scared the president [of the university] who had set it up with me. He refused to take any more government money." A delegation was subsequently sent to then Attorney General Edward Levy asking for its dissolution, said Father Hill, and federal funding was cut off.

"Without this Obscenity Law Center the battle is lost," said Father Hill. "There has to be one source for prosecutors to go to. They can't research these cases, they're too difficult. So we have to fund this law center privately."

In 1975 the Center was reestablished at MM. It was McGeady, said Father Hill, who twice turned the Supreme Court around in obscenity cases, the latest being the Seven Dirty Words. "He wrote the brief that won that case," he said with pride. "And briefs were submitted by the three networks, the ACLU, by the American Library Association, the Motion Picture Association—countless organizations had hired major law firms to submit briefs. And it was his brief that turned the Court and we won the case."

Father Hill is deeply concerned about the youth of this country. He calls much of what the media have to offer, "Paganized, secularized," and he worries about children growing up without Faith. "That's the reason I stay in this thing," he said. "Faith cannot survive in a young mind when it's surrounded and drowned in a media that's inimical to Faith."

5.

Students' Rights

Way back in 1969 a majority of foolish men sitting on the United States Supreme Court cracked school discipline wide open, giving more impetus to students to "do their own thing," at a time when their more radical teachers were encouraging the same. In their decision, the Supreme Court ruled that Des Moines, Iowa, school officials had acted illegally when they suspended several students for wearing black armbands to protest the Vietnam War. "It can hardly be argued," said the Court, "that either students or teachers shed their constitutional rights to freedom of speech or expression at the schoolhouse gate."

The decision was to have far-reaching ramifications for school administrators and parents alike. It would seriously impair former standards of discipline for students and teachers. School boards and administrators who had not heeded the warnings of parents already concerned with the turn curriculum had taken would see their concerns multiply.

Since teachers were also mentioned in the Supreme Court's ruling, they became bolder in expressing their innermost thoughts. If a teacher was an atheist, he could tell his students why. If he was a homosexual, he could openly discuss why he thought it was a preferable position. If he thought abortion was OK, he could bring in organized groups to support his stand. Sex education classes became more rank, if not downright bizarre. Kids grew more uncontrollable. Young girls were flaunting bare and bouncing breasts under see-through clothing. Kids smoked marijuana on the school premises. And just in case they hadn't heard of the Supreme

Court ruling, schools passed out their rights to them on printed cards. Our son got his in the fifth grade. State boards of education spent more of the taxpayers' money publishing more of the same in booklet form, often on glossy and expensive paper with modern artwork interspersed on the pages.

And heaven help those who tried to put any restrictions on the students. With the ACLU sitting at the left hand of the courts, they would become, in case after case, not only the kids' salvation, but their teachers.

Somewhere in between all the rulings that diminished both school administrators' rights and parents' rights, the Supreme Court ruled that school officials could spank children over their parents' objections. There was nothing cruel or unusual about paddling, they said. As if paddling would stop the arrogant ME generation. At best it was a ludicrous decision and meaningless in light of the rights they had already endowed our country's minor children with in other areas.

With all of this in mind, I went to interview K. (Kereazis) KiKi Konstantinos, superintendent of three relatively new high schools located in South Jersey. Konstantinos is in charge of some five thousand students, and a staff of approximately six hundred.

Konstantinos grew up in a small town in Ohio with small-town values. He and his two brothers went to college on football scholarships and went on to coach the game. He is a first-generation American, his mother being conceived in Sicily and born in the States and his father emigrating from Greece. "They didn't have money, but they did preach your good name, your reputation. And geez," said Konstantinos, "you wouldn't do anything to bring discredit to your dad—that was all he had, and he was proud of it."

Konstantinos says he can't remember many "bad kids" when he was growing up. There were no drugs, a pregnant girl out of wedlock was a rarity and the few boys in school that smoked cigarettes, he said, were "considered the bad guys."

As a school superintendent he has seen all of that change. It is not that the schools that fall under his jurisdiction are any worse than any other school. In fact they are typical, in many instances. Today all schools suffer from the same ills.

While Konstantinos more often than not presents a conservative stance, like a politician he is also able to compromise. Throughout the interview he is sometimes a defender of the system, sometimes a liberal, and a superintendent whose philosophy has been thwarted by the courts.

Konstantinos rues the fact that large school enrollments under one roof take away individuality. In troubled times it is more of a handicap, he says. "A kid can do something and walk away with anonymity," he says of the troublemakers.

Trying to relight a cigar that he mostly fails to do throughout the interview, Konstantinos makes reference to the American Civil Liberties Union. "I battle them almost at every turn," he says. "Those people just know that people have all these rights. I believe they do too, individually, but I don't believe the individual right should subvert that of the majority. There has to be a society—that means groups of people—and there have to be rules that groups live under so they can be free of fear. And they [the ACLU] think everybody should be able to do what they want, when they want. The kids," he continued, "will call them every time they get into a bind on a suspension or a policy that we develop, and they'll generally call and harass you with it—take the kids' point of view. I get a little upset with it, because I don't think they're looking at the majority view. I think they're just looking at the individual, and that causes problems."

Konstantinos, who first became a superintendent at the age of 33, is often talked about in educational circles as a candidate for State Commissioner of Education. He smiles when I mention this, chews again on his cigar, and tells me that he and a few other educators regularly spend a few days a week talking things over with the present New Jersey State Commissioner of Education, Fred G. Burke.

What has changed, I ask him, with the 18-year-old student who not only has the right to vote in every state due to the ratification of the Twenty-sixth Amendment to the Constitution, but, in all but a handful of states, is also given various majority rights. These rights enable the 18-year-olds still in high school or college to take command of their academic lives without parental interference.

The 18-year-old may sign his own absentee notes, participate in interscholastic athletics without parental approval, go on a school trip, bar his parents from conferences following a suspension, have his parents boycotted from getting his report card, sign to leave school early, and forbid notification of his parents of any truancy, suspensions or disciplinary actions taken against him. In addition school officials then may, in many states, withhold items of information from parents which in their judgment are of a confidential nature.

Waivers of this nature, says Konstantinos, have been signed by some of the 18-year-old students in his schools. "Parents will call and say, 'Why don't I get my kid's grades?' I say, 'I can't. He's an adult.'"

Konstantinos doesn't like it a bit, he says, but it is the law. "As long as that child is living in my house and I'm supporting him and I'm keeping him and I'm feeding him, he's my child, and if he signs that 18-year-old thing, he should be out of the house on his own. I wouldn't accept it as a parent. But an administrator has to abide by the law. I accept it."

Konstantinos said when these same students "get up the creek," they really need their parents and realize it too late. "He's sitting there and I have no compassion for him because he's in effect said: 'Hey mom and dad, I disown you. I don't want you knowin' anything about me.' And yet, in the meantime, he's like a parasite, living off them. But the parents don't know what to do about it." He has tried to have the waivers signed by the 18-year-olds nullified. "But my legal advice says no. Once they've signed that, they're an adult. They can't give up their rights of adulthood. It's tough," he said.

Because of the law of majority, he said, kids were feverishly absenting themselves from school. To counter this, he instituted a new attendance policy that brought the ACLU and some of the students down on his back. The matter, although in practice, is in litigation. Adopted in 1976 it denies course credits to any student who is absent more than twelve days each year excluding vacation days. The student is able to regain the credits only by attending summer school. When Konstantinos first put the measure in, some ninety kids walked out of class.

Balking students talked freely to reporters. "It's bad for me because I like to cut," said one student. Another girl admitted she spent lots of her cut days at parties. "Everyone had parties and a lot of people went," said still another student. "There was hardly anybody in school. Usually, when there was a party, anybody who heard about it went. We would come before homeroom and find out if there was a party and then we'd leave." Students told reporters that the parties were held in houses where both parents worked or at local picnic areas. When homes were used, they said they would clean up before they left so parents wouldn't know.

Konstantinos' new attendance policy was a success. The absentee rate in the senior class—the prime offenders—was reduced from 9.1 percent in 1975 to 4.6 in 1976. The decline in absenteeism has continued.

From talking to other school personnel, Konstantinos has come to the conclusion that today many parents have given up on their children and have thrown them out of the house.

Along with this faction and the 18-year-old majority position came what Konstantinos called another "dangerous" aspect.

Eighteen-year-olds were moving with other kids into residences in other towns and still coming back to their own high schools. "What some of 'em have done is they've rented an apartment and they get five or six kids from all over. Most of them have been tossed out of their homes. They live there, in the whole drug scene, or whatever, and come to your school and extend their kind of behavior into the school. One way they can make money is selling drugs to support their apartment and their food. That's one of the big problems. We have a number of those," he said.

"Anytime we catch anyone with drugs, we call the police," he said. "So that's hundreds of times in the last ten years. Oftentimes, if the kid doesn't have a record, the police will remand him to the juvenile authorities and he's slapped on the wrists.

"But most of the police now, when you talk about marijuana, and they come in and catch a kid with it—unless he has enough that we can say he's selling it, they just kind of laugh about it. They do what they can, but they know it's never gonna get to court. And if it does, nothin's gonna happen."

Nothing happens, he said, because of the leniency of the courts, and the number of adults who admit to smoking marijuana. "Kids don't think there's anything wrong with it all the way down to fourth and fifth grade," he said of the drug.

I tell Konstantinos that when the drug problem was starting, schools did not want the bad publicity and therefore police blotters and schools protected the minors. Parents knew from their children how many times the ambulance was at the school's door because someone had overdosed, but if you called the school to check, the word was mum.

"Well, that's true, Gloria," he admits. "You talked to the administrators and they said, 'We don't have any drugs here.' And I knew it. The kids were telling me." When Konstantinos decided to finally take action and make the issue public, he said he took a lot of heat because it made the papers. "The first three kids we catch in a group—one of them was a board [school board] member's daughter," he said.

How many parents, I ask him, scrutinize the public school system closely? "Very, very few," he replies.

Without my asking, Konstantinos brings up a controversy that has hit many schools: a visit from Planned Parenthood. I ask him who was responsible for extending the invitation to them. His answer is not unique, nor is what happened. It is part of the destruction of the public schools, the entering into sexual matters, and teachers who brazenly "do their own thing."

"They called," he says of Planned Parenthood, "and one of our physical education teachers said, 'OK. We're on reproduction, birth.' So these people came in and they handed out a comic book kind of thing I wouldn't want my daughter to see." (Konstantinos, married, does not have any children.) I ask him if the comic book was the one authored by the notorious Sol Gordon. He says it was.

"They passed out some birth-control implements. It was a coed class. And the kids were blowing these condoms up and everything. As soon as I found out, I knew what was going to happen. Well, some parents objected. Rightfully so," he said.

Konstantinos countered by inviting in the Right-to-Life people. He also established a policy that required any requests for future speakers to go through two other people and, finally, to him. His conservatism begins to come apart at the seams when he tells me that the statement says, "The teacher is totally responsible for the content and the materials being distributed by that speaker. So I tried to put the onus back on the teachers so they don't invite a lot of these hippies, whippies," he says.

His image crumbles just a bit further when he answers my next question: Have you had Planned Parenthood back since?

"I think we did. They didn't pass that stuff out, they didn't pass the book out. They spoke in terms of what their organization believes in."

Konstantinos says everybody calls schools to speak. "See," he says, "school's a captive audience. Where else do you have all the kids?"

Defending the practice of letting in a variety of speakers on a mountain of subjects, he says he thinks kids' attitudes are already formed at that stage of their lives. No speaker can turn the student around, he argues. "If one speaker can do that, then those attitudinal patterns haven't been inculcated," he says, throwing the onus back on parents and churches.

I suggest that the exposure is so great, on so many levels, it destroys what parents are doing. He argues again that by the time a child is 7 or 8 years old, he is already formed by his parents' upbringing. I tell him I don't buy that, because I have seen too many good kids go by the boards today. He counters with the peer pressure argument.

With no area of agreement, we move on to cursing in the schools. I tell him my reports are that both teachers and students alike swear at will. He concedes that he has had "one or two" teachers who were brought to his attention in this area. One French teacher, he says, "used some words I couldn't believe." She was let go. I tell him the problem is more severe than one or two teachers in any given school.

"You're saying it to me, and I know enough after seventeen years to never say, 'Hey, that never happens.' As you say, do people scrutinize the school program? Not really," he concedes, and therefore these teachers are not reported. And then, falling further to the left of center he says of today's teachers, "You're not going to stop 'em ever from being cute or using double entendre."

Does he think that is right? "Well, I don't know whether I think it's right or not when you're dealing with four hundred people, all of them talking all day long, all being different personalities, all coming out of colleges where you heard a lot more than that and they think that's smart teaching. You know, it's pretty difficult for me to control," he says.

Students, he tells me, swear so unconsciously, that when he reprimands them for their language in the halls, they are unaware they have done it and will repeat the word in their apology to him.

Bemoaning the relaxed dress code for students that he claims was in part instigated by parents who beleaguered the school board for the change, I point out some of the slovenly dress of today's teachers. "Because the court allowed that!" he says with exasperation. Prior to that, he said, he had insisted on jackets and ties for male teachers. He recalled a day, after the court rulings on dress codes, when a teacher, taking off his necktie, said, "Today the necktie, tomorrow the world!" Now, said Konstantinos, it is often difficult to tell the teachers from the students.

"A teacher used to be someone that most of the public held on a pedestal or looked up to. Somebody who had an education and had a mission," he said. "Well, you have to remember in ten years we had them become militant with unions. You had the courts saying you don't have to worry—you can't tell him how to dress, how to cut his hair, when to come to class, what he can learn. And you had them doing the same thing for teachers, because they're not second-class citizens. The whole thing got into a big schmier. You can't expect a kid to really respect a teacher who's out on strike."

"So that whole thing kinda changed," he said with a sigh. Also changed are pregnancies and school. "Now they can stay 'til they have a kid here in the hall. The courts said that. The civil rights say that," he said of student and teacher alike.

Asked if the school houses married students, he says, "There aren't too many married couples, but there are a lot of unwed mothers."

On the issue of schools providing abortion services, Konstantinos said, "There is a law, you know, that came down and said you must provide these services—you must provide this information. It also said there was a confidentiality that if a kid came down and wanted this information, you were to give it to her. And you couldn't tell the parent, even if the child was under 18 years of age. I object strenuously to that, because I think a kid that's not an adult—a parent has a right to know that the child's pregnant, that the child's on drugs, or whatever."

Konstantinos is referring to the 1976 Supreme Court ruling that gives every child in America, regardless of age, the right to get an abortion without parental knowledge or consent.

As to the way his school newspapers are used by the students, he said it was simply another area where the courts once again stepped in. They decreed that freedom of speech did not stop at the school door. And so, he said, he urged his students to use the school newspapers for their views. "And that's what they did. They wrote some scathing articles about school, me, and everything else. But as long as they did it in good, journalistic style and with some class, we let 'em do it. The thing is, if you prohibit them from doing these things, they'll find a way to beat you. It becomes a cause and everybody gets on the bandwagon."

I ask if students in the state of New Jersey can still be excused from certain subjects or books that parents object to on religious or moral grounds. "Yes," he responds, "especially in the area of sex education. It's not mandatory." While it is not mandatory in his schools, it is a policy that is up to each individual school board. Commissioner Burke is now pressing for standard sex-education classes, and if a school board has made it mandatory, the parents be damned if they object.

"That's one of the big problems with public schools," he says, "in that you're operating with all the children of all the public, and you have to be completely amoral, areligious, all these kinds of things, and you can hardly teach anything. So you try to stay somewhere in the middle."

Alluding to the changing face of public education, he says, "Of course all of these things came suddenly and not through the kids themselves, but the fact that society permitted it. Encouraged it. The Civil Liberties Union and the courts and other decisions and parents . . ." And schools—don't you think? I interject.

He skirts the issue by saying he does not believe it is the mission of schools to bring about reform or social change; they are there to maintain and perpetuate the status quo. If they do not, he says, society will overthrow them. "But one of our problems—we have no missions, we have—everybody who comes up gives us a different mission and we're tryin' to be all things to all people," he says.

Is he, I ask, surprised that parents sit still for so much from their children today? "It's unbelievable," he says. "They are afraid of the kid. They're afraid both ways. I really feel sorry for them. Some of them are afraid physically because these kids'll get drunk, they'll get on drugs and the parents are afraid of them and/or they're afraid if they pressure the kid, the kid's going to run away. And it's a real threat, because they could run away with ease. There are places for them to go, there are ways to make money, and they get themselves in trouble. And the parents are cowed. I don't know what to tell them, because at that point it's a little too late. They're blackmailing them—they have them like this," he says of the kids, making a fist.

What are some of the major changes he has observed over the past ten years with students?

"Well," he says, pondering the question before responding, "I find they're more self-centered. They're more interested in pleasing themselves and doing anything that they want to do that will titillate their pleasure centers.

"I think it's part of the whole philosophy that came out of the sixties—everybody do your own thing—not realizing that doing your own thing really affects other people."

6.

From Mousey to Mouthy Mother

Theirs is only a nickel-and-dime operation compared to the millions of dollars Uncle Sam funnels into their opposition's coffers, but it does nothing to deter Jean Garton and Joan McLaughlin.

Jean, a Lutheran, and Joan, a Catholic—both married mothers—are active members of American Citizens Concerned for Life (ACCL). ACCL is a national organization that places great emphasis on education and alternatives to abortion. Together Jean and Joan go into the schools to talk to students about their antiabortion stand. Getting in is not easy. Once there, they often find the students hostile to them.

"First of all," said Jean, who holds top-level posts in the Lutheran Church, Missouri Synod, "we have to establish that across the country, overwhelmingly, the prolife position is not shared in the public school system.

"What we have happening in the area of sexuality, birth control, abortion is indoctrination—a definite attempt to keep out any position that does not conform to that which has been adopted unofficially or however. So any attempt to get into a public school head-on just doesn't work. We have been turned down," she said.

When prolife groups write to schools requesting that students be permitted to hear their side of the abortion controversy, she said, "they either get no response or a firm 'No.'"

"Nevertheless, occasionally we get in." This sometimes happens when parents "kick and scream" (as they did at the school where Superintendent Konstantinos had Planned Parenthood come in) and insist their children be presented both points of view. "I'm thinking of a time when a teacher, in a mixed health class, distributed a sex book that had been banned by this country because of the pornographic content as well as the political material in it," said Jean.

"This teacher had it brought in across the border from Canada. She distributed it in her classes and told the students not to tell their parents that they were reading it.

"They studied it for a week and each day she would collect the booklets. The weekend assignment was for each student to write, in detail, his sexual experiences. So the student went home and that immediately created problems, particularly for those who had no sexual experience. They either had to lie, create something, or tell their parents—which is what two of them did. The parents were furious!" said Jean.

A scuffle with local school officials followed. The matter was carried to the state level with a threat of court action by the parents. At that point the school allowed that a different point of view could be presented to the students, and Jean was part of the team that was called upon. "However," she pointed out, "we were never invited back again. It was to mollify those parents at that time."

On occasion they are called upon when a student is given a choice of subject matter, and is also permitted to provide materials or speakers, and chooses abortion. "This doesn't happen often," said Jean. "It's interesting. These students have told us that if they do a topic on homosexuality, on cigarette smoking, on alcoholism—and they ask to bring a speaker in as part of their report, there's no problem; but when they do it on abortion, and ask to bring in a Right-to-Life speaker, they get all kinds of flak."

The other rare occasion when they are asked in to speak to students is when a teacher allows that her students must make up their own minds on abortion. "And then we're invited in," she said, pointing out that it is a very, very rare occurrence.

But Jean and Joan *do* get into the public schools, and when they do, they preface their session by telling the students to hold any questions until the end of the session. "There is a tendency to have young people shout you down," she said. "The manners of the young people are atrocious. I think there's first of all a lack of respect and acceptance of other people and other ideas. I think the concept of ME first—self-centeredness—extends also to one's thinking. If *I* don't think that, or if *I've* never heard of that, it can't possibly be. There's a very myopic view of the situation," she said of the students' view on abortion.

Recalling one high school where they were to speak, Jean said she was called the evening before by a mother who told her that the students had already been told by the teacher that they were not required to listen to the prolife position and were free to get up and walk out of the classroom.

Jean then planned her strategy to meet the situation head-on. The following day she and Joan entered the already hostile atmosphere of the classroom. When the teacher arrived, said Jean, her smugness and arrogance were showing through, as were the children's. "You could see them all ready to get up and go. I said I was very glad to be there, but I did want them to know that this was a topic only to be dealt with on an adult level. I walked over and opened the door. I said I wanted to request that all of those who felt they couldn't handle this to please leave now. And not a one left. The teacher," she said, "was steamed!"

At another school Jean and Joan had been forewarned by a woman who had preceded them on the prolife issue. "She said she had gone in with a doctor to this school and these teachers had these kids so psyched up that she said they were really afraid the kids were going to hit them. She said the students stood up, they jumped up and down, and they shouted at them and threw things. She said she and the doctor were just glad to get out. This woman would not go back. The doctor would not go back." Undaunted, Jean and Joan went anyway.

"Let us tell you of the evolution of our acceptance," said Jean with a smile. "In this particular school, we went there the first time and the teacher said, 'Well, here they are—Right-to-Life people. OK.' And we were on.

"The next time we went, she said, 'Well, now, I want you to pay attention. There's some things here I want you to know.'

"The next time we went she said, 'All right. Now! I want you to listen carefully. There are things you should be thinking about. Be prepared to ask questions so that you can understand what these people are saying.'"

"Finally, the last time we were there," said Jean, "the teacher stood up and said, 'Well, here they are! What can I tell ya! Two really great broads!' When we left that day, the teacher gave us a bottle of pink champagne." It was, she said, a rare but very real victory.

Jean, born and raised in Brooklyn, N.Y., started out a decade ago as being militantly proabortion. When she turned 40 and pregnant all in the same year, she went from doctor to doctor (before the Supreme Court's landmark decision on abortion) trying to find one that would perform an abortion. All told her she was healthy and could see no reason to terminate the pregnancy.

Jean says she did a lot of agonizing and a lot of crying, and the pregnancy was not an easy one. "I was terribly disturbed because I knew *MY* plans for the future were down the drain." Jean, whose three children were all in school at that point, had planned to return to the world of academia herself, for her doctorate. Instead she carried the pregnancy to term and immediately thereafter joined a proabortion group that was seeking to liberalize the abortion laws. As her involvement with the proabortion group grew, two things happened to her: She became interested in what she called the "double-speak" of the proabortion movement and eventually changed her stand on abortion.

The proabortion meetings she attended were riddled with double-speak, and the use of euphemisms to support the proabortion position. They would refer to the baby in utero as a "blob," or "tissue." Instead of using the word abortion, they used phrases like "terminating the pregnancy," said Jean.

Jean's major at Ursinus College had been English literature. She decided she would develop an argument for abortion that would use honesty and integrity instead of untruths and euphemisms. About that time, she attended her first debate pro and con abortion.

The proabortion debater always talked about the woman's rights, she said, while the antiabortion debater talked about the child's rights. "I really was amused," Jean said, referring to the prolife debater's stand. "I thought: She is obviously a very uneducated person. She talks about that thing in the womb as a human being. So I thought, that's where I will start my project. And I contacted her."

Jean asked the prolife debater for information that would support the position she had espoused at the debate. The woman agreed to send literature to her. Jean said she was expecting gory pictures, dramatics, and "all the statements by the Pope—a lot of emotional crying." Instead she got the latest studies in fetology and a comprehensive package supporting the prolife stand. She studied the package for six months. "And as I studied, I became convinced that we were indeed dealing with a human being with value, but one who was very vulnerable; a human being who had rights, but whose rights were being denied by those more powerful, which is always the situation with rights.

"And so, at the end of six months I came out a convert to the prolife position. However," she said, "still allowing for some exceptions." Today, she said, those exceptions have narrowed down to only one. "And that is to clearly save the life of the mother." It is the position of every prolife group she has ever come in contact with, although it is not a position often allowed the light of print. Its omission makes the prolifer appear to be totally unreasonable.

"They would have us," she said of the proabortion segment of society, "pictured as people who say the unborn child has more value than the woman, and we have never said that. We are saying they are of equal value . . . different degrees of dependence and development, but of equal value."

In the years that followed, Jean was to become a force within the Lutheran Church, Missouri Synod. She would be the first woman appointed to their National Policy Making Board and the first woman appointed to the Board of Social Concerns, which deals with current issues such as ERA, homosexuality, capital punishment, war, amnesty, abortion and euthanasia. She would also be appointed to her church's committee to study women's concerns, chairing that national group. She is, she stresses, not in concert with the aims of the National Organization of Women. Their idea of liberation, she said, is not hers.

As a result of her laudable work, Jean became the first woman to receive two honorary degrees from her church's seminary. The first was a doctorate of humane letters, the second, a doctorate of literature.

The format used by Jean and Joan when they confront students with their point of view on abortion grew out of what Jean first recognized as double-speak. It is this and the catch-phrases that they use as take-off points to discuss abortion with students in the public schools.

EVERY WOMAN HAS A RIGHT TO CONTROL HER OWN BODY: "Not *every* woman has a right to control her own body," Jean tells the students, "because half of those aborted are women. We take driver's ed, get insurance, but even though we've had that, if we have an accident, we don't walk away from the effect on another human being by saying, 'Well, it was an accident. I didn't intend it to happen.' Once involved in a pregnancy, we must be responsible for the consequences of our actions. We say the most effective contraceptive is the oral contraceptive—'No.'"

"They laugh at us," said Joan of the students. "But of course we say it."

Many people in the prolife movement, they tell me, are in favor of contraceptives. "But these young people are really stunned by saying no to sex," said Jean. "It doesn't even enter their minds!"

EVERY CHILD A WANTED CHILD: Addressing the students, they will say, "Every child a wanted child tells us nothing about the child. We have built this whole social policy on the shifting sands of emotions. If I say you are female, I am describing you. You are awake—I'm describing you. You are unwanted. Whom am I describing? Not you! I haven't said a thing about you; I'm telling you a lot about myself. When we say every child a wanted child, we're not saying anything about this child, but we're saying how incredibly selfish, self-centered and unwanting we are."

Touching on the matter of abortion for a victim of rape, Jean said, "If we can get rid of the child, then we have gotten rid of a situation that is probably one of the most objectionable that exists in our society. But in so doing, in aborting the child of a rape situation, we have solved our problem exactly as the rapist has . . . by doing violence to an innocent body. So it becomes a compounding of a sick mentality."

TERMINATION OF PREGNANCY: "We talk about that as a euphemism," said Jean, "because it implies that an abortion is a victimless procedure." In using such phrases as "blob" or "tissue," she says, the proabortionists are using the same strategies applied during World War II to dehumanize the enemy and make killing him easier. The terms then were "Nazi," "slanty-eyed Jap."

"What you call something is so important," said Jean. "But we go on to say that biologically the words fetus and embryo are just medical terms to tell us where a human being is: such as adult, adolescence. Then we go backwards. We say: Is the adolescent less human than the adult, or merely different in terms of development? We go all the way back to let them see that the fetus, the embryo, is not *less* human, but a different kind of human in terms of development."

"Is it size?" they ask the students. "Well then, Wilt Chamberlain is more human than we are. Does being a full human depend on how well developed we are? We're not fully developed in many areas for many years," they point out.

"Does being fully human depend on where you live? And we establish that historically it did if you were black and on a plantation, or a Jew in World War II Germany, or now, if you are an unborn human being in the womb."

FREEDOM OF CHOICE: "We hit home on how American and democratic that really sounds. We give them illustrations: We are free to kick, as long as what we kick is a ball and not our neighbor. Then we say, let's apply that thinking to other areas of human rights. There were people in Germany who said, 'I wouldn't gas a Jew myself, but I support the right of others to choose it.' People in America who said, 'I wouldn't enslave a black myself, but I support the right of others to choose.' In both cases, history has indicated that that's not liberty but atrocity. Now we're into that same mentality with abortion."

A FETUS IS NOT A PERSON: "The leading proabortionists will

admit genetically, biologically," said Jean, "what's in the womb is a human being. But they'll say it's not a person, which means we're not going to give it value."

WHAT IS A PERSON? "Persons can be corporations, ocean-going vessels. You don't have to be a human being to be a person," Jean tells the students. By charts she shows them how the Indian became a nonperson. "We could take his land. How the negro was a nonperson. We could deny him his liberty, take his labor. And now we've said for the third time, another group of human beings are not persons. We can take their lives."

Then they point out to the students that each one of them should realize that they have no guarantee, should this philosophy prevail, that they will always be considered a person. "If we become imperfect? If we become nonproductive and unwanted?" they say, planting the seeds to get the students thinking. From there, they move into the sphere of infanticide and euthanasia.

IS ABORTION A CATHOLIC ISSUE? It is a question, says Jean, that the communications media are always prone to ask. "They will expect me to deny that hotly. I say, absolutely, positively, it *is* a catholic issue, when you understand that catholic with a small "c" means universal . . . that which involves the interests of us all. What could be a more catholic issue than abortion? But, if you're implying that it's a Roman Catholic issue, then I would charge you with bigotry." Jean said they then talk to the students about the history of abortion laws in the United States that were put on the books by Protestants, and go on to point out that 70 percent of all major polls show that Americans oppose abortion on demand.

"So how can you say it is a Roman Catholic issue without seeking to appeal to prejudice or bigotry and insulting so many of us who are not Catholics and support the sanctity and the values of life?" they challenge the students.

When the women are finished with their discourse, I ask them what the reactions of the students are. "A lot of times there are just long periods of silence," said Joan. "Very long periods of silence."

Once the students do start questioning these two women, it usually is along the same lines:

"What do you do when you're pregnant and you know your mother'd kill you?" is a common question asked by students. "We start by saying your mother wouldn't kill you. You don't know your mother as well as you think you do. And we talk about that."

Another frequent string of arguments from the students usually runs something like this: "We really can't have these babies being born. I mean, after all, it's one thing for you, you're married. You have husbands. You don't understand what it's really like. These girls get pregnant. They have no way of raising these kids. They can't finish school. They don't want them. You want these kids born? You know what happens to these kids? They get born, they go on welfare, they get abused. They can't get a job. They become criminals and spend their life in jail. I mean, that's what you want? A million a year! Why, if you let them be born, what would happen? Oh, but isn't it better to abort?"

The women begin first by talking about the students sitting before them in the classroom, telling them many of them also began their lives as unwanted pregnancies, but became very wanted children. It sends the ME generation into shock. "It surprises some of them," said Jean. "The idea that they weren't wanted!"

Nonplussed, Jean and Joan tell the students that the figure of 1 million live births would not be a reality if abortion was not so handy. Instead, abstinence and birth control would be applied.

They talk to the students about the number of marriages that are childless and how adoption agencies cannot fill the requests made by couples that have already waited years for a child.

"We talk about the welfare. They make these quantum leaps in their thinking," said Jean of the students who try to justify abortion. She tells them that given a choice on spending money on welfare abortions or welfare births, they (Jean and Joan) prefer the latter.

The argument that abortion is a one-shot cost is also shot down by Jean and Joan. They tell the students that a teen-ager who has had an abortion has been statistically proven to become pregnant twice more within five years. "Her self-image, first of all, has really been shot through with the abortion," said Jean. "She has to go on and establish her fertility in her own mind, and psychologically, Dr. David Allen, a psychiatrist from Harvard and Yale, has talked about the evidence that shows they become pregnant deliberately to assure themselves they still can. The tendency seems to be to keep that child," she said of the third pregnancy.

"By then," said Jean, "the child is wanted—but for the wrong reasons. It may well become an abused child, despite the fact that the pregnancy was planned." The teen-ager, she continued, sees having this pregnancy as an affirmation of who she is. "She will demand that the child meet certain standards as a reflection of her worth and her value." When the child doesn't comply, said Jean, it often is abused. "Her expectations are often so high because she has such poor expectations of herself," said Jean of the teen-age mother.

Jean talks with enthusiasm of the successful research and programs being done at Johns-Hopkins. They will take a girl through her pregnancy, put her through a two-year program that will educate her and make her independent. These girls, she said, do not become pregnant out of wedlock again. "In the Hopkins' program," said Jean, "they break the cycle. But they all see the need to deal with the problem by continuing the pregnancy. Interrupting the pregnancy just compounds the problem."

The money will continually pour forth, said Jean, if society continues to seek abortion as a solution to teen-age pregnancies. It will be needed for counseling, for psychological purposes and for child abuse.

Facing the students on the issue of population explosion, Jean said the students will often cite outdated literature and the Club of Rome, the international think tank that said some twelve years ago that there would be one square yard per person if population did not decrease. "The Club of Rome has completely rejected its own findings of twelve years ago," she points out. Their position now, she said, is that "we are creating a rapidly aging population where we will not have the young people to provide the work force. And the students cannot comprehend that what they have been taught has now been revised.

"It's like when they said we would have to close the patent office in the 1900s because everything had been developed that could have possibly been invented," she says by way of example.

Discussing the selfishness of today's children, Jean said it is something she and Joan feel strongly when they talk to the students. "We walk into a class and that selfishness is so strong it hits you like a brick wall. It is consuming selfishness and one just stands back and says, 'Oh, the sex generation!'"

Jean has strong feelings concerning the removing of parental influence from the minor. "Whenever you remove the parents' input, advice, direction, involvement, you have not removed advice, guidance, direction, involvement—you have merely replaced the parents with someone else to do those things."

She said it was never more clear to her than when she and Joan went down to observe hearings on the soaring problem of teen-age pregnancies in January of 1977 that were put together by HEW. Dr. David Allen, she said, suggested that school programs teach the teen-ager restraint. "Well! That's heresy!" she said. "It just boggles their minds. They saw that as very unliberated. Unless you just yield to every impulse, you are in bondage."

At those hearings, Jean said, were representatives from Planned Parenthood, Population Council, Zero Population Growth and abortion clinics. Their solution, she said, was that their programs were not working "because they were not starting early enough, they were not explicit enough, parental influence HAD to be terminated; parents were seen as a detriment, as a threat, and the government had to get involved. The solution to the problems of teen-agers rests first with themselves and secondly with the government. There were many calls," she continued, "for government funding or programs, for government making participation in these programs compulsory.

"We have created this attitude that everybody should do his own thing, and as a result, learners—children—have been told that if they really want to be liberated, they must do their own thing. So it's not that there isn't a relationship between parents and children, but there are these outside forces that say do your own thing. Don't bother your parents with it. It has nothing to do with the good relationship. If you really want to be grown up, if you really want to be liberated, if you want to be anything—do your own thing. And that means the last thing you should involve is your parents," said Jean.

"Selfishness" is the key word, she said. "I want more of the good things of life for me. I want more opportunities for me. So I think at the heart and core of the whole thing is that we are shifting from the sanctity of life ethic, which has been the traditional Judeo-Christian ethic, to the quality of life ethic, which is the humanistic ethic.

"I think secular humanism is deeply entrenched in the government programs, in our educational system. I think it manifests itself in the promotion of abortion for teen-agers. Their whole goal when they talk of aborting is: You don't want your educational careers interrupted; you don't want to burden yourself; you don't want to sacrifice."

I ask Jean if those were her feelings when she initially went in search of a doctor who would abort her pregnancy. "At that time? Oh, no! Other people were selfish. *I* was realistic. *My* situation was different from all of those others who were aborting just for convenience. I had reasons! Looking back now, I think there was a great deal of immaturity. I was forty and immature. And I think selfishness is one indication of immaturity. I think what we're doing with this whole concept of 'If it feels good, do it!' is we are perpetuating immaturity and creating this whole generation that we see now, in their twenties, of adolescent adults."

Jean said she and Joan are constantly taken aback when they ask the students if a person who goes into a coma ceases to be human, and the students reply, "Yes."

"And we are the next victims," Joan predicts. "Let me give you an illustration that really happened," said Jean, "that crystallizes this thing that parents are the next victims.

"Governor Shapp (Milton Shapp of Pennsylvania) formed an abortion/law commission in Pennsylvania before the Supreme Court decision. It was holding hearings. That commission was made up of approximately twenty people—lawyers, doctors. I gave testimony at one.

"There was," she continued, "testifying for abortion, a man and his wife. He went on to say that his wife had come to him to say she was pregnant with their fourth child, and he was delighted. But she soon convinced him that he was merely on an ego trip and that she, herself, wanted an abortion.

"Being a very democratic and American family, they decided to hold a family council. They called in their three grade-school children and said to them: Now, mother is pregnant. If the pregnancy is allowed to continue, it will mean that some of you will have to double up on your rooms, depending on the sex of the new baby. It will probably mean that we will not be able to take our camping trip this summer, and it will certainly mean you will not be able to get the bikes you wanted at Christmas. Now—how do you vote?

"Well, the mother, the father and the two boys voted for an abortion," said Jean. "And it was carried out. Majority ruled. Voting against the abortion was the daughter. A member of the commission said to the mother: How could you explain this to your daughter? How could you deny her the right of this brother or sister she was pleading for?

"The mother shrugged her shoulders and said, 'Well, you can't give your children everything they want.' Later another member of the commission wisely observed that this would not be the last meeting convened by this family. For the time would come, given statistics, when mother would be alone. She would need a place to stay. To find room for her would mean that her children would have to absorb her costs. It would mean that they would have to re-arrange their rooms, that they would have to adjust their budgets to reschedule their plans for vacations. They would have learned all too well from mother how to deal with an inconvenient human being."

Joan said she believes attacks on the family unit are the reason things are so out of hand with our youth. "That just didn't exist when I was growing up. I knew that if I got into any kind of trouble, the first thing that was going to happen to me was I was going to get dragged home. That's the last thing that will happen now. There are so many people, whether it's school counselors or agencies, or whatever—government funded things and people that will step in and prevent the parents from knowing anything."

Jean Garton's life has done a complete turnabout. "Up until the time I got involved in this, I was really an at-home mother. Three of my children grew up with me as the traditional mother. But my involvement, because it was gradual, was also gradual for them. They are, today, the three older ones, very outspoken on the issue and very prolife.

"The nine-year-old—the cause of all this—he knows nothing else but me on a plane, me in the audience, me on television. With him, we have had more conversations as to why I'm doing this.

"The three oldest," she said, "can't figure out what happened to that mousey Sunday school teacher mother that they had. I've gone from the mousey mother to the mouthy mother."

7.

The Stoned Generation

As kids turn their parents inside out, as they drop dead from over-dosing on drugs, as they try to fight their way back to a meaningful life, someone is counting the millions of dollars they are making on the destructive drug-wasted children to whom they sell their wares.

Marijuana alone is now one of the nation's biggest businesses, with estimates placed at $48 billion a year.

Every day, in every part of our country, we all see headlines similar to these real headlines I have lifted from daily newspapers: MILITARY DRUG USE 'RISING,' PHARMACISTS CHARGED AS PUSHERS, MARYLAND LEGISLATOR HELD ON DRUG COUNT, $10 MILLION DRUG RAID RING CHARGED AT RUTGERS UNIVERSITY, STONED IN MARBLE HALLS: POT USERS IN CONGRESS, DRUGS LINKED TO TRUANCY, DRUG SMUGGLERS LIVING THE HIGH LIFE IN FLORIDA. Such headlines could fill a large book by themselves. Every newspaper has them by the pound in its morgues.

To our dismay, we read frequently of those whom we would like to think of as being above reproach, cashing in on the drug culture. The *New York Times*, in an article by Leonard Buder, noted that over a two-year period, information from one field associate led to the arrest of thirteen police officers and fifty-four civilians on gambling and narcotics charges. It is not only the police officer, but the family doctor and the school teacher, too. On the other hand there is the calibre of policeman and doctor who is trying to help the drug child.

James A. Forcinato, president of the 6,000 member Fraternal Order of Police, speaking out against reducing penalties for small amounts of marijuana, said, "The psychological dependence on this innocent looking herb may be so strong as to trap our youth into its continued use and force the use of hard drugs."

Forcinato is correct in his assessment. Frances May, director of admissions at Eagleville Hospital in Pennsylvania, an alcohol and drug rehabilitation center, said that 97 percent of the 1,200 to 1,500 drug cases they see each year at Eagleville began with marijuana, and the users moved on to heavier drugs.

Mrs. Maria Yavarone, in a letter to the editor of a newspaper, expressed shock that no public debate had been permitted before the New Jersey Senate Judiciary Committee meeting on the committee's release of a bill for the decriminalization of marijuana.

She said as she was leaving the hearing room she heard Sen. Frank Dodd make reference to reporters that his duty was to make laws, not raise children. "Why shouldn't our elected representatives assist and support those parents who are doing their best to raise their children correctly?" she asked. "On the other hand, shouldn't their interest and duty be even greater for those children who are, unfortunately, not receiving proper guidance and care?

"Sen. Dodd," continued Mrs. Yavarone, "should realize that parents cannot keep youngsters locked within four walls, neither can they alone keep negative outside influences to a minimum. Parents are doomed to failure without the back-up of lawmakers, church authorities and school personnel."

How on target, Mrs. Yavarone. Our children have been cut loose from too many restrictions already. It has set them adrift in a sea of darkness that crests on the homefront as their young, confused and alien lives clash with those of their parents.

Even the once hallowed halls of Princeton University have been touched by the drug culture. In a poll conducted by that university's newspaper, more than two-fifths of the faculty members said they had smoked marijuana at least once—11 percent of the faculty had used harder drugs such as cocaine, hashish, heroin or LSD. Twenty-one undergraduates were arrested on charges of possessing or selling illegal drugs on campus.

So ingenious are those who will profit from the sale of drugs that a "pot dispensing machine" was set up a block from a high school in Denver, Colorado. Students would slide their money through a slot cut in a door, while the pusher sitting on the other side of the door would slide back the marijuana.

Drugs have taken a terrible toll not only on the children, but on the parents and society. Who would want to be the parent of the 16-year-old girl, high on LSD, who slashed her wrists and arms in Hartford, Conn.? When she rushed to the steps of a church, poking a razor to her throat, a crowd of 300 persons cheered and screamed, "Do your thing, sister!" She could be anybody's daughter today.

The 15-year-old boy who hanged himself in a detention cell could have been anybody's son. His father had called the police to his home after his wife discovered their son was unconscious from an apparent drug overdose. Earlier that day the boy had been suspended from school for using drugs. As he left his parents' home handcuffed, he was cursing the police officers.

Three teen-agers died from sniffing canned freon gas inside a closed automobile. They could be anybody's children, too.

When they buried Steve Holtz in Miami, his mother had long since passed the grieving stage. Steve was only 18 when he died, but for the last three years of his life he was spaced out on a variety of drugs—angel dust, cocaine, Quaaludes, mushrooms, speed and marijuana. "I sort of feel like his life with us ended quite a while ago," said his mother. "I think he ceased to exist in my feelings."

The night Steve died was much like other nights. He was stoned on drugs, spoke only incoherently, staggered home and passed out on the living room couch. When his mother got home she snapped: "I won't put up with this stuff anymore. This is the end." She told her other sons to carry him out back to sleep it off in the yard. Three hours later he was dead. His mother won't have to grieve anymore. Drugs, I have found, are worse than death for many parents.

There are other mothers who won't grieve anymore, either, like the mother who asked her drug-infested son to leave the house. He stabbed her 300 times.

For too many parents, the nightmare ends only when the child or the parent ceases to exist in this world.

A mother whose 14-year-old daughter was on drugs told me she had spent an entire year trying to keep her daughter from running away. The following year, she'd had all she and the family could bear. Locks were changed on the house, windows nailed shut. The family tried to keep their daughter out of their lives, out of the house, and from stealing everything that she could turn into quick cash for her drug habit. Now the daughter has done everything to get into the house—including breaking windows. It is a nightmare for any family with a child on drugs.

Many parents refuse to believe their children could be a part of it all. In Warwick, R.I., police placed a camera at the back door of Veterans Memorial High School primarily "to show parents of the kids involved—kids who come from decent homes—that their children are smoking marijuana," said Detective Capt. Frank Ricci.

The National Institute on Drug Abuse estimates that the greatest drug abuse is among children 12 to 17 years old. New York City's special narcotics prosecutor said that even the drug pushers are getting younger and more vicious. He said that the "killer kids" are known by the fancy cars they buy with their money. Some are so young and small they can barely see over the wheel.

It is another unnatural and inhuman feeling that so many parents would rather see their children dead than behaving the way they are today. More than one mother has uttered: "I brought him into this world—I can take him out, too," indicating they could murder their own child. Why? Because like the legendary Dr. Jekyll, who turned into an animal-like Mr. Hyde when he drank the potion, so too do formerly rational and good children turn into something unrecognizable by their parents when they take drugs. They lie, cheat, steal and even commit murder. They are the users and the abusers of drugs, their parents, society.

Since teen-age abuse by parents is also rising, I cannot help but wonder if parents are not fighting back in self-defense, or striking their children out of hurt, anger, frustration and desperation— striking at someone who barely resembles the child they once knew. It is a case of deep love turning to deep hate.

Besides all of the common drugs in use, children have now discovered PCP, or, as it is known in the street, "Angel Dust." PCP is an animal tranquilizer and is often sprinkled on marijuana leaves.

A Los Angeles narcotics squad officer said kids on PCP will march into the muzzle of a policeman's gun or a burning house, or jump off a skyscraper believing they can fly.

It took eight officers to subdue one 14-year-old girl who was under the influence of PCP. Normal-sized men in the throes of a PCP trip have been known to break their steel handcuffs. A young mother dipped her baby in steaming water. Another youth on PCP shot his parents as they watched TV; still another tried to rape his own mother.

Apparently at wits' end with the drug culture and its related crimes, the province of British Columbia has taken a bold step. As the year 1979 was ringing in, a new measure was put underway. Any person considered to be in need of treatment for narcotic dependency could be forced to undergo a treatment program.

The action raised the hackles of the British Columbia Civil Liberties Association. Province officials responded by saying that traditionally health laws have forced treatment and even quarantine of individuals who were ill and posed a threat to themselves or the community. Even though treatment can be made compulsory, the individual may appeal.

Perhaps no drug has been treated so lightly nor used by so many of our youth as has marijuana. How many parents, I have wondered, were faced with the same dinner-table discussions that my husband and I were faced with when marijuana first began to come into common use? How many parents told their children, as we did with no facts to back it up, that the use of marijuana could not be beneficial, it had to be harmful? How many parents faced the same argument from their children that we did? They told us they had discussed it in school and their teachers said there were no studies to support our fears. Many parents, because they could not find another authoritative voice to counter the teacher's stand, or to support theirs, lost the battle early on.

The rumor of the drug's harmlessness persists to this day, in spite of findings to the contrary. "Marijuana poses a substantial risk. Anybody who takes that drug and thinks that nothing is happening to his body has lost his mind. Marijuana is a powerful drug that is influencing his entire body," said Dr. Robert DuPont, Jr., chairman of the World Psychiatric Association's drug dependence section.

Dr. DuPont also noted that marijuana influences the hormone levels of the body, the body's immune response, the way one thinks and the tissues of the lung, and that bronchitis is common in people who smoke marijuana cigarettes. He also said there is laboratory evidence to show that marijuana is more likely to cause cancerlike lesions than cigarette smoking.

In an effort to find out some answers to what elements of family life are associated with drug use by youngsters, a Stanford University research team conducted deep, eight-hour interviews with approximately a hundred families involving about five hundred fifty people. Their conclusion was that drug users tend to come from excessively permissive homes that put a low premium on family life, discipline and self-control. Nondrug users and those who repudiated drugs after experimenting came from warm, relaxed and close families that prized discipline and solid moral values.

The NBC special hosted by Edwin Newman on marijuana brought an avalanche of requests for both the film and the transcript.

Marijuana, the show revealed, is now ten times as potent as that which college students were using five years ago.

Newman ended the program by blaming the government, the schools, everyone, for not telling the kids the facts.

In spite of all the knowledge concerning marijuana that is available, in spite of the horrendous ripping up of the family that has been caused by this "weed," I am disgusted everytime someone tries to decriminalize the offense. I cannot tell you how often I have heard teen-agers say that they would try it if only it were not considered a criminal offense.

The most shocking revelation of the abuse of drugs and the government's disregard for its people in the name of experimentation came in the form of a TV program that I first saw aired in January of 1979. It involved the CIA's interest in sexual behavior and how drugs could be used to manipulate people. Aptly titled, "Mission: Mind Control," it had been compiled through a series of interviews conducted by ABC correspondent Paul Altmeyer.

Dr. Timothy Leary said the CIA had funded, supported and encouraged hundreds of young psychiatrists to experiment with LSD—the fallout being they took the drug themselves. "These people were working on it, and the CIA helped them to do that particular work," admitted John Gittinger, former chief psychologist of the CIA. Gittinger justified the CIA's participation by saying researchers would have been doing the research regardless of who their sponsor was.

Even more horrendous was the fact that private citizens had unwittingly been used in the CIA experiment with devastating aftermaths, including death.

"I know that some of the studies which the CIA supported used as subjects people who later became strong proselytizers of LSD. So in that sense, I think it did sustain the perpetuation of the drug, and it's rather ironic, isn't it?" remarked Dr. Sidney Cohen, one of the country's foremost authorities on LSD.

8.

Face-to-Face With Harder Drugs

After waiting for what seemed an interminably long time for clearance from the Attorney General's office, I was finally given the green light to go and talk intimately to young people who had been on the ground floor in the early '60s, when the drug culture was beginning to make its mark on society.

The now young adults to whom I spoke came from what was classified as a "poor" family by a young man named Carlos, to Valerie's home, where there were maids to do everything. Their median age was 29. Among them were high-school dropouts and college graduates. All of the seven volunteers with whom I spoke, with the exception of one, had begun their drug addiction with marijuana. All had become heroin addicts and were now on the methadone treatment program. The program had been designed in desperation to keep the heroin addict's victims from more muggings, burglaries, rapes and even murders.

I had been cautioned by drug authorities that these subjects might not be reliable—it was not inconceivable that they would lie to me. So it was with great care that I prepared a questionnaire for each one to fill out before the rap sessions began. Then, in two different sessions—one in the morning, another in the evening—I questioned each person separately and then rechecked, for a third time, their answers in a group discussion. With the exception of one, whom I shall call Brian, I found them poignantly candid. Only the things that Brian told me that checked out are printed here.

It was Brian who still wore the garb of the '60s, as if he had been caught in a time warp. His dress was faded, skin-tight blue jeans.

On his cap of the same material was lettered his mode of travel: Harley-Davidson. His long blond hair and beard were scraggly. With financially affluent parents, he had spurned society to serve King Heroin. A brain that had been wasted time and again on drugs was able to recite a lengthy poem by that title for me from memory. "King Heroin" told of the hell, the torture and the magnetic pull of a drug that rules supreme once ingested.

When I met Brian, he had gone on and off heroin for the seventh time. The last time he had stayed away from the powerful drug for twenty-two months. When I asked him why he had gone back to it after such a long span of time, he said, salaciously, "Because I love it!"

An addict, he said, is always searching to recreate the unmatchable high of his first experience. The closest Brian ever came to his first experience, he said, "was when I overdosed. That's the way dope is. It's so bad."

In his young lifetime, Brian has carried a pistol, joined a nationally known terrorist motorcycle gang, and done it all in the way of drugs . . . sniffing cocaine, "shooting up," marijuana, heroin, you name it. He has been in and out of jail for everything from robbery to violating parole. His first wife was also, in his words, "a dope fiend." When she became pregnant, Brian went off drugs. When she lost the baby, Brian went back to "shootin' dope."

"And once you shoot dope, you're gonna go back the second time," he said. "You're not just gonna do it once, I don't care who you are." There was a time that Brian went through $6,000 in three months to feed his habit.

Prior to coming to the methadone treatment center, Brian's weight had dropped over a hundred pounds. "I almost died," he said.

Brian began his addiction when he was 9 years old. He was hustling drugs at 11.

Prior to his first encounter with jail, he said he "was shootin' as much dope as I wanted to. I'd speedball all day. So when I got busted, I got busted with seven pounds of speed, a quarter ounce of pure meth [methadone], and I knew I was goin' away for a l-o-n-g time."

Less than twenty-four hours after he was jailed, Brian began suffering from withdrawal. "And they come and took me out and took me to the nut house. The only way I can tell ya how I felt, it's like somebody's inside ya tryin' to cut his way out. You throw up, you're hot, cold. You curse yourself and say you'll never do it again. As soon as you get through it, you're gonna do it."

When Brian was 16, he was walking home from school, thinking

all the while about the drug he would take when he got home. Sitting
on the front steps of his house, his head resting on crossed arms, was
his friend, "Gumps," another drug user. Brian recalled going up to
his friend, pushing him and saying, "Hey! Gumps! What's hap-
penin'?" "Gumps" keeled over. "He was dead from overdosing."
Showing no remorse, Brian said, "He got greedy and he shot my
dope and he OD'd."

As to why young people take to drugs, Brian said, "This is how I
seen it happen. Their older brothers or their peers get high, so
naturally they want to be cool. So usually they start out with smokin'
a little bit of pot. Then maybe in a month—maybe the next day, you
can't put any time on it—however his peers go he'll follow, to be
accepted. I would say eight out of ten cases, they'll go on to harder
drugs."

At one point Brian worked in a drug rehabilitation center, going
around to schools talking to kids about drugs and their harmful
effects. "You know what kicks my ass?" he asks of me without
waiting for a reply. "Every one of these movies [in schools], there
was only one movie that was any good. It was called *Not Me*. It
showed a junkie, a thirteen-year-old Spanish kid in Harlem. It
showed what he did, how he lived every day and how he died at fifteen. He overdosed. But all the other movies I seen might show a girl
freakin' out—but it's so flimsy and fake. Understand what I'm
sayin'?"

Brian's relationship with his parents has, predictably, taken a
nose dive. "I try to avoid seein' my parents," he said. "They blow
everything completely out of proportion."

I suggest that perhaps they have been through too much, with
three children on drugs. "Really, yeah," he says, admitting that
trust, broken so many times, is difficult to repair. "They treat me
with less respect than they would a dog," he says. "If I have to keep
payin' for the rest of my life for things I've done to 'em there's no
reason to go around there—because it makes the situation worse.

"You know who they fight with the most?" he says of parents in
general who have children on drugs. "Themselves. 'Where did I go
wrong?' I had a beautiful home," he says with sadness in his voice. "I
never had to want anything in my life." And then, recovering, he
says staunchly: "But I wouldn't live there and I wouldn't be around
them because my parents' morals and the way they look at life is so
different from the way I do."

Given a choice of his lifestyle or that of his parents—knowing now
what drugs have put him through—I ask him if he thinks his
parents' lifestyle is really all that bad. "Oh, everything that my

parents ever told me in life, I don't think they ever told me anything wrong at all. I just couldn't listen to anything they had to say. I wouldn't. I refused to. And that's where I was wrong . . . all my life."

Brian has come from a home where his father, back when Brian was growing up, was making $30,000 a year. He slips in and out of street language. He can either speak "straight" English or "street" English. As the interview progresses, his English improves.

"Parents nowadays happen to be too into themselves," he says, assessing the parent world. "They're so worried about the money. Back in the old days you didn't have TV—you had to do everything as a unit—as a family. Everybody shared and worked together. You don't have this unity in the nowadays. Usually if you go to a home where there's ten or twelve kids, there still is, 'cause they're poor and they do have time for one another."

Brian has remarried, but he and his wife are pretty much loners. A social life, he said, is taboo, "because if I go around anybody that gets high, it's gonna pull me down." This is his first time at the methadone treatment center, he says.

The methadone treatment center where we have all converged to talk is on a street mixed with small, rundown businesses and equally rundown and faded houses. The location: Anywhere, U.S.A. I have changed all of the real names of those young people with whom I spoke, because, in truth, they could be anyone's children.

After talking face-to-face for hours on end with these seven drug users, I shall never again believe that an untrained person can tell a drug user by looking into his eyes, unless the person is obviously high. Nor will I ever again believe that you can spot a drug user by the way he/she dresses. Other than Brian, all were neatly dressed— what my generation would call the clean-cut look. It frightened me not a little that I would have welcomed any of these people, on face value, into my home as friends of my own children.

All of them had the physical beauty that shines only in youth. At one point, during the evening session, I had had it. I felt so ripped up from the human waste of it all, I simply broke down and cried. "You're all beautiful looking!" I said. "Dear God in heaven, you all look healthier than I do!" They grew quiet as I fumbled in my handbag for a tissue to wipe my eyes. And then, after a few minutes of stilted silence, one of them said: "You should have seen us when we first came here." They told of emaciated bodies that had been wasted on drugs, like a cancer.

I was amazed to find that these people came every morning to the methadone clinic for their "treatment." For an hour and a half, the drug is dispensed. It was a source of complaint for them. They all live with the daily worry that they will either not get to the clinic on time, or will not get to a phone to give the required half-hour notice that they will be late. If they fail to show or notify the clinic, the doors are locked and they do without. "They had one guy here, he's in prison now for murder because he didn't get his medicine. He went to another town with a gun and killed somebody," said Jerry, who lives with Lola and her 6-year-old son.

Another source of complaint is that the counselors are not former drug users. Lola said she felt it was just a job for most of them. "They're not really into your problems or [don't] care about your feelings," she said.

As the hands on the clock turn, I am educated. I learn that a "shooting gallery" is a far cry from my definition. The best shooting galleries on the East Coast, they tell me, are found in Harlem. They are usually located in abandoned buildings. "It's dark," said Lola. "You can't see where you're going, so you can get ripped off and killed, or anything." Lola sits close to Jerry. They are trying to make it back together. Both are detoxifying—trying to get off methadone by gradually cutting down on their dosages under the clinic's supervision.

Shooting galleries are so well known in the drug culture, they tell me, it is not unusual to see people from your home town there. They tell me of people who have been shooting dope for so long their arms are five times normal size. They talk of arms covered with blisters, oozing pus, and, in the summertime, flies sticking to the arm. And they tell of the frustration of veins that have collapsed and of not being able to get a "hit" any more. All agree that it is not unusual to have a gun put to your head in the shooting gallery by another addict. "Ah, some of the things in Harlem you wouldn't believe. Well, they're buildings that aren't fit for animals, much less people," said Lola.

Lola, once married, started her drug addiction because she was dating a dealer. "I didn't know he was a dealer at the time I met him," she says. He gave her her first drug. When her habit grew too expensive for him, he dumped her, and she was on her way. Three years later she remarried another drug pusher. When he was finally caught by the law, with jail pending, he began to take drugs himself. "I think I hated him more," said Lola, "because when two people are shootin' up, you can't get along. You only got enough money to get one bag. One bag and two people . . . it's not enough. So he's gotta have it and you've gotta have it."

Lola, who has been on the methadone treatment program for two years, said if people really love you, they won't stand for your taking drugs. Turning to Jerry, who has been on the program for nine years, she said, "If I were to cop one time, it would be over between us. And I think that if somebody really cares for you, they're not going to go along with it."

Lola's habit, before going on methadone, was costly. She recalled getting a $1,500 settlement on a car accident, "and within a week it was gone." She had rented a hotel room and gone on a drug binge.

Lola was eventually caught by the law for using stolen credit cards to pay for her drugs. She had come from a broken home with a mother that she says was always "confused."

Four times Lola was hospitalized for her addiction. "My mom would put me in. They put you in the psychiatric ward. I couldn't last any more than two days. I just signed myself out." One of her hospital stays was precipitated by shooting up, which resulted in a huge and swollen arm. That time, she spent four weeks in the hospital. But she didn't do without drugs. "I had people slippin' me stuff in the hospital," she said.

Lola says her mother did a lot of crying over her. "She tried to get me the best doctor. One doctor was charging $75 a day— psychiatrist. She tried her best, but she knew I was gonna do what I wanted to do." Rehabilitation, she said, is not something you can force someone into.

All except Brian felt that the drug movies shown in the schools not only told the kids what to use but how to use it, and Lola pointed up the fact that they will stimulate kids who are already using drugs— to make them want to "get it off," as she put it. "Just talking about it," she said, creates the desire, "or seeing a movie. I know that when I went to see *Lady Sings the Blues*, just seein' her get off—each time I saw her get off I wanted to go and do it more and more and more. I went back and saw the movie thirteen times."

Jerry, who came from a family of comfortable means, began his addiction in the U.S. Army with marijuana. After a dozen times, he jumped right to heroin. He was finally "busted" in civilian life. Missing from home for a week, he was afraid to call home and tell his father he was in jail. The night he was scheduled to go to court, the authorities called his parents. "When I went to court, they were there," he said of his parents. "My father started hollering and cursing."

This was the second time that Jerry had been "busted." His parents knew he was taking drugs. He had stolen from them many times for drugs. They had tried to help him by sending him to a therapeutic community, but he ran away. In 1969 he heard of the methadone clinics. His father offered to pay his rent for him if he moved out of the house. He did. All along, he said, "it was a hassle for my parents."

At the clinic he met Lola. Both were in the detoxification program when they spoke with me. They both told me that the first rule, if one is to successfully detoxify, is to stay away from anyone who even smokes marijuana.

When Lola's 6-year-old son came home from school one day with drug-related material that had been handed out in school, a pamphlet called "A Reason for Tears," he asked Lola point-blank if she had ever put a needle in her arm. She told him she had. She said she was sure, young as he was, that he had memories of her preparing her arm for the needle.

"It's amazing," said Jerry. "We cannot talk about drugs. It creates feelings." Lola agreed. She said even when she looks back at the type of company she once kept, and she and Jerry talk about it, they have to stop. "I look at him and I know—cut it—don't say any more," she said.

"The book that her son brought home," said Jerry, "I couldn't look at it."

While both are looking forward to being drug-free, Lola says there is an underlying fear of failure. "I've seen so many people come back to this clinic that detoxed, and it scares me to think," she said. Lola and Jerry have also cut out the morning breakfast gathering with the other methadone patients. "We had to cut that loose. New people come in here and it's still, the whole conversation, methadone, heroin, pills. The pills are still bein' sold, you're still gettin' high," said Lola.

Sam is late in joining the group; he has been consulting with the clinic psychiatrist. Sam didn't start on drugs until he was twenty, although his wife and brother used drugs. At a party one night where everybody was getting high, Sam decided to try drugs too.

Eventually, he and his wife were arrested together on burglary charges. Agreeing with the others, Sam says of the films in the schools: "It gives them ideas, really."

Divorced from his first wife, Sam is now separated from his second wife, also a heroin addict. They are, he said, working at getting their marriage back together. His three children have spent years going from one foster home to another. After not seeing his oldest child for three years, he learned that his 12-year-old son has started smoking marijuana. It upsets him. "Do you wanna wind up like me?" he asked the boy.

In the morning session I spoke with two young men, Carlos and Tom, and a young woman, whom I shall call Valerie. Carlos is as tall and handsome as Tom, only he has jet-black hair and Tom's hair is blond. Both are neatly and conservatively dressed. Valerie, her dark hair curling at the temples, is braless under a gauze blouse. She wears rings on almost every finger. These three began their drug experiences to either feel they "belonged" or as an "experience." Each, eventually, in different time spans, moved on to harder drugs.

Valerie confesses that her two children, six and nine, are both into marijuana. "They smoke pot. They know it's illegal. They know it's a secret. They don't tell anybody," she says.

When her children ask her about heroin, she tells them it just makes her sleepy. They have, she says, seen her smoke coke (cocaine). "And I've told them that it's just a drug that keeps me awake when I'm driving." Valerie's is the only voice that is thick and slurred, and in her own language, she seems to be "out of it" to me. She sometimes has difficulty in following what we are talking about.

When I point out to her that researchers find that 90 percent of the hard-drug users started on marijuana, she says, "I never used to believe that. I believe that now. I never used to believe that," she repeats, twice. "I was of the generation, I guess, where it originally became popular," she said with a New York accent. "And I bought it like crazy. After I saw myself into harder drugs I saw there was definitely a pattern. I was always looking to get high. I was always looking to change my consciousness. The transgression is your body gets used to the drug—you have to keep doing more and more in order to get high on it. All it does is keep your body straight."

Knowing that, I ask her why she would permit her children to smoke pot. "Maybe because they're seeing it now, they won't smoke it when they get older," she reasons. Valerie still does not get the point. I am beside myself thinking about her children. I drop it.

All those I spoke with said the main reasons they all went on to harder drugs was twofold: The high is not enough, and once they become involved in the drug culture, other drugs become available.

"I killed my parents," said Carlos. "I stuck 'em with bills and stole from 'em." Carlos was the only one who had put down "poor" beside his parents' income. Only after talking with him for a long period of time did the realization come to him that it was he and his drugs that sent them into the depths of poverty. "I wanted to buy a car and I needed a co-signer," he said. "And from using drugs every day I couldn't hold a job. When I lost my job they had to pay off the car loan or they'd lose their credit or their house. It happened more than once," he says. In fact, three times they put their misplaced trust back in Carlos and co-signed for cars. "I guess they didn't learn their lesson," he says. "You keep promising and promising your parents: This time it'll be different," he said.

Of parents Tom said, "It seems they're paying more than we're paying. It's hurtin' them more than it's hurtin' us."

"Still, to this day," said Carlos, "I'm twenty-eight years old and they co-signed for the car sittin' out front . . . really."

Tom had been gearing his life to go into the priesthood until he tangled with drugs. When his parents found out he was involved with drugs, they offered to get help for him. "And after the part where they seen that I was so stubborn, that I didn't want any help, they just completely lost all sort of trust in me, you know?" This is Tom's second try at the methadone treatment center. "I didn't want to tell them I was back on the stuff again because of what I put 'em through the first time." Eventually he shared his misery with his parents. "I just broke down."

Carlos' parents never knew he was on drugs until he was arrested. "My mother cried," he said. "My father seemed like he lost all respect for me. And my mother, she tried to help; you know, comfort me, do anything she could for me. She still does. Maybe she feels it was her fault that I turned out this way, I don't know. It wasn't their fault. They brought me up fine," he said.

While Valerie and Carlos were never thrown out of the house by their parents, Tom said, "I wasn't thrown out, but I was asked to leave." All three of them laugh at the way Tom has tried to add dignity to the action. "And then told to come back when I was better," he adds.

Carlos said he still does not get along with his father, but of his mother, he says, "Oh, my mother, I'd do anything in the world for her!" Carlos tells me he is married now and has a young son himself. Backtracking, he says, "Don't get me wrong, I love my father."

"I can understand why some parents can throw their kids out," said Valerie. "I can understand why some kids' parents beat their kids, too."

"Well, I'll tell you one thing," said Carlos. "If I had all the money my parents borrowed for me to get me out of debt and all the cars they've paid for, I wouldn't have to work no more. That's how much I cost them."

Carlos is also on his second try at detoxifying. His first attempt lasted only three months. "I couldn't fit into society. I went right back to dope. And three, four months after that, I'm right back here." There is an aching drive, he says, for the drug. "Ya gotta get it, ya gotta get it, ya gotta get it. This won't leave you alone."

"Your body's craving it," said Valerie. "You're physically ill. You can't function."

Both Carlos and Tom would "cop" drugs. This, they tell me, means going to a pusher, buying a lot of drugs, selling some and keeping some for yourself. I suggest they could really help the police by telling them where they get their drugs. They tell me it is the law of the streets not to "rat."

All three talk of "ratters" who have been beaten up or murdered. "Yeah," said Tom. "I know people that have been murdered because they dimed somebody out just to beat a court case."

"A junkie always has at least four, five connections," said Carlos. "Because if he only had one, he'd never make it. If he couldn't find that one person, then he's done for the rest of the day."

These three also speak of Harlem. "You'd have to get a black person to take you to Harlem," said Carlos. Harlem drugs, they all agree, are cheaper. "What you'd pay fifty-five dollars for there, you'd pay a hundred twenty-five here," said Carlos.

They, too, talked about how sick they would get from the "Jones." The "Jones," explained Tom, "is when you get strung out and you stop takin' dope for like maybe a day—withdrawal symptoms. Your nose might run and you sweat cold sweats." "It could be ninety degrees out, you're freezing," said Valerie. "That's where you get to the point that you want to get a gun and just stick somebody up, take their money. You don't care," said Carlos.

When they talk of how expensive the habit is to maintain, Valerie says, "Three weeks in August, when my husband and I were in between programs (drug therapy) we spent fifteen hundred dollars."

"Where you gonna get a hundred dollars a day if you don't steal it?" said Carlos. "I gotta admit it, I've beaten my friends, you know, taken their money, told them I'd cop for them and come back with nothin'." Facing the friend with empty hands after he has put up the money for the drugs, said Carlos, does not bring fear to the heart of the addict. "You're thinkin' of gettin' off; you're not thinkin' of gettin' beat up or anything. You just lie," he said, and tell the "friend" you were either beaten up or a policeman stopped you and you threw the drugs out of the car window. "You gotta be a good liar and a good con artist," he said.

Valerie has resigned herself to the fact that unless there is a miracle cure, she will be on some form of drugs for the rest of her life. My heart sinks when I think of the two young children that are in her custody. "In my mind, right now, I think so. I think I'm gonna be a lifer, either on methadone or something," she admits.

Talking about his recent marriage, Carlos says his wife knew he was on heroin when she agreed to marry him. He promised her he would give it up. His wife's parents, he says, call him a bum. "And they won't help us and they won't lend us a dime," he says bitterly. But his parents continue to help, even buying them groceries. His mother, he tells me, thought that when he married he would turn over a new leaf. That didn't happen.

"I used to literally take the food off the kitchen table to go buy," he said. And then he grew quiet. "My mother, I guess she really spoiled me. I can always turn to her and get whatever I want. And I knew that when I was on the streets." He tells me he doesn't think this is a good thing. "That's why I'm tryin' to tell my wife to get away from that with our son . . . that he can't have anything he wants, you know?"

Valerie chimes in. She never had any responsibility, she says. There was even a maid to make her bed when she was growing up. By now Valerie is really "out of it." While she agrees with Carlos, she mumbles that she doesn't really know what she has agreed to.

Reflecting on all the cars his father has paid off for him, Carlos tells me his father never owned a car of his own.

Of these seven young adults, all told me that they thought stopping the traffic of drugs was "impossible." In fact, Lola said, "The best stuff I ever had was from a mayor of a small town." They all talk about organized crime and corrupt politicians and policemen. All told stories about themselves or people they knew who were arrested for drug possession only to have the police report read a lesser amount of drugs than what was actually confiscated from them.

All have found it difficult to hold down a steady job. One of the seven admitted to having over twenty jobs since he began taking drugs.

"I've got a Rolls-Royce in that arm," Tom said, pointing to his right arm. "And ten-thousand-dollar Cadillacs in that arm."

All but Valerie—who moves in a circle of fast and affluent friends, and who says: "I never had to struggle for money. It was always available to me"—have obtained the money for drugs by stealing from their parents and "dealin'" and "stealin'" in a variety of other ways. They tell me of some of their scams.

Lola explained the process called "noting." "You go into a store or a gas station. You give 'em a dollar bill and you tell 'em you gave 'em a twenty. And you get 'em all confused and they get to the point where they really think you gave 'em a twenty, and they give you change back."

Another means for obtaining cash, they said, was to obtain check-cashing cards at a variety of supermarkets. They would spend a whole day taking around worthless checks—writing each one in the amount of $50, to each supermarket. They could, on a good day, net $500.

It was credit cards that eventually did Lola in with the law. Before she got into drugs she said, "I had never, never even stole a candy bar in my whole life."

She and another girl had another supermarket scam cooked up. They would go, in separate cars, to the supermarket and head for the meat counter, looking for the shopper who had left her handbag in the shopping cart. Lola would engage the shopper in conversation as her girl friend made off with the handbag. By the time the woman noticed that her handbag was missing, Lola's accomplice had long since left the store. Lola would console the woman and then leave. Before the police, banks, or credit companies could be notified, the two were out on a spending spree, making purchases they could "fence," and cashing any checks that were in the handbag. "We would do that," said Lola, "several times a week."

Sam and his first wife worked "shorts." Shorts, he explained, were breaking into cars to take anything of value that was left in them. "I was from New York, so we used to go down near Macy's, Gimbel's. People put their cameras and things in the car and we'd take anything out of the cars that was worth money. We'd go up Fifth Avenue," he said, using coat hangers in broad daylight to gain entry to the vehicles. "You'd be surprised at how many people leave their wallets in the glove compartment," he said of the theatre district in New York City.

Sam also burglarized apartments. While he was "burglarizin'," he said his wife was "hustlin'." "She would go up to a room with a guy, and when he got undressed or went into the bathroom, she'd grab his wallet and split."

Did she prostitute? "I don't say she never delivered. But sometimes, if you don't have to deliver, you don't deliver," said Sam.

I ask all of them to review their lives—to look at what they have done to their parents and themselves. I also ask them what advice they have for parents who have children on drugs.

Brian says he thinks parents should spend more time with their children and not chase money. Jerry said he thought parents give their kids too much money—it makes them a mark for pushers. All agreed that parents do not keep enough of a check on their children's whereabouts and friends.

Recalling that his parents bailed him out of jail twice, Jerry said,

"My ideas have changed." He now thinks the child must be made accountable the first time around. "Many times," he said wistfully, "I wish we had been livin' back when we didn't have what we have now." Reflecting on the time his father cursed him out, he says he wishes he had listened. All seven said kids are left alone too much today.

Carlos, whose parents paid for a host of cars for him, said it was a mistake. "After the first time, I wouldn't have done it again," he says, if he were the parent.

Valerie said she was never given any responsibility—she thinks that's wrong. But both Valerie and Brian seem to love their drugs too much to ever give them up.

Lola and Jerry are trying to lead a new, drug-free life, even though the odds are against them and it is all uphill. Just talking to me has obviously been taxing for them.

Sam still has a lot of personal problems to clear up, he says, but he is proud that he has held his present job for five years now.

Tom and Carlos are articulate when they look back on their lives and assess them. Both said if they could turn back the clock, they would never have taken that first drag of a marijuana joint. "I would have stayed in high school and gone to college and made something of myself," said Tom. Carlos says he wishes his father had not just beaten him up once, but instead "stayed on it," and made "sure I wasn't hangin' around with those people again." If his son ever smokes marijuana, he said, he would "beat his rear end."

All seven cried for more parental discipline. "I think, instead of bailin' 'em out more, I think you should, no matter what shame it might bring to parents, they should let 'em like if they get arrested, let 'em spend some time in jail, instead of bailin' 'em out all the time. Let 'em take the rap," said Tom. I say it would be a tough thing for a parent to do, but Carlos counters by saying, "It could be the best lesson for them."

It was a consensus that a parent was truly expressing his love for a child by making him stand on his own two feet and facing punishment for his actions—that interfering in any way only perpetuated the problem.

When Tom asked me at the close of the morning session what my book was going to be about, I told him it's what parents are up against today in trying to raise good children. Carlos shook his head and said, "It's a big battle."

9.

They'll Drink to That!

Steadily rising into yet another full-blown disastrous epidemic is the teen-age consumption of alcohol.

The youth of our country prefers a mixed drink. The recipe: Alcohol and "wheels." It is spelling doom for our youth, who are dying on the nation's highways in ever increasing numbers.

By 1974 alcohol and our youth began making headlines. It was estimated that 1.1 million kids between the ages of 12 and 17 had serious drinking problems. The figures showed up in a report to Congress by the National Institute of Alcohol Abuse and Alcoholism.

The following year auto accidents accounted for 65 percent of all accidental deaths among youths aged 15 to 24. By 1976 the number of deaths by auto accident among that same age group climbed to 24,000 fatalities. By 1977 the FBI reported that 155,693 persons under age 21 had been arrested for driving under the influence of alcohol.

However, prior to the lowering of the drinking age in many states, which followed the lowering of the voting age, there were only 17,807 persons in that age group arrested for the same offense.

We see these kids hoisting cases of beer onto their shoulders at various resort spots, and we see the litter of their beer cans strewn all over the nation's highways, city streets and suburban lawns. Could this be the same generation that screams so loudly about ecology while tossing nonbiodegradable beer cans out of car windows?

By 1978 the American teen-ager was turning more and more to

alcohol. Three out of four teen-agers were drinking alcohol and one of every five was getting drunk at least once a month.

All too often the car that was given as a graduation gift turned into a coffin, as did the family car when teen-agers, drinking, were behind the wheel.

Our teen-agers were already "flying high" on drugs, alcohol and sex, but it wasn't enough—they also had to fly on "wheels," and doting parents saw to it that many of their children had that privilege, even if it strained the budget—high insurance costs be damned.

Kids today are also coming to school stoned—not only on drugs, but on alcohol. They have been caught sneaking bottles into washrooms and drinking during the school day.

One high school pupil sent his solution to the problem to a local newspaper: "I think the answer would be better education in the schools." Unaccustomed to turning to the home or the parents, almost like a knee-jerk reaction, the student was running once again to one of his "surrogate parents" for the answer . . . the schools.

Many believe the older teen-ager is supplying the younger children with alcohol—for a price. Counselors who work with teen-age alcoholics say that the young drinkers defy definition. Once again they come equally from stable homes, broken homes, families with and without histories of alcoholism, from the slums and from the affluent sections of the country.

They were, said many of the experts, drinking because of their inability to cope with emotional and psychological problems . . . problems that every parent knows are more prevalent in today's atmosphere of unprecedented permissiveness.

Canadian children and their parents are going through the same traumas. In 1978 the rate of alcohol-related accidents among teen-agers dramatically increased there also.

In New Jersey, Senator Lee Laskin began pushing to raise the drinking age back up to 21, citing the thousands of licenses lost, the grim head-on collisions and fiery crashes typical of alcohol-related accidents. "Twice as many young people below 21 die in car accidents than die of cancer, diabetes, or the other serious problems we hear about every day," he wrote in an article explaining his move. He touched too on the people who were fed up with the rising number of drunk and disorderly youths.

"Parents," wrote Senator Laskin, "unable to stop the flow of alcohol to their children, feel powerless. The legislature seemed to forget when it lowered the drinking age that it is tough enough being a parent today. Instead, they had to let experience show us that teen-age drinking makes it even more difficult for caring parents to guide their offspring."

As support to raise the drinking age back to 21 rose, the chief lobbyist for the New Jersey Licensed Beverage Association, Sal Pollina, said he didn't think it would curtail teen-age drinking. His solution to the problem seems stupid, when one looks at the undernourished curriculum and atmosphere of today's public schools. But Pollina insisted the solution was better educational programs on alcoholism in the schools.

There is absolutely no way, Mr. Pollina, that schools—which cannot keep order in the classroom, whose philosophy is that the individual child must make up his own mind as to what his actions on this planet will be, that there is no right or wrong—can do anything about the drinking problem.

Where do your sympathies lie, Mr. Lobbyist? Do you really care about the bodies of the kids that are rolling around on the highways until they are inert, or do you care more about the big bucks the kids are bringing in for the alcohol they buy?

Parents may not be able to keep their kids from drinking, but they certainly can keep them from driving. Perhaps the answer is in raising the driving age. Parents still hold the keys when it comes to driving for minors. If they would but insist that their sons and daughters work and earn the money for their own car and its insurance, it could have a great impact on this problem.

When I was working as a reporter for the *Philadelphia Bulletin*, a woman who was on one of the local governing bodies in a township that I covered called me one day to talk about some pending legislation but went on to tell me she was "very upset" with her son, a freshman at a college facility located less than two miles from her home.

Her son had been driving to college every day using her car. He had also been drinking. Finally he was picked up for drunken driving. The local chief of police called this mother into his headquarters, told her he could rightfully revoke her son's driver's license, but because he knew her, her son would only receive a warning. She told me she was so glad that he was let off, otherwise he would not be able to continue college without his driver's license.

"Couldn't he have a friend pick him up, or better yet, couldn't he walk to school?" I suggested. "If he really wants that education, he'll make those concessions," I said.

"Oh, I wouldn't want him to do that!" she said. "It's too far for him to walk. And you know how these kids are," she went on; "once they get wheels under them, they don't want to give them up. Besides, all the kids that he knows drive to college."

I could understand her not wanting her son to have a strike against him on his first charge, but I also told her that it was a serious offense. She asked me how I would handle it. I told her I would have told my son that his license was revoked, keeping the license myself, and then I would have read him the riot act. I told her I would make him walk to school or ride a bicycle. It was my feeling that to let such a serious infraction go by with no punishment was a disservice to her son and to any person who might be driving on the road should it happen again. She told me in no uncertain terms that my methods were "too harsh."

Several weeks later I read in the local newspaper that her son had been involved in a serious accident, along with some of his teen-age friends. He had been drinking and driving again.

I also know of another family where the son was exceeding the speed limit on a major highway by over 40 mph. He was not drinking; he just wanted to "open up the car and see how fast it would go." At the hearing before the local judge, one known for his toughness, the judge refused the 19-year-old any chance to alibi for his actions. While the judge went to a leisurely lunch, he had an officer of the court put the boy in a holding cell with a homosexual who told the boy to prepare himself for homosexual activity if he was going to stay in jail.

When the judge's lunch was over and court recessed, he recalled the boy to the courtroom. As he stood before the judge, visibly shaken, he was told his license was being revoked for three months. The judge also levied a heavy fine and gave him a stern lecture.

This boy's parents, on learning what their son had done, had already taken away the privilege of driving their car. Since he had none of his own, he had already been grounded. They also dropped him immediately from their insurance coverage, telling him he had violated a privilege. When he returned home from court that evening, he told his parents what the judge had done.

The parents then wrote a letter of thanks to the judge for enforcing the actions they had also deplored and acted upon.

One of the state troopers who witnessed the courtroom incident said, "The judge thought he looked like a good kid, but he wanted to be sure he never did anything like that again." Commenting on the visibly shaken youth's appearance, he said, "I don't think that kid will ever so much as jaywalk."

A year later I got in touch with this young man's mother to see how it had all turned out. She told me that he had gone to work, saved and bought his own car. His insurance, she said, because of his speeding record, was almost four times the previous cost of insuring him. And he was paying for that too. She said while he had been driving their new car, he now settled for a ten-year-old model. It was all he could afford. But, she said, he takes great pride in it.

"When he was using our car, he put several dents in it and never kept it clean," she said. "It was a wreck when we finally claimed it back as our own. I can't thank that judge enough for backing us up as parents. If our son had been given the easy way out, he would never have learned. He was beginning to get wild. That calmed him down. I can't thank that judge enough."

I opt on the side of the parents who stood firm in refusing to cater to a child who was running amok on the highways just for his own pleasure and daring. People say that "scare" tactics don't work. Well, they do. If you have no fear of recrimination for your actions, then you are without respect for yourself and anyone around you.

As it stands now, Montana and Michigan voters have approved proposals to raise the minimum drinking age from 18 to 19 and from 18 to 21, respectively. While the New Jersey senate passed a bill that would raise the state's drinking age from 18 to 19, Assemblyman William Dowd (R., Monmouth) said at the conclusion of the hearings: "Drinking is a right, not a privilege, and one who proposes to take that right away from a class of people has the burden of proof to make sure we're doing the right thing."

The kids'll drink to that, Assemblyman Dowd!

10.

Moms and Dads

Many poems and songs have been written about them; special days are set apart each year to honor them. They are called mom and dad.

Philoprogenitiveness. It's a $50 million word, or a William Buckley word. It means, simply, love of offspring.

If parents today have been guilty of one thing in the last two decades, it has been too much philoprogenitiveness—overindulgence. Their motto was: "I want them to have everything I never had."

Their predecessors said it differently: "I want them to do better than we did. If they behave, and try to help themselves, they'll make it. We will give them our love."

Each group of parents wanted something better for their children, but their philosophies were worlds apart. Where prior generations of parents encouraged their children to strive, themselves, for the better life, the modern parent would hand everything to the child, trying to anticipate in many instances the child's every want and desire. It happened for the first time in poor, middle-class and upper middle-class homes almost simultaneously.

Parents, for the most part, stopped behaving like parents. Today it is the kids in almost every home who to some degree pull the strings, as parents dance like puppets for their children. It is, indeed, role reversal at its worst. In many cases these parents got only what they deserved. Not only do their children not love them, they no longer have any respect for them.

What is the image of today's teen-ager? What words spring

immediately to mind? Selfishness, sassiness, spoiled, sexuality, stoned. They are youth so inarticulate they have to use sign language in the form of the "finger" or verbal vulgarities to tell somebody off.

We know from headlines every day that they are breaking records daily in contracting social diseases, sleeping around, getting pregnant, taking drugs, loving suggestive lyrics and movies, and using and abusing anyone they can to get their own way.

With inflated grades and diluted basics in the public schools, one wonders if, without the computerized cash registers or battery-operated calculators, most of our youth could subtract $1.11 from $5 and come up with the right answer.

Parents have told me of children who think nothing of coming in and devouring half of a pie that was intended for dinner dessert for the whole family; of empty cereal boxes left in the cupboard by children who are too lazy to throw the container out; of insisting on brand-name jeans to wear, or nothing—they issue the ultimatum and cowering parents give in. Of calls from college on Mother's Day—collect, even though the parents have provided the child with an allowance. It is a picture of a modern-day parasite, of children who think nothing of wasting parents' hard-earned money on colleges they are "bored" with. Or presenting their parents with a 4.0 average only to have them find out that the enviable score average was achieved because their son or daughter dropped every subject but one during the term—all that money wasted for subjects that will have to be made up. Of college graduates who don't want to pay back the money they borrowed from the government who initially financed their academic venture. The signs of selfishness are endless.

I have also found that the child is constantly putting the parent into a crisis type of situation, and I have found parents all too often helping to feather the unbearable beds their children are lying in, by stepping in, catering to the child, softening the blow or stopping it altogether, instead of making the child suffer any consequences for his or her own unsuitable actions. It is but another crutch offered by parents that perpetuates adolescence.

Where did it all begin? The first time a child asked for a cookie before dinner and mother said emphatically, "No," and then, "Well, OK, but only one!"

By the time they are teen-agers, it is no longer a cookie they are asking for, it is "wheels," their favorite expression for a car.

A father told me the following true story about his young

daughter. For months, prior to his daughter's 17th birthday, mother, father and daughter looked for a suitable car as a birthday present. "We spent a thousand dollars on the car," he said. It was one that his daughter had picked out herself. Along with buying the car for her, the parents bought new tires and paid for the car insurance.

"But here's the story now," he said. "This is a stick-shift car. She doesn't drive a stick-shift car." He said he felt too involved with his daughter to teach her, so he offered to send her to a driving school. "She didn't want that," he said. Her girl friends offered to teach her to drive the car. "She didn't want that!" he said. "Finally, after the car is here now—licensed, insurance, everything, she doesn't want this car," he said with annoyance.

Disgusted, he told his daughter to sell the car and list her private phone number in the advertisement. ("She has her own phone," he says.) "And you don't have a car," he told her, "unless you pay for it totally, out of your own money." It sounds as if this father has made a good and sound decision concerning his ungrateful daughter. But this was not the end of the tale.

"Then she's not driving?" I asked. He falters, and then says, "She takes my wife's car now because she can't drive the stick-shift car." He gets a minus in my book.

As we continue to talk, he mumbles that maybe, after all, he'll buy her a car with an automatic transmission. I give him another minus. "Listen," he says to me, "I feel guilty about having my daughter sell the car. Listen, I'm thinking: Sell the car and go buy one with an automatic transmission." I tell him I think he will regret it.

So he says, "Nah! No way! I'm going to keep the money. I'll do that. Obviously I have overdone it with her. We're so easy with kids. There's no appreciation if you get something for nothing. It's always been that way," he says.

As I draft the final copy of this book, I give him a call to see how it has all turned out. His daughter has not gotten another car, but he is still thinking about it. He is going to issue her an ultimatum. The ultimatum? A new car or college. And yes, she does continue to drive her mother's car. In the end, she got what she wanted, even if it meant taking it from her mother.

Another father was charged with beating up the school superintendent because his daughter failed an exam and was not allowed to graduate. He did this in full view of the entire senior class during graduation ceremonies. Explaining to the police why he beat up the superintendent, he said he had spent $3,000 on graduation presents for his daughter and could not see why she could not graduate. Three thousand dollars for a high school graduation gift!

While mothers have traditionally had a way of smoothing over family troubles, many mothers today, I have found, have acquiesced to the children over the wishes of the father to the detriment of the child.

"I've had incidents where I would feel that if my wife stood with me on these things, these kids might have a rougher time. But my wife ameliorates it and we do come to compromises," a father told me. "I don't like the compromises," he said. The longer he talked with me, the more I realized that it was not compromise he was talking about, but total abdication to the child's wants.

"I didn't believe in simple things like allowance, you know. My wife felt like they [the children] should have an allowance. But I don't subscribe to that. But," he sighs, "those are the compromises that we've made about that. As far as giving kids too much money, I don't think a child is entitled to 'get' anything. I see it the other way—that he should be giving things to his parents if they are exemplary parents. He should show his appreciation to them."

Thinking for a while before he made the next confession, he pointed out the "used" feelings many parents have today. It also points up for me just how much these children think of their interceding mother.

"It is very, very unnerving to have to remind your children that it's their mother's birthday. Now that's the kind of thing all children knew—when their mother's birthday was, and they dreamed about it. They wanted to do something for Mamma. Today they let it go by—and you think: My God! How could they do that? But my wife says, 'You shouldn't make them.' I say, my God, I'm gonna make them pay attention to their mother's birthday, because if they don't appreciate it, I appreciate it!"

There is no question in my mind that the mother today, more than ever in recent history, has helped to do her child in by permitting him to bargain, nag, cajole, pester and whine until he gets his own way. It is an area in which today's child is very proficient. Parents may think they can "buy" the child, but in the end they will lose them.

I cannot tell you how many parents complain about the condition teen-agers leave the family car in (usually the mother's). They complain about everything from candy wrappers and beer cans to leftovers from a fast food chain littering the interior. If the teen-ager dents or scratches the car, the child is often able to convince the parents they should be glad it wasn't a major accident.

I rarely hear the parent insist that the child wash and clean up the car. I rarely hear of a parent relinquishing that child's privilege by asking him to turn in the car keys if he doesn't shape up. How many homes would fall in and out of warfare if parents told their children: 1. They could no longer use their parents' car? 2. They would have to pay for their own insurance, car repairs, and wash and clean the car once a week? 3. They could not drive at all until they saved their own money for a car?

Parents in the suburbs reason that a youngster needs "wheels" because there is no mass transportation. But this argument does not really hold water. One only needs to go into any major city to see that parking, which has always been at a premium, is now an impossibility due to the teen-age population that has its own cars. Even when public transportation is available, it is shunned for the most part by today's teen-ager. Parents also reason that their children must get to work. Heaven forbid if you were to suggest they ride a bicycle or even a moped. That simply isn't "cool" enough for most of them. Even where children have school buses, they shun them for "wheels." Just look at the parking lot of any high school.

For their "giving" moods, parents are now paying an even higher toll—this time in the way of physical abuse. In New York a man was sentenced to ninety days in jail for beating his mother. The mother wept openly in court when her son was sentenced for beating and robbing her. She had hoped he would stop the beatings without having to be jailed.

This is a growing phenomenon. An 81-year-old Chicago man was chained to a radiator by his 19-year-old daughter. She had stolen $2,300 from him. He refused to press charges.

Another 19-year-old was arrested for hitting and robbing his mother. As police led him away he said, "Aw, come on, Ma. I only hit you a couple of times."

Sue Bienemann, director of a new coalition of eighteen Pennsylvania projects for battered wives, commenting on this relatively new outbreak, said that mothers want to protect their children. Therefore they are often reluctant to disclose that their children beat them. "They don't want to get them into trouble," she said.

One of every ten children in the U.S. attacks his parents each year with everything from fists and clubs to knives and guns, according to a nationwide survey of Americans conducted by Dr. Richard Gelles, a University of Rhode Island sociologist.

This episode—told to me with great trepidation, and only with my consent that no names would be used—highlights my observation that mothers will go to unhealthy lengths to spare their children their due.

Mrs. Smith's 20-year-old son had left high school without graduating and obtained, in what seemed to her a remarkably short time, a job, a big and expensive car, and an equally expensive girl friend. This mother reasoned that her son was a good boy because he was working. She assumed he was paying off his car in installments. Like most mothers, she felt only pride that her son, who had been in and out of petty trouble all through high school, was finally making it in the working world.

However, she was to find out by telephone from the local sheriff that her son was in jail for transporting illegal drugs in his new and shiny car. Jumping to her son's defense, she asked the sheriff if there wasn't something she could do to keep him out of jail. The sheriff told her to come to his home that evening, and they would talk it over. That evening she met with him.

The next day she and her husband took out a loan for $1,200. Following the sheriff's instructions, she put $400 in each of three blank envelopes and took them personally to the sheriff's home.

When her son went before the local judge, he was found "not guilty." As he left the courtroom with his parents that day, his mother told me he had a smug look on his face and commented to his parents: "See? I have friends."

To this day this son's smug attitude and disrespect for his parents persists. They have never told him why he was judged "not guilty." His mother is still hanging in there, hoping, she told me, that he will eventually grow up. "I did the wrong thing, didn't I?" she asked me. I nodded my head in assent.

Mothers are the most loved because they martyr themselves for their children—however wrong the reasons. Drug users especially love mom, because she can always be counted on to give more chances than anyone else for redemption.

One New Jersey mom was given a suspended jail term for smuggling heroin in to her son when he was in a correctional institution. What they do in the name of love seems to know no bounds.

The public defender said to the judge hearing the case: "What you do to this mother means a thousand times more than what you do to him. Spare him the horror of going to bed in that hellhole knowing that his mother is locked up in another jail." Where was this son's concern for his mother when he asked her to smuggle drugs into jail for him?

The young man's mother, in tears, told the court: "I did it because he was in trouble and I didn't want him to get hurt or killed. I did it and it was wrong." She did not go to jail; however she suffered a nervous breakdown.

I thought back to my meeting with young people at the

methadone treatment center, and more poignantly, to Brian. I remembered that he told me that the first time he got out of jail on drug charges, his parents asked him to come home and try to straighten himself out. "And then my mother walked in the bathroom and I was shootin' dope and she started cryin' and I said, 'Look Ma, there's no reason to cry. I've been doin' this *so long*.' Those people [his parents]," he said, "you know, they've really been through a lot. Mom was always behind me. Even in jail she'd still write me and send me five or ten dollars. You know how moms are."

A group of mothers who had given too much to their drug-addicted children decided on a turnaround. Without any federal or state aid, they banded together to help themselves and their kids. Through trial and error, they found that by disengaging the parent from the crisis and making the child responsible for his actions, there were big dividends to be made.

Jim Nicholson wrote an article about these mothers for the *Philadelphia Daily News*.

At one time these mothers had carried their money around in their bras, or had walked from room to room in their own homes with their pocketbooks under their arms so their kids wouldn't steal their last penny from them for drugs. "Most of these kids were overprotected; they got too much," said one of the mothers whose son was successfully rehabilitated.

Their philosophy is shape up or ship out. They have thrown the stealing and abusive children out of the house, telling them they could only regain entry if they went to a drug rehabilitation center. These were the same kids who had cried to their mothers that if they didn't give them money they would be beaten up, or go to jail and perhaps fall prey to homosexual advances.

"We tell the parents to give their junkie child one choice—go to a rehabilitation program or stay on the street and drop dead," said another mother. "A mother isn't helping a child by supporting him while he or she is on drugs."

Realizing this is a wrenching experience for a mother, the mothers in the group tell new mothers who balk at the suggestion: "You don't love your child. You're helping his drug habit by keeping him home. He's out on the street laughing at you for being a sucker."

So adamant are the women in sticking to their method of solving their children's drug problems, they refuse to acquiesce when parents want to bring their drug addicted kids to the meetings. "No way," said one of the mothers. "We tell the mothers, you help your kid after you first help yourself. We are here for the parents, not the kids."

Ultimately they are there for the kids, and they have been successful with these tactics.

Other parents, who have vacillated for too long in every area that is upsetting the home today, find themselves little more than hostages—and the ransom demands made by their selfish, inconsiderate, amoral children are incredibly high mentally, physically, financially, morally.

Better to make a decision not to have the entire family suffer—to force the child into crisis, with a sink or swim attitude, or to let him take to the streets—than to wind up as Marilyn Dietl in Vermont did. With tears in her eyes, she told the judge that she took her 18-year-old daughter, Judy, for a drive in the family car and shot her to death to keep her from running away to become a prostitute.

The mother told the judge it all began when her daughter went away to college. She eventually became involved with a pimp and began her new and sordid life.

Once the decision to kill her daughter rather than let her lead such a life became paramount, Judy's mother said, "It was as if she was already dead. I felt so relieved she was safe." In spite of Judy screaming, "No, mama! No, mama!" Mrs. Dietl continued to fire the gun until her daughter's body was inert.

So disenchanted with today's youth are so many parents, that some are beginning to take advantage of a process called emancipation. It is a legal way of disavowing responsibility for your child's actions.

A mother who had tired of her son's behavior was able to convince a municipal judge to agree with her request that her 21-year-old son be sent to jail for stealing $1,800 worth of stereo equipment from his own brothers

The mother told the judge she "could not tolerate the kind of life my son is putting me through." She said he had a record of juvenile arrests for glue-sniffing and intoxication.

So it is that still more phenomena spin off from all that has been done to our youth by a society that has encouraged them to "do their own thing," and by parents who are going against their own upbringing by engaging in illegal actions for their children. What kind of a world are we living in with parents killing their children, parents throwing their children out of their homes?

A wise person once said that to spoil your child is to open the door and invite heartbreak to live in your home.

11.

Terror in the Streets

Not only are the children of our country committing crimes in their own homes, they have also taken to the streets, and the drug culture cannot be blamed for it all. What I have found again is the child who craves excitement, bent again on doing "his own thing" with no concern for his victims.

More than half of all serious crimes in the United States are committed by children 10 to 17 years old, and that includes murder, rape, aggravated assault, robbery, burglary and car theft. Youth crime is rising twice as fast as adult crime today. From 1970 to 1975 girl offenders increased 40 percent.

In a recent year United States schoolchildren committed 100 murders, 9,000 rapes and 12,000 armed robberies, exhibiting an almost depraved indifference to human life in the process.

"Vandalism is the way juveniles vent their frustrations on society. A lot of kids are spoiled and get everything they want," said Police Chief John Baugher, of Maple Shade, N.J.

But the crimes of our children go far beyond vandalism. Three youths—two of them 16, one 17—armed with handguns, were arrested for raping and sexually assaulting a woman and her 8- and 10-year-old sons. One of the young intruders attempted to sodomize the 10-year-old and failed, according to police, but another youth forced the 8-year-old boy to perform oral sex on him.

Another 17-year-old, in confessing to robbing and slaying two elderly women, said he did it because "I couldn't give my baby nothin' for Christmas."

We are all too familiar with our youth who prey on the elderly—

beating them up and grabbing their wallets and purses. But when I read a report on a new "sport" taking place in Miami, Fla., I was outraged. Teen-agers were trying to scare the elderly by coming at them at top speed on bicycles or in cars and then laughing as they missed their petrified victims by inches.

Another sign of our times is the printed messages posted in many store windows stating that no more than three children under the age of 18 are permitted in the store at one time. How sad that so many of our young people are so feared and hated.

More and more authorities are coming to recognize that the juveniles who commit crimes are neither necessarily disadvantaged children nor children from a poor home environment. Instead, they are coming in increasing numbers from what they call "good homes."

"The statistics on juvenile delinquency are alarming and growing worse," said John Rector, administrator of the Law Enforcement Assistance Adminstration of the U.S. Justice Department. Arrests in the 15-to-18-year-old bracket, he said, have tripled since 1963.

The cost of the entire juvenile justice system is now costing the taxpayer $1 billion a year and is increasing at the rate of $50 million a year.

Brenda Spencer, 16, took a .22-calibre rifle and some 500 rounds of ammunition, reportedly given to her for Christmas by her father—an audio-visual specialist at San Diego State University—and fired forty shots into a crowded school yard. Dead were the principal and a custodian, and wounded were nine students and a policeman. "I just did it for the fun of it. I just don't like Mondays," she told reporters. Brenda also bragged that she had been in trouble before for burglary and shoplifting, "but it never went to court. I always got off."

So critical has the situation become that we see the so-called "liberal" turning conservative. What was it that Philadelphia's former mayor Frank Rizzo said? A conservative is a liberal who just got mugged.

Former New Jersey Supreme Court Justice Richard J. Hughes is a case in point. "I've become a hawk on juvenile violence. I don't like little old ladies getting battered around by teen-age thugs. I used to be a great reformer on this issue," Hughes said. "I used to say, 'Give the kids a break; don't ruin their lives.' But I've turned into a hawk on this issue," he repeated.

Unquestionably the courts have, in too many cases, been lenient with juvenile offenders. A 15-year-old boy who held a gun three inches from a subway rider's temple, squeezed the trigger and killed the man was later picked up for pickpocketing and shooting another man in the back. He was also charged with beating up a psychiatrist and spitting on an assistant district attorney while his lawyer was trying to get the judge to release him in the custody of his mother. (Good old mom.) Explaining the killings the youth's cousin said, "He got a kick out of blowing them away."

Police say their hands are tied in many cases. And they are absolutely right. When residents in one city asked for more foot patrols to deal with underage drinking, drugs, vandalism, curfew violations, urinating in the open, and open sex, a police captain said that the underage drinkers cannot be arrested if the beer is not in their hands when the police arrive.

Kids are street- and law-smart today. They put down the beer can, drop the drugs, sometimes throwing them arrogantly on the ground right at the officer's feet, with no attempt to conceal their actions. Because the policeman cannot say the substance was found on the person, possession is impossible to prove.

Commenting on the courts, one East Coast police chief said that police are "disgusted." He said officers "go to court, spend their time and nothing is done. They [juveniles] are spanked and let go. It's all a waste of time."

Dr. Thomas Brooks, a school psychologist, is another liberal turned around. Dr. Brooks cited homes where both parents work and fail to put much control on their children, schools, and a society that says, "do your thing," as some of the causes of the problem. "There has been a liberal establishment rampant in the country for ten years now. This so-called progressive-liberal philosophy is bankrupt. As an ex-liberal myself, I feel we have to get more conservative," he said.

So frustrated is society with the actions of our youth, that various areas of the country are taking legal action by passing ordinances requiring parents to pay for the vandalism perpetrated by their children.

"We must get after the parents of these children," said Police Chief Joseph Leedom of Evesham, N.J., who favored such legislation. "You can't dump the responsibility on the schools or the police if the kids are not getting any ideas about values at home," he said.

Often no matter how good and moral and caring parents are, their children will turn on them, too. I think of John White, the Cleveland, Ohio, father who was shot to death in a contract killing that police said his 14-year-old daughter and 17-year-old son had confessed to setting up with a 19-year-old. "He wouldn't let us do anything we wanted, like smoke pot," a police detective—who asked not to be named—quoted the children as saying. Police said the children paid the 19-year-old $60 to kill their father.

The detective said investigators have no doubt the two were involved in the killing. "You could call it a confession if you want to," he said. "They told police the whole story of what they did, how it happened, how they used the money and credit cards. They told the whole thing."

Besides objecting to his children smoking pot, the father also opposed his children's desire to quit school, and set an evening curfew for them.

In a meeting with parents, Burlington County, N.J., Court Judge Anthony Tunney told parents why he opposed a law that would make the parent responsible for the child. "Some kids might like nothing better than to embarrass or bankrupt that SOB sitting in the front room with the cigar and would not be deterred from delinquent actions by that type of a law.

"I am convinced," said Judge Tunney, "you must be a super parent to be able to deal with the problems of today."

12.

Working Mothers

What will salve the conscience of the working mother who leaves behind everyone from infant to teen-ager? A slogan: "It's the quality, not the quantity, of time spent with the child that counts." Baloney!

I came from a home with a working mother and obviously I myself am a working mother . . . so what am I doing downing the cause?

When I was a child of 12, my mother worked because my relatively young father had such a debilitating stroke it rendered him incapacitated for the rest of his life. The difference for my sisters and me was that our father was always there when we got home from school.

As for my own working, I have been fortunate to be in a business where I can work around my family. So I don't really object to the working mother 100 percent, but I do object to the mother who leaves her infant or toddler with relative strangers and her teen-ager alone.

A recent study demonstrates the vital part parental care plays in a child's development. Children from the age of 12 to 17 were observed over a five-year period. At the conclusion of the study, the evidence proved to be "overwhelming" that the 17-year-olds who were friendly, more balanced, effective and valued by others were those whose parents had spent the most time with them.

"Let the fathers share in the home work load," scream the working mothers. A good father always has! He may not scrub the floors every week or prepare the dinner each night, but he will mow the lawn, do some remodeling, work on the car to save some money, paint the house, drive the children to various activities, and help with the homework.

But when both parents are working at full-time jobs, no one can ever convince me that you do not have two exasperated, tired, grouchy, irritable people with little time to spend with their children. If anything, working mothers are becoming aware of just how tired their husbands have felt lo these many years when they finished up their working day. When mother was home on a daily basis, the atmosphere for the entire family simply had to be more relaxed and enjoyable.

Schools today, for emergency purposes, list not only the parents' names and telephone numbers; because so many families have both parents out in the working world, the top listing is often a neighbor who is not working.

Many times over the years I have gone to school to pick up sick and feverish children who could no longer make it through the school day. They were the children of parents who were both out working. There were times when the fathers and mothers, both of whom I called at work, asked me if I minded keeping the child until they got home. They didn't think their boss would let them leave work early—they were simply piled up with work and couldn't get home—I understood, didn't I? Well there were times when I didn't, because the child was so sick. It broke up a few acquaintances. Naturally I did everything I could to make the child comfortable, but the real look of relief only came to his face when his parent came for him.

I clearly remember one icy, snow-covered afternoon when one of our sons came home from his kindergarten class and asked if he could bring his little classmate home. She had forgotten her house key and was locked out. I said, "Sure."

My son and I walked a distance to the child's house. No one was at home and the doors were locked. We found her outside, knee-deep in snow, her teeth chattering. Her snow-encrusted mittens pinned to her sleeves hung below her little red hands. She really did not know me, and told me her parents said she wasn't allowed to go with strangers. The thought of staying inside our house spread panic on her face. It was a dilemma. It would be four and a half hours before anyone would come home. If she stayed out in the whipping wind, she would suffer. If I brought her home, I would be going against the wise teachings of her parents. Besides, she wasn't coming with me.

Only with a lot of coaxing did she agree to let me make her a cup of hot cocoa, if she would agree to at least stand in our garage. The door had to be left open on her insistence.

I watched this child grow and her parents prosper financially. They owned big cars, a boat, threw expensive parties, bought their own business. Her name was always on the honor roll at school. As she grew she was shuttled from one after-school activity to another—always with no one at home when the school day ended. She got pregnant, married, and dropped out of school . . . all in her sixteenth year of life.

That incident happened over ten years ago. Today there are many such children. They are called the "Latchkey Children," for the house key that dangles from a string or a ribbon around their necks. Fifteen million mothers are working today. One-third have children under age 6, one-third have children from 6 to 12 and one-third have children 12 to 18.

Capitalizing on this growing trend, *McCall's* magazine, in October of '78, debuted a publication entitled *Working Mother*.

Recognizing the emptiness, the void and the problems that become a part of the lives of children who come home from school to a house devoid of parents, a Willingboro, N.J., minister, the Rev. Kent Pipes of the Presbyterian Church, is trying to do something about it. He is setting up a pilot program to have nondenominational centers provide planned and supervised activities for these children until their parents return from work. He has received a $15,000 two-year grant to develop this after-school day-care program for children from the first to the seventh grade.

"The empty home," he said, makes youngsters "open targets for drugs, alcohol, sexual abuse."

"What are the kids doing now? It's anybody's guess," he said. While his intentions are good, if his program is successful it just means that we will have more surrogate parents involved in the rearing of children.

Rev. Pipes might not know what the kids are doing in the interim, but a truant officer, who went to a home looking for a high-school girl, had his knock on the door answered by a teen-ager who was dressed only in her underclothing. He found her and her friends partying. No parents were at home.

In a recent nationwide study of the sex life of unmarried girls 15 to 19, the Pill and working mothers were cited as contributing to the sexual freedom of the young. Many feel the prostitute has been replaced by the girl next door.

Dr. Melvin Zelnik and Dr. John F. Kantner of Johns Hopkins University, who conducted a study on teen-agers and their sex lives, said many of the teen-agers are saying, "My house or yours?" since no one is home to check on them during the day. They can, and do, said the doctors, have intercourse in the luxury of their own homes. "It's got a refrigerator, a bedroom, radio, hi-fi, and the price is right," the doctors said.

For many parents Get Set Day Care, established by the federal government in 1969, seemed an answer. It was funded by federal, state and local school monies. Its main purpose was to provide dawn-to-dusk child care, freeing parents to work, look for work, or learn to work.

When parents found out in 1973 that there would be a cutback in the federal funds for day-care centers, they protested by taking their children to work with them. And nationwide, mothers with their children traveled to the nation's capital to take part in a protest rally outside HEW offices.

In a 163-page report that was the result of government auditors interviewing some sixty-seven randomly selected Get Set families in 1976, it was found that "many of these parents used Get Set services for the education and development of their children, rather than for work-related reasons," that "there was little improvement in income and financial stability of parents who continued working," and that "Get Set had little effect on the unemployment status of welfare recipients using the service."

They also found $5.9 million in "questionable expenditures" that included children who were clearly ineligible, and money appropriated for larger numbers of children than were actually enrolled.

By 1976 the cost to the taxpayer to provide one child with Get Set services was estimated at more than $4,300 annually per child compared to $1,674 for educating a child in a public school.

William Prosser, chairman of a federal interagency task force, estimated that total public and private spending on Day Care was $10 billion, with $2.5 billion in federal money and $6 billion from parents, and the rest from state and local governments.

The average cost per child in a nonprofit center is about $175 per month, and in those run for profit, about $125. The magazine *Everybody's Money* estimates that about one-third of all American children spend from ten to thirty or more hours a week in such facilities.

In Philadelphia's Get Set day-care centers, almost a third of the children enrolled were supposed to be eliminated from the program unless their parents found work or enrolled in work-training programs. A government audit accused the school district of wasting $12.2 million since 1975 by mismanaging Get Set funds.

President Carter's welfare bill in 1978 set aside a minimum of $400 million in the jobs section to provide day-care for children of low-income working mothers.

Children today go to various types of day-care centers—some nonprofit, others for profit. The centers range from no regulations for a woman who cares for children in her home to questionable regulations. In one daily local newspaper that we subscribe to, under Situations Wanted, over 75 percent of the ads I counted were people offering to watch other people's children.

Spencer Rich of the *Washington Post*, writing about a private home that furnished day-care to children of working mothers, pointed out that there was one attendant in charge of sixteen children. He noted that half a dozen children died when a fire broke out. In another day-care facility, he said an infant sleeping on a couch, because no crib was available, was struck in the head and killed when an older child dropped or swung a heavy toy.

In another newspaper was the account of a nursery school owner who disciplined a child less than 2 years of age by putting tabasco sauce on his tongue. The owner said it was only a tiny drop and she had the parents' permission to do it.

When inspectors from the Bureau of Licensing, State Department of Human Services, paid an unannounced visit to that nursery school after receiving complaints, they found no sheets or blankets provided for the youngsters. While a complaint was registered that youngsters under the age of 2 were being given improper care at the facility, a spokesman for the bureau said the law they operated under "does not give us jurisdiction over children under two years of age."

I remember stopping at a woman's house when I was soliciting door-to-door contributions for the Heart Fund. She asked me to come in while she looked for her pocketbook. "These kids aren't all mine," she said of the half-dozen preschoolers. She was a private day-care center unto herself. The house was bedlam!

When one toddler clung to her slacks, she ripped his hand away and then told me she was "out of it, thank God," because she had taken Valium. At that time I was not that well acquainted with the tranquilizer, so what she said didn't really register with me. It is estimated today that about 5 million children go to the homes of other people who watch them for a fee.

With both parents working today, what will become of daytime parent-teacher conferences? Who will go to see the children in the school play? Who will take care of them when they suddenly feel ill?

Who will listen to them when they come bursting through the front door to an empty house? Who won't be too tired to help them with their personal problems? Who will wait up to see that they are not breaking curfew? Who can really dig to see why our troubled children are so troubled? Who?

For the last decade, government statistics have recorded a steady rise in the number of women entering the job market. The reasons most often cited are: that women are having fewer children, they have become more career-oriented, and inflation.

Just because women are having fewer children does not negate the responsibility someone must take for those children—are they of lesser worth than those children who come from a large family?

I know too many families where both parents are out working. Oh they complain of inflation, but their kids start out with a minibike and graduate to a moped or motorcycle (even when they're too young to be licensed for it, parents let them drive it in their back yard). Parents see to it that they get expensive cars and have a CB that is guaranteed to infringe on a neighbor's TV or stereo reception; they send them to Europe on class trips, and then off to a college of their choice. These same families, still complaining of inflation, have three and four cars, expensive vacations, and try to deny their children nothing that involves money.

To compensate for the lack of attention and time they can give the child, they dole out material things instead, all the time complaining about the high cost of living and how their children are turning out so badly.

There are many keys to the Kingdom but I don't think both parents working full-time will necessarily unlock the door to a better life for their children or will solve the problems society is inundated with.

"A lot of children are frankly neglected by parents who give them too much freedom and independence," said Dr. John Bowlby, the keynote speaker at a conference of child-care experts in Canada. Dr. Bowlby cited such things as children's camps, day-care centers and baby-sitters who only put more of a gulf between the child and the parent, producing, he said, "conditions unfavorable to family living," and has had disastrous consequences for many children.

13.

"Talking" T-Shirts

Somebody said, "You are what you eat," which makes me wonder if our children are a reflection of what they wear. It appears to me that the popular T-shirt worn by many teen-agers is but another badge that blares out a philosophy they have adopted. These are the "message" T-shirts. The raunchier, the more suggestive the lettering, the prouder the wearer.

After going through a summer of idly and occasionally watching teen-agers gather at a concession that was set up for the sole purpose of printing anything (and I do mean anything!) that the buyer wanted printed on the T-shirt, I had had it.

And so, when I was browsing around a department store that my family frequents and pulled out from a circular rack what I thought was a black blouse, I flew into a rage. What I had mistaken for a blouse was a T-shirt with the wording "I am a Virgin" on the front, and on the back, the update: "This is an old T-shirt," I wrinkled it up in a ball, threw it on the floor, kicked it under the rack, and headed for the manager's office.

On the way I encountered a man in a business suit who wore the label of the store on his lapel. Livid with rage, I spouted out my outrage over finding this type of a T-shirt in a store I and my family had patronized for years—a store where families freely brought their youngsters in to shop.

The man with the store label shifted uncomfortably as I vented my spleen on him. The manager was not in, he said, but he would tell him of my complaint when he returned to the store.

I went immediately to the checkout line, aborting my shopping trip. In my mind, I swore that I would turn in my charge if something wasn't done about those T-shirts. As I was standing in line, the smoke pouring out of my ears, a man tapped me on the shoulder and said, "Ma'am, would you be willing to give us your name, address and telephone number in relation to your complaint?" Would I! I was ready to go to the executive offices to register my complaint I was so furious.

That evening I received a call from the manager of the store. I railed on about a decent family store carrying this type of merchandise. I told him if I ever found such trash there again, I would turn in my charge. He not only thanked me, he told me the complaint would be carried higher, lamenting that such clothing even existed. He said if there were only more parents complaining, it would eventually freeze these items out of every store. A father himself, he said, "It's so hard to raise good kids today." It is a phrase I have heard over and over again from parents.

I can truly say that I have never seen that type of T-shirt in that particular department store since. And I thank them from all of us who care about our children.

The following summer I was shopping in the once fashionable area of Chestnut Street in downtown Philadelphia. I stepped into a shoe store to try on a pair of shoes I had seen in the window. I could hardly believe my eyes. Stapled to one entire wall of the shoe store were lettered T-shirts that said everything from "Smile if you're horny," to "Eat at the Y" (a number that showed a torso clad in tight jeans whose creases formed a "Y" at the crotch), to others that are not fit to repeat.

One parent, whom I talked with while putting this book together, reacted when I told him that today's children are called by some the "ME generation." Sheepishly, he said, "Guess what my son's new T-shirt says on it?" "What?" I asked. "In capital letters," he responded nervously, "it says just one word: 'ME.'"

It's not enough that these kids buy these obscene and suggestive T-shirts, but they brazenly wear them to school. And because the courts and students' rights uphold the youngsters' right to wear whatever they please, no disciplinary action can take place.

A student who felt very strongly on this issue took pen in hand and wrote his feelings to the editor of a newspaper. Reflecting once more the "do your own thing" philosophy, he said, in part, "I disapprove of students not being allowed to wear T-shirts which have any kind of saying on them." Everybody, he continued, "has his own opinion."

But most of all I love the following true story of how a coach in

Fort Lauderdale, Fla., handled a young man who was wearing a T-shirt that said, "Help stamp out virginity." It was reprinted in Ann Landers' column:

After striking up a conversation with the young man who was wearing the T-shirt, the coach said, "Save that T-shirt. When you feel that you no longer want to wear it, wrap it up and put it away in a drawer. Maybe in three or four years you'll meet a girl and fall in love and get married. If you're lucky, within a few years you'll have children. Maybe you'll be fortunate enough to be blessed with a little girl. She'll be the apple of your eye. That little girl will grow up. Then one day you and her mother will be anxiously awaiting her first date. It probably will be some awkward, gangling kid you never saw before. That's the time, my friend, for you to go to the drawer, unwrap the T-shirt, and hand it to the kid so he can share your philosophy."

14.

The Runaways and the Castaways

You see them hitchhiking along the major arteries all over the country, usually with nothing more than a knapsack on their young backs. They go singly and in pairs, many of them shivering in clothing too light for the season. Some look disheveled and dirty. These are the runaways who have left home of their own accord, and the castaways, those whose parents have cast them out of their homes because they can no longer tolerate their new lifestyles. A quarter of a million teenagers a year run away from home.

Many will become involved, if they are not already, with the drug culture and prostitution, stealing, mugging. Some will fall victim to rape and murder. Nationally, more girls than boys run away from home.

There are some 10 million women with tranquilizer and alcohol addiction today. The National Institute of Drug Abuse in Washington puts some of the blame on their runaway children.

Who can forget the heartrending story of 15-year-old runaway Mary Vincent, who became the victim of a rapist who chopped off her forearms and left her for dead. Mary, like so many other teenagers, ran away simply because of "a few problems with my family." After treatment, Mary dispensed advice to her peers. "Don't run away from home. I learned the hard way."

To learn more about the runaway and the castaway, I traveled to YES, an acronym for Youth Emergency Service, a runaway shelter for kids up to 18 years of age.

YES was opened during the Bicentennial year in Philadelphia. By its second birthday it was threatened with bankruptcy when its treasurer embezzled nearly all of its funds. YES was bailed out by a $149,000 federal grant and survived.

Under his rumpled, navy-blue wool shirt, John Adams, the assistant director of YES, wore a T-shirt with the lettering: "YES—A friend in Philadelphia." The day I spoke with him, his offices reeked with the chemicals used by an exterminator. "We don't go around with a butterfly net and pick the kids off the streets as some of the parents have accused us," said Adams.

I tell him that maybe parents feel the "butterfly net" comes in the form of social services groups, radio and TV spots, and flyers, all telling the child that he can find bed and food at these shelters. If they didn't exist, maybe the kids would try to iron out the problems they are having with their parents.

Adams concedes that in some cases that could be a possibility, but he says, "In other cases the kids would be dead in an alley."

Shelters across the country, he said, are unofficially allied. There is work afoot for a central office that would join the various services, but he said they must proceed with caution. "I think in the early sixties there was a push for government to do this, and this, and this . . . to provide all these services, because all the services are needed. But," he warned, "you have to consider who is going to provide the services and what is the consequence of those providing you the service."

YES is not funded, as many runaway homes are, through HEW, he says. It is currently being funded by the Law Enforcement Assistant Agency as a crime prevention measure.

Since they have been operating, YES has seen an average of 900 youths a year. With an open-door policy (as most are), most runaways, he says, stay seven days. "If they don't like the service, they can leave," said Adams. "They can leave at three in the morning if they want."

The problem YES deals with most frequently, said Adams, "would come in the area of just disagreement with the family about the process of the family." Those disagreements, he said, cover "not being able to have their friends over, drug and alcohol situations [which he said can involve the parent or the child], school problems, grades." I had been told earlier that there is always a large influx at YES at report card time.

Today's adolescent, he said, lacks the training and maturity to deal with the problems and "doesn't particularly like the reaction of an authority figure. Then you've got the problem," he said.

While drug and alcohol problems are seen frequently at YES, Adams said these two substances often will eventually become the problem itself. "A lot of those things are symptoms. Alcohol unfortunately, and drugs, from symptoms tend to become their own problem."

Symptoms of what? "Mostly symptoms of the fact that the process of the family isn't working for them." The family isn't working today, said Adams, often for two economic reasons: low employment and economic pressure in one group and affluence in the other, where, he said, parents are out "hustling" all the time. "We get those parents quite a bit, calling us up. They say, 'My kid couldn't have run away. He's got everything!' They got a sailboat and a car in the driveway," he said. What parents don't have, he added, is the realization that the major part of their lives is revolving purely around economics.

I ask him if one of the problems is that kids today have too many choices, which totally confuse them when they are pressured to make up their own minds. "There are a lot of choices," he agrees. "The choices are not always ones they can relate to. The choices are often foisted upon them, too."

It is the adults of the society, he says, who decide what is best for kids. This, he feels, makes kids rebel. They are unable to take direction or advice from an authoritative figure. "But the idea that somebody else can make a decision for you," he tells the kids at YES, "you have to accept that to a certain extent." He said they are more likely to accept it if they are permitted to join in that process.

"All the time," said Adams, they see runaway girls who are pregnant and don't want to tell their parents of their condition. Here again the young person is given more "choices," but Adams calls it "options counseling."

"We will sometimes coerce and push hard, but we will never do it to a point where we are fooling or deluding the youth—or making the decision for her." Should the decision be abortion, they will refer the young girl to an abortion agency.

Adams said YES gives the child twenty-four hours "to sort things out" or to aid them in sorting things out, before parents must be notified. Other runaway shelters, he said, will give the kids up to seventy-two hours without parental notification.

Adams says YES encourages youngsters to return home. They will bring in families, he said, so the kids "see what the contractual basis of the return home is."

"For sure," Adams said, more parents are throwing their children out of the house and more kids are running away from home at earlier ages.

Who, Adams wonders aloud, puts such pressures on kids for sexual freedom?

The runaway shelter is a relatively new concept, coming into being in the last decade or so. YES is still in its infancy. In its first annual report, dated 1976–77, YES saw 945 youths. Roughly one-third had come from out of the state. One hundred and ten were either listed as abused or neglected children. The highest figure was listed simply under runaways—407.

Years ago many a child might have entertained the idea of running away, and some did it. But they would more than likely go to a relative's house, a friend's house, or walk around the block until they cooled off. Today they know they can go cross-country and their "relative" Uncle Sam will dig into the pockets of the parents to provide this service.

Since many runaway homes work with an open-door policy, which means the child can leave at will, it is not inconceivable that a child could stay from one to three days to "refuel" before he hitchhikes to the next runaway shelter, traveling hundreds of miles without being forced to notify his parents. If the child is in a vindictive mood, the parents will be the ones to lose sleep and worry while Uncle Sam finances the propulsion of their progeny clear across the country.

There have been cases recorded of the runaway child who will say he is abused. On close questioning and checking, he relents and confesses to making up the story as a bid for sympathy and justification of his behavior.

When the National Runaway Switchboard Service was a year old, HEW awarded a $152,080 grant to Metro-Help of Chicago to continue the project. The toll-free number, with round-the-clock volunteers manning the phones, has a list of two thousand referral services for our children. The average caller is 16. Only when the child is ready to let the parent know that he is alive and well, does the child call that number. The message is then relayed, second-hand, to the parents.

While parents are often relieved that their child is still alive and well, Freya, a switchboard volunteer for the service, said, "Others get very upset and want to know where the runaway is. But we aren't allowed to give that information."

Here the parents are treated as outsiders with no power over their minor child. Even columnist Dear Abby, widely read by our youth, writing about the runaway hotline, said: "There will be no lecturing or counseling. No attempt will be made to bring you home, regardless of your age."

It is an incredible age in which we are living—where Uncle Sam and many of his supported agencies take away the right of the parents to reconcile their differences and bring their child home again themselves. Again, the child is pulling the strings, and as a parent even of a minor child, you must be content with crumbs . . . a second-hand call to let you know your child is well . . . at least for now.

In a letter from HEW in response to inquiries on how much federal funding has been poured into yet another project that prevents the parents from acting in behalf of their minor child, I was informed that in the four-year period from 1975-78, in federal funding alone, the American taxpayer has shelled out $29,306,512 to these shelters. That figure excludes state funding and other sources of revenue.

This is your government at work against the parent once again. Instead, Uncle Sam has given the trump card to the child.

15.

Teachers' Unions Strengthen, Academics Weaken

The face of public education over the last two decades has been considerably and seriously altered, leaving its ugly imprint on our children too.

Charging the schools with academic malnutrition, parents are demanding more school discipline and a move back to the basics. "I'm fortunate enough to be able to give my daughters a quality education and we're certainly not turning out quality education in the public schools," said William Klenk, a mayoral candidate for the city of Philadelphia. Klenk was one of four candidates seeking the mayorality who are sending their children to private schools. Another candidate called the public schools "a mess."

Parents everywhere deplore and dread the annual interruptions of study as cordons of striking teachers leave the classrooms and abandon students and studies.

In a study headed by University of California (Los Angeles) Professor Alexander Astin, for the American Council on Education, it was discovered that freshmen arrived at college campuses in the fall of '78 with the highest high school averages ever—nearly one in four with an A average, compared with one in eight in 1969. Only 17.6 percent of today's freshmen had C averages in high school compared with 32.5 percent in 1969.

It all sounds as if the schools are doing an absolutely fantastic job academically—as if all the screaming about the public schools ignoring the basics is nothing more than hyper parents screaming about nothing. The bottom line of the study is another story.

"When these grade increases are considered in light of declining scores in college admissions tests," said Professor Astin, "it seems clear secondary schools' grading standards have been declining since the late 1960s." Put more simply, teachers are giving students inflated marks. It is but another smoke screen to get the public off their backs.

In May of 1978, HEW released yet another devastating figure concerning the world of academia—some 42 percent of 17-year-olds in America were illiterate when they graduated from high school.

After a full year of being hidden from the public's eye, although it had been distributed among government officials and educators, a study conducted by Frank Armbruster, a senior staff member of the Hudson Institute in New York, finally saw the light of print.

The study revealed that the decline in student achievement scores was more serious than had been reported to date. Armbruster called it "the tip of the iceberg." Discipline, he said, declined sharply in most schools and crime mounted; homework was being emphasized less and less, and more and more decisions were being left to the students, who were treated as adults although they were still children and adolescents.

Armbruster blamed the current educational debacle on a lack of classroom discipline, teacher laziness and the fad of relevance, open classrooms, new math, busing, and the acceptance of street language.

Parents are fed up with all of the new programs, the new breed of teacher, and the product the public schools are turning out. They hunger after a back-to-basics school. Only on parental insistence was such a school set up in Marin County, California. A few back-to-basics schools have shown up in a few other states.

So eager were California parents to sign their children into such a school, they slept willingly in sleeping bags to guarantee their children's registration. In the end, over a thousand children had been signed up for a school that could only accommodate four hundred.

The school had promised to stress not only the basics, but discipline, a dress code and parental involvement. In other words, it was a resurrection of a policy that had been practiced until twenty years ago by every single public school.

Not only have teachers been overloaded with teaching subjects that interfered with the basics, but they were becoming more militant. The National PTA, long used by the educational system as a rubber stamp of approval for "innovative" programs, is now seriously considering dropping the initial "T" for teacher from its name. Happy Fernandez, co-chairman of the Parents' Union for

Philadelphia public schools, said she does not believe teachers are as purely interested in education as they were in the era before the National Education Association became the menace it is today.

Once called the Sleeping Giant of organized labor, the NEA, with a total membership of 1.8 million, makes many quake as its rumblings are heard in the halls of Congress and the chambers of the Senate, and as it stoops to new lows as it enters the doorways of local public schools.

"An integral part of the NEA design is to siphon ever more control of public education from the grass roots to Washington," warned Rep. John Ashbrook (R., Ohio), "closer to its own powerful lobbying influence, farther from the parents and taxpayers who elect the school boards and pay the bills."

I believe Rep. Ashbrook's words are prophetic. We are fast heading for federal control of our schools and the total dissolution of local school boards who are already beset with complying with federal regulations that began in 1965 when Congress passed the Elementary and Secondary Act, which involved the federal government for the first time in the education of our children. If parents think it is tough getting through on a local level, can you imagine how impossible the Washington bureaucracy will be to crack?

By 1971 the NEA began organizing for political power. With an annual budget that is more than ten times that of the AFL-CIO and PAC (Political Action Committee), who can doubt that they are, indeed, a formidable threat? They are pouring their money into political campaigns and giving the politicians countless man hours.

Is the unionization of teachers paying off? In dividends! Educators were appearing at the Capitol in large numbers in 1975 for the enactment of a $7.9 billion appropriations bill. President Ford's veto of the bill was overridden 88–12 by the Senate.

The following month then Governor Milton Shapp of Pennsylvania signed into law a bill that boosted teacher pensions and liberalized benefits for employed teachers. The press hailed passage of the $24 million bill as a victory for the Pennsylvania State Education Association, the teachers' union that lobbied hard for the increases.

Politicians are not impervious to favors strewn in their paths, and they know when they "owe" one. It is commonly called a political payoff.

Following the reelection of N.J. Governor Brendan T. Byrne, who had received strong support from the teachers' union, Byrne commuted the jail sentences imposed on striking teachers, flying in the face of the justice meted out by Superior Court Judge Merritt Lane, Jr.

Back in 1971 at the hundred and third annual convention of the American Association of School Administrators, Mrs. Helen Bain, president of the NEA, was agitating for a reorganization of President Nixon's cabinet to include a Department of Education that would be separate from the Department of Health, Education and Welfare. The department would consolidate federal school programs and create a separate budget for education.

Nothing happened until Presidential candidate Jimmy Carter came out in favor of creating the new department, which would add a thirteenth Cabinet member, employ sixteen thousand and have a budget of $13.5 billion. Then, for the first time in its 102-year history, the all-powerful NEA gave its first Presidential endorsement to candidate Jimmy Carter. Now he has paid the piper. In the summer of 1979 the House approved, by a narrow margin, Carter's plan for the separate Department of Education. In the fall of 1979, with a swirl of his pen, Carter gave birth to the Department of Education.

Has the unionization of teachers and their subsequent political clout paid off? Not for our children.

The irascible Max Rafferty, educator and syndicated columnist who writes against the abominations of the present educational system, gives this advice:

"In any election year, the candidates endorsed by the teacher unions are the ones to vote against," and, "Anything the education Establishment ardently believes and aggressively pushes is always wrong."

16.

A Different Kind of Teacher

As standards of education fall, so apparently has the calibre of teacher in the public school system. What is tolerated in the name of teacher is nothing short of deplorable.

Of course there are still excellent teachers, but I fear the great majority no longer fall into that category. So horrendous is the school curriculum and the type of teacher, that many teachers are quitting or taking early retirement.

If a teacher swears, little is done about it because the student does the same himself, or at least tolerates it. All too often when a teacher is called down for conduct unbecoming a teacher, he is not fired, but another slot is found for him in the educational system.

We must remember that we are, in many cases, looking at the teachers who were the former children of the '60s. Like many of the young college students today who are studying for the teaching profession, they were taught in a permissive atmosphere. They refuse to feel thwarted by a system that used to insist on standards of behavior. They too are hell-bent on doing their own thing and in transferring this attitude to the students.

In Massachusetts parents were livid over allegations that at least five high school teachers provided female students liquor, marijuana and a trip to Bermuda for sex.

Mayor Jean Levesque, of Salem, Mass., said parties involving Salem High School students and teachers were discovered when a mother found the diary of her teen-age daughter after the girl had been in an auto accident. The story was broken by the *Salem Evening News*. The newspaper said the teachers kept an apartment outside of Salem for the sex parties.

In Pittsburgh, Pa., the Commonwealth Court upheld the Pittsburgh school board's firing of a former high school math teacher who allegedly boasted of his sexual conquests to students, provoked physical confrontations with them and used profanity. The three-judge panel reversed former Education Secretary John Pittinger's order to reinstate the teacher. Yes, if it had been left to members of the educational establishment, that teacher would have been reinstated.

It has become apparent that teachers feel their conduct outside of school should have no bearing on their teaching job. One such teacher told the judge her wife-swapping activities had nothing to do with her teaching competency.

But Superior Court Judge Charles H. Church did not see it her way. He refused to reinstate the teaching credentials of Elizabeth Pettit, a former instructor at an elementary school in Orange County. The judge made specific his reasons:

> The intimate and delicate relationship between teachers and students requires that teachers be held to standards of morality in their private lives that may not be required of others.

If teaching employment were to be based on Judge Church's wise words—across the board—one can only wonder how many teachers would be barred from this once honored profession.

Which brings me to the issue of the homosexual teacher. It is something I have agonized over for a long time before coming to a decision. I have known homosexuals intermittently for short periods throughout my life, having interviewed or worked with them. But after all of my research, after looking at the host of problems that exist in the schools today, at the "freedoms" that run rampant under the banner of "a free flow of ideas," I have come to the conclusion that a homosexual teacher is not the role model our already confused youth need.

There is a strong and growing opposition to gay rights. Voters in several states have gone four-square against the homosexuals. Commenting on this trend, Dr. Harold Voth, senior psychiatrist and psychoanalyst at the Menninger Foundation, said, "We are seeing a grassroots backlash against further moral decay in our society. People are now eager to take a stand against any form of unnatural behavior. They think there's been a sliding morality in this country that's gone too far. They want to draw the line."

I agree. Maybe we all had homosexual teachers when we were going to school, but we could only suspect, we could never be sure. If they seemed different we labeled them eccentric and let it go at that. Today, with the homosexual "out of the closet," and the topic freely discussed in schools, the picture of course is more volatile.

I know that Anita Bryant is right when she says the homosexual cannot reproduce so he/she must recruit. I am thinking back now to the time when a good friend of mine was a nurse at a fashionable summer camp for children in the Pocono Mountains. The weekend that my husband and I went to visit our friend, the camp was in turmoil. One of the young male counselors had admitted to having had homosexual relations with a ten-year-old boy—the son of an editor of a prominent metropolitan newspaper—only after he had been caught with the child. He was promptly fired but was given a clean reference to seek out another camp counseling job. Why the good reference? So it would not ruin the business of the camp where the incident took place. The same has happened in schools in the area of sexuality.

But the worst infraction of all was that the parents of this young boy would never be told their son had been accosted. They would never be given the opportunity to talk over the horrendous experience that had been foisted on their son. Did he return home a troubled youth? Did it affect his masculinity? Perhaps only he knows the answer to that.

In the news in recent times has been what has been called the worst mass murder of the century. It is the case involving a 36-year-old contractor named John W. Gacy, who, police have said, acknowledged killing up to thirty-two boys and young men after he lured them to his home to have sex with them.

Equally horrendous was the homosexual torture ring involving the bodies of twenty-seven young boys and men who were found in shallow graves in Houston, Texas.

The words of Anita Bryant ring true. Miss Bryant's conviction comes from her religious beliefs. I am not a student of the Bible, and therefore cannot evaluate the homosexual's activities on that high a plane. I can only go by hard, cold facts.

To bar avowed homosexual teachers from public-school classrooms became a cause in California's Nov. 7, 1978 general elections. While the measure failed, its sponsor, Senator John Briggs (R-Calif.), has vowed to introduce Proposition 6 again in 1980. Senator Briggs claims that there is a national movement afoot in the country to teach homosexuality as an alternative lifestyle, and that homosexuals were trying to put down the American family. One can only wonder just how much further down the American family can be pushed at this point in our history.

As part of a sex education package, homosexuals appeared before 13 to 15 year olds at San Francisco's Roosevelt Junior High School and described in graphic detail "how they do it," according to a piece written for the *San Francisco Examiner* by Guy Wright. The homosexuals became so anatomically explicit in describing their sex techniques, said Wright, "that some students were soon in imminent need of air sickness bags." Parents complained, the principal passed the hot potato to the supervisor of Family Life (sex education), and he called the Gay Counseling Service. No, of course they weren't going to stop the program. The supervisor of sex education simply told them to send a higher class of homosexual next time.

Do not believe for one minute that the account written in the *Examiner* is isolated. It is being repeated again and again, across this now tainted school land.

Homosexuals do molest children. Such goings-on were reported in an Associated Press release that told of "homosexuals upset by a sensational child molestation case who are trying to convince the public that there is nothing inherently wrong with sex between men and boys."

The effort, in this case, was led by a group who called themselves the Boston-Boise Committee. The group felt the news sensationalized the arrest of twenty-four men for alleged sexual conduct with adolescent boys.

While Boston-Boise has not officially endorsed man-boy sex, its leaders say such encounters are a fact of growing up for many teenagers, according to the AP account.

The group attached "Boise" to its name to recall prosecutions of homosexuals in Idaho in the 1950s.

The Boston-Boise Committee wanted to:

• Lower the age of consent from 16, possibly to 14.
• Change the child molestation laws so there is a difference between the penalties for statutory rape and forcible rape of boys.

Thomas Reeves, a history professor at Roxbury Community College in Boston, admitted to being a "boy lover." Reeves said, "I feel it is important to say it is possible to be a man and have a variety of relationships with adolescents, including sex, and still be an ethical, upstanding individual." He said there was "nothing wrong" with adolescents and men having sex. "Boys between the ages of fourteen and sixteen just need sex all the time," he continued. "They need to get it out of their systems."

No matter what those people might say who would support the

right of homosexuals teaching our children in the schools, Reeves has said it all. To me, sex between two people of the same sex is a contravening of nature.

Still think it's OK for a homosexual teacher to teach your children?

Let us step outside the world of the schoolroom for a minute and enter the macho world of the U.S. Marines. Today even the marine's image has been tarnished by the homosexual. Twelve marines were discharged and thirty others are under investigation in connection with a homosexual male prostitute ring that operated at Camp Pendleton. An officer on the base said the organizers of the ring approached "fair-skinned, young looking kids." We have to remember that these young men complied, since there was no mention of force. Should we expect otherwise? They are being taught in the schoolroom that homosexuality is but another lifestyle, another choice that is available to them. This type of teaching is unwittingly encouraged by parents who do not object to the subject.

For years controversy has been brewing over what makes someone take up the homosexual lifestyle. Little, surprisingly enough, has been done in the way of research on this lifestyle.

However, well-known gynecologist and sex-researcher Dr. William H. Masters, addressing a convention of the Associated Church Press in St. Louis on the subject of homosexuality, claimed that after ten years of research on the issue, he is convinced there is no such thing as a born homosexual—or heterosexual. Sexuality will be determined by culture, by learning, and by accepting society's customs. "You were born with sexual facility," said Dr. Masters. "How you use it is something you learned."

Did I still hear you say that you wouldn't mind a homosexual teacher in your child's classroom? You still don't mind that this deviation is being taught?

Rabbi Abraham B. Hecht, president of the Rabbinical Alliance in America, addressing himself to homosexuality, said, "Accepting this lifestyle would be misleading to young people who will grow up believing that [it would be] an equally acceptable alternative in choosing one's sexual preference."

Pointing out that most people want to be fair to homosexuals, Dr. Charles W. Socarides, clinical professor of psychiatry at the State University of New York's Medical Center, had this to say on the subject: "But the activists among the gays want the right to teach school children that homosexuality is 'normal.' They want to encourage homosexuality among the youth. They even want to censor textbooks which list homosexuality as a disorder."

Not only do they want to do all of the above, Dr. Socarides, they are doing it. If not a homosexual, then one or more of the new breed of teacher is carrying this message to the students, always with the banner that the student has every right to make his own "choice." This type of teacher too should be excised from teaching.

A book that I found in one of our local high schools, titled, *Modern Sex Education* by Cloyd J. Julian and Elizabeth Noland Jackson, discusses homosexuality. Under the chapter entitled, "The Misuse of Sex," they back up Anita Bryant and every caring parent when they write: "Adult homosexuals sometimes attempt to lure unsuspecting children and minors into their way of life. The best protection against this unfortunate condition is to realize that such deviants exist and avoid them." This is the kind of material homosexuals would like to see censored.

Still feel your children should be taught about or by homosexuals? Well then, you deserve the consequences.

17.

Battle of the Books

Across our land, a battle has been raging over the types of books being used in the public schools. On one side of this war are the educators, who want their students to have what they call "a free flow of information." On the other side are the parents, who say they will be the final arbiters in the material their children will read in the schools. No matter that what the educators are giving the children in the way of reading matter goes against the grain of the parents by including passages littered with profanities, obscenities, and philosophies unacceptable to them. Justifying the profanities strewn throughout much of the objectionable reading matter, the educators point out that today's young people are less likely to be shocked by such language than the parents who are complaining.

But does that make it right, just because parents want this desensitizing stopped? On this score I go along with Abraham Lincoln who said: "To keep a man down in the gutter, you've got to get down there with him." Our educators should be trying to elevate our youth, not condoning gutter language by using it themselves and advocating books that have to resort to these measures. This too has taken its toll on the final product our children will become.

As we begin to examine the battle over the books, it opens the door to one aspect of the new type of teaching and the new types of literature and philosophy that are being perpetrated on our public school children.

Edward B. Jenkinson, head of the National Council of Teachers of English Committee Against Censorship, said that censorship over the last fifteen years has been growing and is creating a blockage of the free flow of ideas that is dangerous for the nation. Once educators get a phrase going, they will use it time and again. In this case it is the "free flow" of ideas or information.

"The absolutists say we cannot draw any line anywhere," wrote William A. Stanmyer, an associate professor of law at the Indiana University School of Law, Indianapolis, and the father of four. "This is patent nonsense. In a democracy, why should the minority who cannot distinguish between art and trash dictate the education—through magazines, television, and schoolbooks—of the children of the majority, who *can* tell the difference?"

"The whole philosophy of education has changed," said Norma Gabler, a Longview, Texas, woman and one of the chief advocates of book banning. "The aim is no longer to teach fact, skills and knowledge. The aim is to change the thinking and values of children.

"The aim is to change the social values of the child and any time you do that, you're going to step on people's toes. Parents," she continued, "are spending more money on education than ever before and they have less to show for it. Whenever you choose materials with offensive language and no academic value, I think parents have a right to complain."

It is important to note that the publishing houses take their cue from the education establishment. They are the ones who dictate what will appear in print.

With raw tenacity and guts, parents have begun to step forward and say, "Enough!" The most publicized battle over books took place in Kanawha County, W. Va. It was the parents who refused to surrender their children's minds to books they considered unsuitable for them. It was the parents who brought clearly to the rest of the nation, via newspapers, TV and radio, the plight of parents who try to have a say in what their children will be exposed to. They refused to give up their arms until the school board agreed to split the schools in their districts into "traditional" and "nontraditional" schools, giving parents a choice. In the end, all but the least offensive of the 352 books that parents objected to were removed, and those that remained on the shelves of the schools could only be read with a parent's consent.

There the children stood firmly on the side of their parents. At one point, fifteen thousand students boycotted the schools. The coal mines, an interstate highway, a construction site, a food warehouse, railroad lines, trucking companies—all were shut down in the fight over the books that these parents called "un-American, antireligion, profane and filthy."

When the dust had settled, the new rules for school books would include a parents' screening committee, and the books to be permitted would have to comply with the following:

- Must recognize the sanctity of the home and emphasize its importance as the basic unit of American society.
- Must not contain profanity.
- Must encourage loyalty to the United States and emphasize the responsibilities of citizenship and the obligation to redress grievances through the legal processes . . . (and must not) teach or imply that an alien form of government is superior.
- Shall teach the true history and heritage of the United States . . . Must not defame our nation's founders or misrepresent ideals and causes for which they struggled and sacrificed.
- Shall teach that traditional rules of grammar are a worthwhile subject for academic pursuit.

In spite of the outcome, there were still thousands of parents who felt compromises had been made. They opened Christian, private schools for their children to attend.

And the NEA shook with rage over the battle that had been waged, calling it "the tip of the iceberg." In terse wording, their report said: "Below the surface lies a right-wing-sponsored nationwide book-banning campaign which jeopardizes the education of millions of American school children."

The conservative element can never be called reactionary. If anything, they are too slow to make a judgment on any issue. First they must study it, mull it over, be sure of their facts, and then act. It is the sure-footed liberal faction that leaps immediately to the fore, grabbing the golden ring the first time around.

That same year book banning in various degrees took place in New York, New Jersey, Texas, Indiana, Delaware and other areas. But none forced their school boards to go as far as Kanawha, W. Va., parents had.

A national revolution was predicted, but it never came to pass. In fact, when parents in one town complained that the textbooks being used in their schools were immoral and anti-God, a thousand students walked out in protest. It was the children rising up against the parents. Nothing could have better suited the educational community.

One of the parents in the Kanawha County battle said of the books: "There are some leading phrases in these books that will change a person's attitude toward his family, the way he's raised. We don't teach this at home and we don't want it in school." But much of what is taught today in school is not taught at home—and that is where parent and child will eventually clash.

Some of the work sheets that accompany the controversial books—the teaching manuals, those that are kept from the prying eyes of parents—read in part: "Most people think that cheating is wrong, even if it is only to get a penny. Do you think there is ever a time when it might be right? Tell when it is. Tell why you think it is right." And another: "I think it must be lonely to be God. Nobody loves a master." Another involved having intercourse with your mother.

Back in 1973 Erica Carle wrote an article entitled, "Truth in Education," for the *Milwaukee County News*. She wrote of books in schools in that area. ". . . there are many books in the junior high school libraries which give a complete catalogue of the drugs available and a description of the effects of each. There are books which show all the equipment necessary for injections, and there are books which show drug addicts actually injecting themselves." There were also books, wrote reporter Carle, whose main point was stating that marijuana should be legalized. It was, she pointed out, a course in drug education—not antidrug education.

Back in 1972 in a seven to two decision, the Supreme Court let stand a lower court decision upholding the authority of school officials in Queens County, N.Y., to ban from student libraries *Down These Mean Streets*, a book containing explicit descriptions of drug and sexual activities in Spanish Harlem. What would the Supreme Court's decision have been, I wonder, if it had been parents who wanted the books removed?

In spite of the ruling, which should have set a precedent, in 1976 the Sixth U.S. Court of Appeals said, "A library is a storehouse of knowledge" and ruled that the Strongville Board of Education in Cincinnati could not keep the books off the school shelves. Justice is indeed blind and not very even-handed when it comes to our children.

But then again, we must not forget the enormous profits made in the sale of books to schools. Textbook publishers sold $632 million worth of books just to elementary and secondary schools that same year.

While interviewing an artist for an art column that I was writing for a newspaper, the artist, a mother, suddenly departed from the interview to ask if I knew anything about the local schools. She said the family had moved from a "less desirable" area into what she had hoped was a better area. But she was having some reservations. At the core of her worries was a school book that her daughter had used to do a report for school on VD. Unhappy because the book dealt more "with contraceptives than VD," and with some of the wording, such as "Protect your lover—wear a rubber," she began discussing it with me.

I know immediately that she is not referring to a book, but a comic book. What a source of reference for VD! The comic book first grabbed national attention when it was passed out to children at the New York State Fair. It is authored by the king of this kind of trash, Sol Gordon. And now, I find, it has infiltrated the school system.

"My point is," she tells me, "they're constantly telling parents they [the teachers] aren't allowed to moralize. Whether it's moral or amoral, they're introducing moral concepts," she says, and then adds, "or amoral."

Whether her daughter got the comic book in the school library or from her teacher, this mother is not sure. "I wonder too," she mused, "if even the principal or the librarian is fully cognizant of what kind of material comes in. I really don't know. I really don't know how this stuff works, and maybe I should make it my business to find out."

Referring back to the comic book, she said, "It's not the kind of language we use at home. I moved into an area where I hoped that my children would be elevated. Instead I find that ghetto kind of stuff in their reading material. Why did I pay the taxes to move into this place if I'm going to get the same thing I could get in a ghetto," she wondered aloud. "I think a lot of parents are disappointed that they've made such efforts to pull their children up out of a situation they thought was bad for them, and move into what they consider a better situation, and find out it's not a whole lot different. We just have more places to play and fancier houses," she said.

"My rights," she went on, "are getting smaller and smaller. I was always under the impression that until age eighteen I was the responsible parent—what happened to my right to decide what my child will be given and what she won't be given? My daughter may grow up to have views directly opposite to mine, but not without me giving it a good, damned try," she said, warming to the subject of today's schools.

"It seems so insidious sometimes," she said to her captive audience of one, "almost like a form of brainwashing, and you don't realize it's been done until it's been done. All right, they can turn around and tell me that I'm not a responsible parent because I'm not aware of what my children are involved with—well, I can't be in school all day," she reasoned.

From the comic-book issue, this mother went on to tell me that her 11-year-old son told her that if children are not happy at home, all they had to do was get an adult to say this was not a good home and they could be removed from their parents' custody. "Where do they learn this! Who tells them this?" she asked of me.

Only because comic-book writer Sol Gordon, with a comic-book mentality, is writing this trash, and our children are being exposed to it, am I taking the time and space to talk about it. I have looked through much of his material. Of one thing I am sure. His work, in many instances, severs the parent-child relationship by wording and illustration, and fuels the disastrous sexual revolution that swirls around our children.

In his introduction to his paperback book, *Facts About Sex*, aimed at our youth, he says to the young reader in his opening line: "Parents are not always clear on how much their children know—or should know about sex. Parents have a tough time when they discuss topics like sexual intercourse and masturbation." Right away the young reader has a graphic vision of an ignorant and uncooperative parent. After all, this book is written by an adult and a psychologist at that. The young person has not lived long enough to know that title alone does not make someone's words the truth.

Gordon goes on to say: "Many parents feel that knowing 'too much' too early leads to sexual misbehavior, but most experts have the opposite view." Again, on a sliding scale of one to ten the parents are at the bottom. Who are these "experts"? They are the ones who have helped to alienate your children from you and the family concept.

Giving license to street language, Gordon writes: "It is very important for young people to understand sex and to know the language associated with it, including 'street' expressions which we have used in a few instances to explain the meaning of difficult words."

Putting parents aside once and for all, and at the same time belittling morality, he recognizes the academic inabilities of today's youth, as he writes: "This book is purposely brief because the average young person to whom it is addressed will not read, or may get confused by, a long, detailed or 'moralistic' presentation. Most books about sex are written to please uptight parents."

In his comic book, *Ten Heavy Facts About Dating*, Gordon writes: "Teenagers who are afraid to get help because parents might get upset should seek counseling at a local Planned Parenthood or at a county or hospital family planning clinic. They can help you prepare for a baby or arrange an abortion, or refer you to a place that can help you." And then, almost as an afterthought, he adds that it's still "a good idea" to communicate with your parents. It is apparent from the whole theme of his writings that the parent remark is thrown in just to cover himself from further attacks by his many critics. It does nothing to diminish my feelings of his flagrant destructive drive against parents, and ultimately the child.

"You may run into a few cold people who act as if you should be punished," he tells his youthful reader. "Don't let such insensitivity influence you—one way or the other," he says of their sexual lives.

Gordon writes a whole gaggle of garbage, guaranteed to gag any decent and discriminating person.

And you wonder, dear parent, why your children are not learning the basics, and why there is a lack of discipline, and a sexual revolution? Look deeply into your public schools for the answer.

Yes. These works are being used in the schools across the country. One of the recommended readings at a New York school is *You*, a paperback that contains Gordon's four sex comic books scattered through it.

How many other schools are using this type of material and other material with the same philosophy? Just about every public school in the country. However, they are not always exposed. Were it not for Pennsylvania State Senator Richard Schweiker, the American public might never have found out that foreign-aid monies were used to buy ten thousand copies of a birth control comic book for distribution in South America. On the cover of this comic book is a picture of the Virgin Mary with this caption: "Little Virgin, you who conceived without sinning—help me to sin without conceiving."

Planned Parenthood, which also subscribes to Gordon's comic books, went a step further in the comic mentality. It fashioned comic strips, which it sent to Chicago-area newspapers under a cover letter signed by the public education director of the Planned Parenthood Association in Chicago. One of the cartoons clearly shows a Catholic bishop holding matches and a can of gasoline. The bishop is saying: "Now we're losing the flock on the subject of abortion—but we're not worried . . . we've got the faithful out burning down the clinics."

In another comic strip, which was an apparent stab at Anita Bryant, a woman is drawn standing next to an orange tree branch. She is saying: "Sex, sex, sex. That's all they think about. Homosexuality, abortion, promiscuity, premarital sex. It's wicked and against the will of God. Everyone knows what's normal— normal is what my husband and I did after we got married—all 3 times." (Anita Bryant and her husband have three children.)

How much venom was put into the pen of the persons who dreamt up those cartoon strips! How frustrated the Planned Parenthood people are with goodness, morality and those with strong religious convictions that constantly block their way, causing them to expose their feelings so openly!

Obviously heady with the incursions they have made with our children with the aid of our tax dollars, they believed that they had won the war and that their cartoons would be accepted on the open market. It must have come as a terrible blow to Planned Parenthood when it found out otherwise.

18.

This Is an Honor?

One afternoon when I entered a hobby shop, I found several mothers embroiled in discussions of the public school system. The owner said, "Talk to her. She's a reporter," pointing to me. The mothers' complaints ran the course of reading materials in the schools to grade curving—which means that in a test, if the class has mostly failed, the student that scored the highest has his grade subtracted from a mark of 100. That differential is added to the grades of every other student's final test mark. It is just another way to give an inflated grade.

As I listened, one mother suggested I talk to her daughter about the books she was required to read in her honors English class. I told her I would be happy to talk with her if she could get her daughter to agree to the interview. By telephone several days later, the matter had been settled—I thought.

But once I got to the home of the parents, it was questionable that the interview would materialize. The mother told me that her daughter had changed her mind, was upstairs in her bedroom and was adamant about not coming downstairs. I asked her if I might try to convince her daughter to talk with me. She agreed. I called to Jean from the bottom of the steps leading to her bedroom. I was able to coax her into coming down by telling her that if she didn't like any of the questions I posed, I would not be offended if she refused to answer them. The interview was to begin with Jean as a "hostile" witness.

I was to spend a total of two hours talking to her and her parents about her honors English class, a course that is offered by invitation only to those students who are considered to be the crème de la crème in English.

That interview is printed here for the first time, in abbreviated form. It poignantly points out the fears expressed by parents who fight the literature they see as unfit for their children. It screams of the tearing apart of a young girl when the values her parents have taught her are challenged in the classroom and disparaged in the materials she is required to read. It reeks of the havoc that these materials thrust onto the once peaceful coexistence of family life. Only the name of the 16-year-old high-school student is changed, because she is already suffering from ulcers and nervous attacks due to the pressures exerted on her by the public schools and the conflicts it has caused to her relationship with her parents.

As we sit around the kitchen table, I find I am in the center of the hurricane of what has been called the Battle of the Books. I feel privileged to be a part of parents and child opening up to a stranger, just so others will know they are not alone and perhaps our educators and government will see that they have torn and fragmented once wonderful family relationships into ribbons.

Jean, the student, begins: "If it [the book] has some foul words in it, she," she says, gesturing toward her mother, "gets upset over it. I was reading this magazine and the teacher told us there were going to be some bad words in it, you know?" While reading the magazine, Jean came across a word that was unfamiliar to her, so she said she asked her teacher the meaning of it. "That was my first mistake—to ask her what a word means, 'cause she got a little upset then."

I ask Jean what the word was. She hesitates and her mother steps in: "Trojan. They went to the drugstore to buy a Trojan," she offers.

"It was required reading," Jean continues when she sees that I do not blanch. "We were supposed to have a discussion about it the next day."

I ask Jean if she thinks the magazine story, that was sexually explicit, could have been told just as effectively without being so graphic. "It didn't bother me, it bothered her," she said, looking again in the direction of her mother. "Because you hear the students use it in the hall. It's like common, everyday language," she said of the four-letter slang term for intercourse.

"Hearing foul language in the halls of a school," her mother says, is objectionable in itself, but teaching it in the classroom "is something else!"

"We had one class where we had a substitute—boy!" said Jean, her eyes rolling skyward. "I'd never tell you about that class," she says addressing her mother.

Would she tell me, I ask. "No. I'm not going to tell you either," she said with an embarrassed laugh. After some gentle prodding on my part Jean will tell me only that "that word" was used constantly by the substitute teacher. Eventually Jean tells me it is the four-letter slang word for intercourse that used to be reserved for public bathroom walls and now is apparently bouncing off the classroom walls. She also reveals that the teacher assigned them a book that was replete with "that word."

Her mother is livid at the revelation she is hearing for the first time. "It's not to be taught in a classroom!" she says with measured emphasis on each word.

"The teacher said it was for mature readers," Jean says in self-defense. "Mature readers pick their literature," her mother shoots back.

I feel the strain between mother and daughter and I ache.

Confronting her daughter, the mother asks: "Do you have the same amount of respect for a teacher who is using gutter words?" shoots back.

I feel the strain between mother and daughter and I ache.

Confronting her daughter, the mother asks: "Do you have the same amount of respect for a teacher who is using gutter words?"

"No. Not really," Jean replies. "No. A couple of the teachers, when they get upset, they use words like 'damn,'" Jean offers.

"We had teachers who used to get very upset too, but they never, never came down to that!" said her mother.

I ask Jean if she does not consider it degrading to the image of an educated person to use such base language. After all, I ask her, isn't education supposed to elevate one?

"The way I feel about it is that in order to get something across, the teachers come down to the students' level—so I just take it at that," Jean answers.

Jean's school is not in a ghetto. It is in a highly fashionable area of the country with most of the people in the area in professions.

I quote Abraham Lincoln to her. It was Lincoln, I say, who said, in order to keep a man down in the gutter you have to get down there with him. And such justification for a teacher using base language, I point out, will just keep the kids on a gutter level. I also point out that in her honors English class, one could rightly assume these students would have a better vocabulary than most. On that basis, there would seem no real justification for it—would there?

"No," says Jean, mulling it over in her mind. And then, "No, I guess not!"

By now Jean tells me she is comfortable talking with me. After telling me about her fears in facing a reporter, she suddenly decides on her own to tell her mother and me the story she had previously said she would "never" tell us concerning the substitute teacher.

"There was a poem we had to read. And this girl just couldn't read it. She got upset over the few choice words that were in it. So they had a boy read it. It didn't bother him. This girl said it was disgusting."

I ask Jean how she felt about the poem. "A lot of people felt it was disgusting, but I'm not going to say, 'Oh, I think it's disgusting!' because they [the kids] would think, 'Boy, she's one of the weirdest!' "

"Don't you think it's better to be called a weirdo and an intelligent person?" her mother prods. Jean does not answer. I step in and say to Jean that she is telling us that there is peer pressure. "I just let it go in one ear and out the other," is her only response.

When I ask Jean's mother if she feels parents' input in schools is diminishing, she responds by saying, "I have felt that way ever since my daughter got out of the lower grades."

When I ask both parents and Jean if these base books and teachers are splintering their family relationships, all three quietly agree.

"They [the teachers] have no respect for the students, and therefore the student has no respect for them," said Jean's father, who has been nervously pacing between living room and kitchen throughout the discussion.

When Jean's class read *Hamlet,* Jean said that because of the language used in Shakespeare, all of the kids were saying Hamlet was "weird." "And the teacher," said Jean, "asked the students if they would agree that he would be like—in a manner of speaking—like a faggot. And everybody agreed with her."

"This is only one teacher's opinion," said Jean's mother, "and I think she used a poor word when she used the word 'faggot'." "The word shouldn't be used in the classroom," agreed Jean's father. "Dad, then don't ever come into our high school during the changing of the periods," shot back Jean.

Jean went on to tell us that the "cleanest" book she had read that year was *Green Mansions.* Referring to the selection of books the teacher had given the honors English class as required reading, Jean called them "stupid." "They're not going to improve anybody," was her assessment. Her own preference for reading, she said, was mysteries.

"I thought that when I got into high school people were going to act mature," she said with obvious disappointment in her voice.

"Every year it gets worse," her mother muttered.

By now Jean was loosening up and began to voluntarily talk about

other classes in her high school. She chose first the subject she called
health, which I shall call by its right name: sex education. "We had
debates on abortion in health. Now I was against it, and some people
were for it—but I couldn't see their point of view, and they couldn't
see my point of view. It's just like in English. But why should I stand
up and say I disagree? I'll sit in a neutral zone before I'll take a
stand, because somebody will come up to you afterwards and say,
'Why did you take that point of view? You're nuts!' or 'That's a stupid
point of view. You shouldn't do that.' So I'd just sooner be neutral.

"I'd say," she continued, "that it's pretty close to the truth that if
you don't share a teacher's point of view on a controversial subject,
she'll let you know it. In English class we were discussing
marijuana, and we were supposed to discuss the pros and cons of it.
They were talking about legalizing it, and I was against it. You can
always tell by the way the teacher looks at you that she doesn't agree
with you and it's not her way of thinking.

"In one discussion, a lot of kids were quoting the Bible and I
thought—why don't I do it?" Jean called her pastor, told him what
she was looking for, and he gave her two quotes from the Bible. "I
threw those in at her [my teacher] and I would say that's when she
got turned off and she gave the impression of 'Here we go again—
one of those religious freaks starting up.' It was just a strong feeling
I had."

Getting back to the discussion of the books on her required
reading list for honors English, Jean said, "The teacher says these
are terrific books—these are required to get into colleges. My
mother looks them over and can tell you every despicable thing
about them. That's one reason I wouldn't want my mother and this
teacher to come face to face, because I think it would become a cat-
and-dog fight. They'd claw each other's eyeballs because they're so
opposite."

"I would hope to be a bigger person than that," her mother puts in
softly.

I ask Jean what her opinion is of the majority of her teachers. "In
plain English? Well, in plain, clean language, some of them are
really queer. And the way they dress—you would expect a teacher to
set an example for the dress code, right? They come dressed worse
than the students come dressed. When I was brought up my mother
always told me to respect the teachers, that they're the know-it-all.
How can I do that when they get into school and they look worse than
I look?"

"I started my daughter off to school that way," her mother admits,
"but I've changed my mind. Now they should only get respect when
they earn it."

Jean says that if she were a mother, she would never tell her child the teacher is always right.

Talking about the conflict between her parents and the teachers, Jean really opened up and pointed out first-hand the damage being done to our youth by the direction education has taken today.

"I always thought..." she began, "my parents always told me that it's this way. The teacher says, 'Well, that's not the way it is anymore. It's not right.' How can the teacher tell you one thing and your parents tell you another thing? You're on a tug of war. You're being pulled at both ends. So you don't know which one's wrong and which one's right. So you wind up you can't believe your parents and you can't believe your teacher. So I'm just stuck in the middle and let it all go in one ear and out the other, 'cause I don't believe anybody at this point; because if your parents tell you something and you're ridiculed by a teacher because of this..." Her voice trails off leaving her thought hanging, momentarily, in midair.

"I thought I had good standards," she begins again. "And then all of a sudden you have a teacher who says, 'Well, I think that's a very rotten thing to go by.' I don't think it's right," said Jean shaking her head slowly from side to side. "It does more than upset you. It makes you think the teacher wasn't right, but I don't know if my parents are right. So I just don't believe either one."

Jean paused and the room was quiet for a spell. Then her mother said quietly, "I've always tried to impress on Jean that the reason I do what I do is because I care. And a parent that cares, loves a child. Listen, we used to be able to sit down and relax as parents. Today when you sit in your home, you can't." Jean's honors English class, she says, is, in her opinion, no honor at all.

At this point I am looking over Jean's teacher's list of required reading for honors English. I point out the fine print at the bottom of the last page. It is a disclaimer. It reads: "Neither the Department of English nor its members, the school or the district, endorses all these books."

Mother, father, daughter are all stunned. They had not noticed the disclaimer. Jean breaks the silence: "Then why does she make us read it?" I suggest it is a good basis for ending this mess once and for all in this particular class.

"I can see it if you want to read trash—you can do it on your time— but not as a homework assignment," says Jean.

"I've spent all year trying to get that out of you," her mother says with a smile on her face.

As I pack up my tape recorder and notes, it is Jean who thanks me for coming. "I was scared when you came here," she confesses. "But you're nice. You understand how my mother feels."

19.

What Do Our Kids Read on Their Own Time?

In just about every area of society we are experiencing an eroding of morals. And now a new type of columnist has sprung forth on the pages of just about every major newspaper in the country . . . the columnist who answers questions on sex-related matters.

These columns are widely read and quoted by our young. If they don't read anything else, they will read their horoscopes and these daily column offerings. Oftentimes these columnists are doctors, other times they are sex therapists or writers who are expressing nothing more than their own preferences in their replies.

If your children are not finding approval for some of their sexual behavior at home, they will not only find it in school, but now they can find it in their daily, home-delivered newspapers.

When Abigail Van Buren, who writes the Dear Abby columns, guested on Phil Donahue's TV program, he called her "just an old-fashioned girl." But Abby herself admitted that five years ago newspapers would not have printed some of the letters she answers in her columns today.

If I can judge by the printed letters to the editor, surprisingly few parents have lodged written complaints concerning this relatively new aspect of writing.

I can foresee the day when these columns will jump from the printed page onto the TV screen, coming on as a five-minute feature spot with the six and eleven o'clock news.

While an entire book could be compiled on the questions and answers sent in by our youth to these sex columnists (and I'm sure eventually more than one of these columnists will do just that), I shall give just a few examples of what I am concerned with.

Just as in the public school classrooms, no subject is taboo for today's columnists.

A mother wrote that her son, whom she described as being a fine and upstanding student, contracted VD when he was in his teens. The mother found out later that instead of coming to her or her husband, he went to a doctor without their knowledge. She felt the doctor had no business treating her minor son, and if this was the law (and it is in most states), it should be changed.

The columnist's reply said, in essence, that the ideal situation would be for the child to confront the parent with the problem; however, it was his feeling that many cases of VD would go untreated if the child had to tell his parents.

Most will argue that if the parent-child relationship has been a good one, the young boy would have turned to his parents. That's a lot of malarkey! As long as the child has been taught (and he has been—in school, in newspaper articles, by columnists and by TV and radio spots) that he need only turn to Uncle Sam for help, why should he face his parents? Why should he go through the painful experience of letting his parents know of his sexual encounters? It is another clear-cut case of the "surrogate parent" usurping the natural parent.

"But parents would hit the ceiling if their children told them they have VD," is the other argument. So what if they do? How else does a child know he has done something wrong? But I forget. In schools and in today's philosophy, there is no right or wrong. Wrong has been obliterated from the vocabulary of the sexually active children—thereby obliterating also conscience.

Eventually the child of today must become more hostile toward his parents. Everyone is supporting his school-taught philosophy but his parents. So logically, he begins to believe there is something drastically wrong with their reasoning and that his is sound.

Writing to a columnist, a young girl said that she and her boyfriend went "all the way." She asked for a quick reply as to what she could do and asked what the odds of her getting pregnant were.

Without any moralizing, the person writing the column gave as one alternative to the possibility of a pregnancy developing—abortion. Abby was right. Five, ten years ago, a newspaper would never have printed the letter. Would that it were still so!

In another major metropolitan newspaper someone wrote asking about his family dogs licking the genitals of their children. The writer specifically asked the columnist to answer in print. Without hesitation, the request was honored.

In part the columnist said that sexual stimulation of humans by animals was common in adolescence and perhaps a year or so past the teens. The columnist never suggested that the animals be made to stop this repulsive practice.

It brought my memory back to a visit to "Old Town," a section of Chicago, Illinois, where artists display their works in quaint, little shops. I had picked up, on that visit, what turned out to be an underground newspaper. When I read the paper on the plane on my return home, I discovered that there were ads placed by people looking for animals for sexual gratification. Today this topic is fare for a regular daily newspaper.

I also remembered discovering in the vocabulary of one sex education class the definition for the sexual attraction to animals. Is it any wonder our children are so messed up?

Ann Landers really took to task a girl and her boyfriend who indignantly wrote to her about a policeman flashing his light into their parked car and ordering them to put on their clothes—amazed that they were being harassed for "doing what comes naturally." Landers said they should have been arrested. But my gripe is that a syndicated column, read by thousands, showed poor taste, to say the least, by giving valuable newspaper space to the subject.

It is rare, but every so often the readership will come down hard on a columnist's response to a letter writer. Such was the case of the columnist who responded to a woman, with two young daughters, whose male friend was spending nights with her. The columnist advised the mother to tell her youngsters that the relationship was "special" and was a combination of "love and sex."

The flak that followed berated the columnist's response, calling it "disgusting." The columnist was told she had also misused the word "love." Others wrote in and praised her response.

A 14-year-old asked a columnist's opinion on whether or not she should "go all the way," even though her parents had advised against it.

The response, in part, told her not to do anything she didn't want to do. (That also transcribes to: you can do anything you want to do simply if you feel like it.) The columnist did not say it would be morally wrong, but said, in part, that the girl was not quite ready, in her opinion, for a sexual relationship with that much involvement.

The question is—when? Next year when she's all of 15? The columnist never said he thought she should listen to her parents— that they were giving her good advice. Heaven forbid! A moral stand, and in print? How unliberated.

A mother asked the opinion of two writers who share a column if it was "right" or "wrong" for her daughter to live with her boyfriend.

So many parents are caught in this terrible tunnel thanks to the so-called experts who have even confused parents on this moral issue. Their reply was basically the same thing our children are taught in public schools. They said there was no "right" or "wrong"—it was just a question of "values." It is the daughter's decision, the columnists replied. Living together, they agreed, is a product of our times. They urged the mother not to show rejection should the daughter go through with the arrangement. I say phooey!

A young girl wrote in to a columnist and said she had contracted VD from two different boys and come to the conclusion that sex before marriage was now taboo for her.

Instead of lauding this girl's good decision, the columnist went on to recommend Planned Parenthood and to make a point of saying that treatment in most states is available for VD without parental knowledge or consent.

An 18-year-old wrote to a columnist and said she and her boyfriend could not complete intercourse. She asked for advice.

Again no moralizing to an apparently unmarried couple. Instead the columnist gave a clinical explanation of why the act could not be completed. He then suggested the boyfriend needed "a good dose of self-confidence," and proceeded to give the young woman some "hints" to make her boyfriend "perform."

My research on this topic is replete with how healthy masturbation is, to urging a daughter to defy a father who has forbidden that daughter to go to a baby shower for her pregnant, unmarried friend.

It is always the parents who are either chastised or asked to adjust to an immoral situation, to compromise, to do anything to keep the lines of communication open between them and their children no matter what their offspring's sexual appetites or desires. And once again, the child is told in many ways to "do your own thing."

20.

Leadership Sets an Example?

Back in August of 1976 President Gerald Ford stood before a crowd of a hundred thousand persons at the closing ceremony of the Roman Catholic International Eucharistic Congress in Philadelphia. While not coming out for a constitutional amendment on abortion, he said he shared the church's concern about the "increased irreverence for life."

Bishop Miguel Rodriguez of Arecibo, Puerto Rico, said the President was merely courting the Catholic vote. "It was opportunism, the same old thing," he said with justifiable cynicism.

Three days later Ford's wife, Betty, on the TV magazine program "60 Minutes" told an audience of millions that the Supreme Court's decision to liberalize abortion was "a great, great decision."

On the same program, when asked by interviewer Morley Safer what she would do if her daughter Susan came to her and told her she was having an affair, Mrs. Ford responded that she would not be surprised and she would "want to know pretty much about the young man that she was planning to have an affair with—whether it was a worthwhile encounter . . ."

Here was our First Lady engaging in the same rhetoric our children were being inundated with from other quarters. Here was "First Mama" not passing any moral judgment.

As to the question of drugs, she said of her children: "I'm sure they've all probably tried marijuana," and went on to say that had drugs been popular when she was younger, she might have tried marijuana herself.

The roof fell in on many households across America, and the

following day Mrs. Ford's remarks were plastered all over the newspapers and columnists wrote extensively about them. Using her position, it was inevitable that she, like so many others, would undoubtedly create chaos in many a home with young people and their parents.

Interviewed on the street the next day by a reporter, one woman said, "I can't imagine any mother feeling that way." Another woman pointed out that the remarks would bring more conflict between child and parent. After all, the First Lady thought it was all OK. Still another said, "I have trouble getting my kids to keep their curfews. And now this? My 16-year-old heard it all right, and I haven't heard the end of it ..."

The final mail count at CBS showed that viewers opposed Mrs. Ford's remarks by about three and a half to one. It would have been a safe bet that most of those responding were parents already embroiled in discussions and arguments on these topics with their own children.

In fact, a 17-year-old wrote a letter to a newspaper to "compliment" Mrs. Ford on her stand. "Having an affair is part of life. Also, experience makes it all the better, physically and mentally." The letter was signed "Self-Experienced."

One newspaper's editorial said that in spite of the uproar, the reaction was "largely favorable." The editorial found Mrs. Ford's remarks to be "an admirable example" for today's woman.

Shortly after Mrs. Ford's disgusting, amoral and permissive stance involving her children, Nancy Reagan, wife of former California Governor Ronald Reagan, brought some dignity back to politics when she addressed a group of Michigan Republican women.

She defined morality as "a word whose meanings we should instill in our children, even though some will tell us it is chic to do otherwise. Society needs morality to keep it from flying apart.

"Moral standards are needed for they encourage the most vital asset of civilized people—self-restraint." Mrs. Reagan went on to denounce welfare programs that make abortions available to underaged girls without parental consent. She called it "government at the highest level interfering in family relationships."

Apparently flushed from all the attention drawn to her after her appearance on "60 Minutes," big-mouth Betty was not to be silenced. Twenty-four days later Mrs. Ford told reporters: "I've never seen an X-rated movie. I'm dying to."

Just as tasteless were the remarks of Joan Mondale, campaigning in 1976 for her husband, Walter, then the Democratic vice presidential candidate. When asked on a television show in Seattle, Wash., about the Wayne Hays sex scandal, she said: "The two scandals in Washington are Watergate and waterbed. The Democrats are doing it to their secretaries, and the Republicans are doing it to the country."

By 1978 the country's newest President was baring his soul publicly. He let us all know in *Playboy* magazine that he had "lust" in his heart.

Not only what the politicians were saying, but what they are doing, is hitting the newspapers on an almost daily basis. It would be impossible to mention all the politicians who have been jailed or engaged in less than savory activities. Covering this wide spectrum was one columnist whose column was titled, "So much for morality." He wrote of a confessed adulterer, the father of two illegitimate children, and Wayne Hays, who all handily won reelection.

Harold Stassen said recently that in the past twenty years more congressmen have been convicted of crimes than in its two-hundred-year history.

The ledge of decency demanded by those who elect our politicians to office grows ever narrower. To find out that someone has done a criminal or immoral act while in office, and to be foolish enough to reelect that individual again, shows that our level of tolerance for immorality is widening at an ever-frightening pace.

21.

The Yellow Scourge

"It's just like being prepared for war," said a school-district security director. What he was referring to was the forced busing of public school children out of their neighborhood school and environment to other schools in order to comply with government orders to desegregate.

In 1954 the Supreme Court handed down a decision that stated in part: "The opportunity of an education, . . . where the state has undertaken to provide it, is a right which must be made available to all on equal terms."

It was interpreted as busing. There were other methods suggested, but busing became the password. Once put into effect, it was to cause billions of dollars of tax revenue to be spent contrary to the wishes of many parents who contributed unwillingly to it. It would also begin to spin the wheels of hundreds upon hundreds of school buses, and would erupt in state after state into acts of civil disobedience bordering on a civil war, which has continued to this day.

As parents assured their children they would not be bused and sought to fulfill that promise, the battle was on. It was, in many cases, reminiscent of the hand-to-hand combat our soldiers engage in during street warfare, only in this case our children were being forced to side with the enemy and against their objecting parents.

As our nation was celebrating its two hundredth birthday, the right of parents to determine the shape of their children's lives educationally was being slaughtered. Busing was but another area.

The battle over court-ordered busing was never fought harder than in Boston, where it took four years for federal controls to be lifted in the strife-torn South Boston High School. U.S. District Judge W. Arthur Garrity, who had ordered the busing, called it the "four most difficult years" in the city's history.

Feelings had run so high that a black man was pulled from his car and beaten to death. The turmoil literally rocked the Cradle of Liberty as parents fought for their rights. The press referred to the calamity as the "Battle of Bunker Hill." Sixteen hundred policemen were called out, the disruption was so massive. The year before the Bicentennial, federal marshals moved in with riot gear. "It's too late for us now," a Boston father mumbled half to himself. "Who's gonna fight against a thousand cops?"

But fight they did. Even the birthplace of the late President John F. Kennedy was damaged in a fire apparently set to protest Boston's school desegregation. Antibusing slogans were written on the sidewalk in front of the two-and-a-half story structure.

Eventually the police went on overtime (more money) and the National Guard were called in (more money); 50 FBI agents entered the scene (more money); and 100 U.S. marshals and 550 state troopers marched in (more money). The civil disobedience, begun in 1974, finally subsided to a whimper as our country began to outgrow many of the notions that had once made it so desirable.

All over the country parents fought this measure. They promised in one state after another that they would not be bused. They promised their children they could stay in their neighborhood schools. And they promised them that they knew what was best—and busing was not in their best interests. If they would have to war against the bureaucracy, then war they would.

And they lost. Now what kind of an image do those parents have, their tails between their legs, defeat etched on their faces? Our children got the message: Your parents no longer have any control. Their judgment is poor. Who is the "relative" that is the strongest? Who has the manpower, the means, the strength to make your parents buckle under? Altogether now, shout, children: Uncle Sam!

Our already confused and disenchanted children would be further confused and grow more skeptical. They were learning about pollution. Wouldn't all of these buses add more pollution to the nation's highways? How many would remember parents waiting in long lines at gas stations during the 1973-74 oil embargo, just so they could get to work to support their families? And then, when the price was right, the fuel shortage disappeared, and attendants pumped gas till it almost overflowed just to make the figures at the pump come out to even money.

How many children would remember putting on sweaters and coats in the classroom because the President said there was an energy crisis and we would all have to sacrifice? If the children learned anything else about busing, it would be cynicism over a fuel shortage. How much gas is gobbled up by the yellow scourge that now rolls across our land?

By the 1976–77 school year 23 million, or more than half of the nation's children, were riding the yellow bus at an annual cost of $2,666,466.83. Each year that figure will rise, taxpayers paying out all that money for a program that defies any grounds of common sense be it socially or academically.

No matter that we are facing still another fuel shortage. Uncle Sam will take care of his charges. He will provide them with shiny new buses, and their gas tanks will always be filled. These buses will take them further and further away from their stupid parents who don't know how to win any wars for their children.

Glenn Barnhill, whose child will be attending a private school because he is determined to beat this federal intervention, said, "Every time I turn on the television, that simple son of a——— Carter is smiling at me and telling me there's an energy crisis. And here we're going to spend two point four million dollars on some buses that use gasoline. Taking our son out of public school is just our way of standing up to this federal takeover."

Barnhill is one of the parents who have balked at school-ordered desegregation in the state of Delaware, a program that the press has called "highly successful" and a "model." In reality, it is neither.

Russ and Carol Cross of Delaware decided to teach their son, Wayne, at home rather than have him bused fifteen miles. They, like parents in other states where busing was being forced down parents' throats, have gone to alternative means of education. For some it may have been a clear case of not wanting their children to go to school with black children, but for the great majority, it was simply the straw that broke the camel's back. In a way, forced busing has had a positive side. It forced parents to seek saner methods of education away from schools that they were already unhappy with. By asserting themselves, they could break federal control over the lives of their children through absenting them from the public schools.

Over fourteen hundred students in Delaware chose alternative methods of education rather than give in to the busing demon. Other families moved away before the court order became a reality. School enrollment declined another six thousand. Six private schools have sprung up in Delaware. And the press and the administrators still insist on calling Delaware a "model" and "successful."

Headmaster Kenneth Weinig of the Independence School, the largest private school to spring up in the state of Delaware, said the formation of the school was more than a reaction to busing. "We're going to return to teaching methods that have been successful in the past. This will be a school where discipline reigns and patriotism flourishes. We're going to put emphasis on the three Rs. We're going to stress grammar, spelling, penmanship and the old math."

The fact that many would be branded racist bothered Peggy Settle, who said, "The only thing that bothers me is explaining to our friends that we're not racists." Her husband, an associate professor of economics at the University of Delaware, said of his young daughter, Christine, "She would have had a thirty to forty-five minute drive in to [and back from] a neighborhood where I wouldn't want to spend a day."

Don't worry, Mrs. Settle, black mothers and fathers are not happy about busing either. What could be more insulting to them than to have the government tell them their children couldn't learn unless they were sitting next to a white child?

My husband and I fled a neighborhood and a home that we had grown to love because of busing. It was probably the first busing program to take place in the nation. Only the students were not bused, they were "trolleyed" in by public transportation.

Soon new and unfamiliar faces in the way of the trolleyed students converged on our neighborhood and flooded the junior high school that was three blocks from our home. Families of children had followed each other for generations into this school. But the good feelings and the neighborhood school concept began to crumble, and pride in the school diminished as busing took place. Both internally and externally, the school would be marred. From without, graffiti would be swirled across its bricks. Internally, academia was swept away as knife fights broke out in the halls, and policemen were called to patrol the once serene school.

In the short time it took these trolleyed students to walk to and from school and their transportation, they left their marks everywhere. We all knew each of the four shopkeepers who owned small stores along the route. Most were women and widowed. The trolleyed students eventually caused these shopkeepers to bolt their doors when school was either convening or letting out for the day. The "new" students would go in droves into these stores, packing the interior from counter to door. They would steal sodas, comic books, candy, anything within their reach. If the owner of the store would call out, "You didn't pay for that!" they would shout back obscenities and make off with whatever their hearts desired or their hands could grab. And animosity grew.

On their way to and from school they would pass our home. If it was a trash collection day, they would arbitrarily kick over the cans along the way. The girls as well as the boys spat on our pavements, and if you were brave enough to go out and tell them to stop, they just shouted obscenities at you or stood their ground and challenged you physically.

The same thing happened at the high school I had attended. One of my former English teachers had been stabbed by a pupil.

And so it was, with great reluctance, that we decided this was not the atmosphere we wanted for our children in the way of schooling. Nor did we want them exposed to the filthy language and the uncouth pupils who showed no respect for any authority.

Five years after we moved away, a special study was done by city officials to quell the gang and racial violence at that school. In 1979 yet another teen-ager was stabbed.

In those years I was too busy with "babying" to even know that "busing" was going on. We only knew what was happening in our alma mater. And it wasn't good.

The most important thing that was brought to national attention was that schools in poorer sections of the country needed upgrading. It was a fact that few either knew or thought about, unless they had children in those schools. But busing is definitely not the answer.

Parents have marched three thousand strong chanting, "Wake up America, wake up!"; they write letters to the editor of their local newspapers and rail that we are living in an Orwellian society in which "Big Brother" dictates to parents, telling them that their children will adhere to the ride on the yellow bus whether they like it or not; and they even go mad because they feel so impotent in decisions concerning their children. Some, like Neal Bradley Long, took matters into their own hands. Bradley, who shot and killed an Ohio educator who was appointed by a federal court to devise a plan to desegregate Dayton schools, said, "I did what I had to do."

They may kill a man, but they have been unable to kill this mad scheme that has been dictated to them. So parents simply acquiesce, admit defeat, knowing the "enemy" has the money, the power and the troops to defeat them. And their children learn, at an early age, that their parents are impotent against the bureaucracy.

In one state parents are being threatened with legal action because they refuse to comply with forced busing. Their child is asthmatic and has already suffered a near-fatal attack on the bus.

Minutes count for her young life, but still the advocates insist that she must attend a school far from her home. No matter if, as in this case, it means life or death; the dictator has spoken; knuckle under!

If schools do not comply, they are blackmailed. Federal funds will be cut off. The Philadelphia School Board said it had no choice but to force transfer twelve hundred of its teachers to meet federal desegregation guidelines on the teacher level.

Had it refused to comply, HEW would have refused to release the $6 million needed to implement the voluntary pupil desegregation program just beginning; and HEW also held the threat over the Philadelphia schools of taking back $100 million the School District was to receive for other programs. School board member Philip Stahl said the disruption of students and teachers "just plain wasn't worth it. We have lost sight of the purpose of education. We are diseducating the children," he said. Philadelphia's school desegregation calls for the moving of more than nineteen thousand pupils during the first three years of its implementation.

"I oppose any busing that disregards the right of the parents and takes children from their neighborhood schools for the sake of racial balance," wrote one columnist. "As good as such a goal is, even more important is the preservation of parental rights. The court decisions on busing leave out those rights."

In 1978 the Senate tried once again to limit the authority of federal judges to order busing of pupils to desegregate public schools. On a vote of 49-47, the amendment went down in defeat. Senator William Roth (R., Del.) spoke on the issue: "In the guise of achieving a supposedly ideal racial mix in our schools even where no discriminatory intent has been found, the courts have reached deep into the once private confines of family life to engineer social change that separates families from their communities and children from their families."

Over a hundred studies on busing for integration have been conducted since its inception.

One ten-year-long study of the impact of voluntary school desegregation in Riverside, Calif., revealed that not only had busing failed to improve the self-esteem of minority children but it "did not gain in achievement, either absolutely or relative to national norms.

"We expected to document the successes of the whole program: busing to achieve ethnic balance in school, the rising competence and ambition of minority children and their subsequent academic rise to equality with whites. We have been profoundly disappointed," read the report that was conducted by psychologists Dr. Norman Miller of the University of Southern California and Dr. Harold B. Gerard of UCLA.

Not only did the grades of minority groups fail to improve, but the psychologists discovered that the grades dipped and even after several years there appeared to be no change in minority achievement motivation.

As to the social mix that was hoped for, they found instead that "the children in each ethnic group became more and more cliquish over the years and less accepting of those outside of their own group."

Sociologist James S. Coleman, whose study in the mid-1960s was widely used to support school desegregation, is now in the position of other apologists who have disrupted family life. Coleman now admits that it is a "mistaken belief" that black students learn better in integrated classrooms.

He said research has borne out his changed conclusion. "Thus," said Coleman, "what once appeared to be fact is now known to be fiction."

Originally Coleman supported the theory that the social-class composition of a school had more impact on student achievement than either resources or teaching methods, and he claimed that black children scored higher on standardized tests in schools with a middle-class white majority than they did in schools where all of the children were poor and black.

Coleman then carried his theory before the congressional committees and to school-desegregation cases in the courtrooms.

Coleman now admits that for minority children there were "no overall gains," and that mandatory busing programs in many cities have been "counterproductive."

Which brings Mr. Coleman belatedly over to the side of the parents, too late to halt what he so strongly helped to set in motion—the yellow scourge.

22.

Changing Your Child's Behavior

"Sex education is probably the most volatile curriculum in schools today," said one district coordinator of health education. "It's being questioned constantly in every school district."

In the mid-1960s sex education began to flood the nation's schools, muddying the feet of kindergarten children right on up into the college level, leaving a mildew stain on the nation that would indelibly continue to mark those generations who had waded into it.

It was also at this point that the public schools turned away from intellect and skills and turned instead to social issues. Through conditioning, they eroded and then inured our children to the meaning of morality.

It would also mark the first major battlefield involving parents against the educational establishment. Some fifteen years later, the concerned parents have proven to be prophetic when they claimed it would wipe out the family, religion and moral values, would create generations of sexually active and selfish children, and would show a drop in the basics.

In the face of all these predictions come true, those committed to the programs and those who are making money from it (and it is big business) continue to preach that what our children need to stop the sexual revolution is not less sex education, but more. And so the artists who continue to paint our children's minds a dark and ominous color draw even broader strokes.

When first polled, 71 percent of the American people favored the program. Now, realizing it has brought about all the damaging effects predicted, the polls are reversing themselves. When a thousand women from all parts of the United States were asked: "How do you feel that children should first learn about sex?" 87 percent said it should come from their parents. What do the children think? Another recent study showed that nearly 90 percent of adolescents preferred the mother or father as a source of sex information.

But the schools, unwilling to admit they have made the mistake of the century, brazenly push on, and the building domino effect, as predicted, continues to act fatally on family life.

Whatever hangs heavy over the homes of America today—teen-age pregnancies, VD, abortions, ad infinitum—the solutions from various special interest groups is the same: "We need to step up the sex-education program" or "It needs to begin earlier" is the stock answer. How much earlier than kindergarten, one asks?

As Jean with her honors English, her French and health classes illustrated so well, the subject is interwoven into every single subject and left to the discretion of the teacher. The philosophy of this new teaching is riddled with such words as "values," "the right to choose one's lifestyle," "there is no right or wrong to a sexual action," "you need not be responsible to anyone but yourself," "it is your choice."

The programs grow more base each year. Not only are students in the state of Pennsylvania expected to discuss birth control (including abortion, withdrawal and the use of a diaphragm), according to State Rep. Martin Mullen, but they are expected to discuss noneffective methods of birth control, including sex during menstruation, sex other than lying down, and the use of Saran Wrap as a substitute for condoms.

Teacher language grows more vulgar by the day. In one sex-education class the teacher prefaced his talk on teen-age pregnancies with: "Now, this may turn you off, and you may think this is a lot of Honky bullshit," and then went on to tell his class, "There are too many fourteen- or fifteen-year-old fathers and there shouldn't be with birth control." Not abstention . . . birth control.

Widely used in the elementary schools are pictures showing a naked, prone female with her knee raised—lying opposite a male figure in a position for intercourse.

Posters distributed to schools show a penis with hands putting on a condom and a picture of the uterus with hands inserting an intrauterine device.

The *San Francisco Examiner* told of the father of a 16-year-old who has promised to wage a fight against pornography all the way to the Supreme Court because of five films that were scheduled to be shown to his daughter's class. He termed them "absolute filth," saying the films showed lesbian acts, a human being having intercourse with a goat and several scenes of oral sex.

Meanwhile, our children, numbed to any moral values, treat these encounters with their teacher/sex educators lightly and scorn their parents for being so "old-fashioned."

In Maryland, an article stated that if your 16-year-old son or daughter comes running home one afternoon and shouts, "Hey, Ma! I just learned all the characteristics of a successful honeymoon," it may well be that he or she is enrolled in the course called "relationships" being offered in the Montgomery County Public Schools system.

But more than likely Ma isn't home. And more than likely when she comes home from work, she'll be too tired to even listen—or maybe she's just tired, period, of fighting the system anymore.

When parents initially warned that the type of sex education in the public schools would stimulate the pupils, they forgot to include that it could also stimulate the teachers. There is no question that this no-holds-barred type of "education" has had a destructive effect on all of society.

A newspaper account told of a junior-high sex-education teacher who recruited teen-agers directly from his sex-education class. One source said: "They had sex orgies in house trailers, tents, houses ... just about everywhere except cemeteries." The teacher has since been charged with kidnapping, taking indecent liberties with a child, and conspiring to take indecent liberties with a child.

I had appeared on television in New York City talking about the horrendous liberties taken in sex-education classes by teachers who were trained to do their "own thing." Prior to my coming, the TV station had sent out a crew to film a sex-education class in progress. Of course it was such a mild program it made everything I said seem like a woman gone mad. I was told by the moderator that the things I was talking about were not happening in New York City. And that, of course, is what all people including the educators say about their schools on the subject.

Did the TV crew really expect the teacher to show the world what was taking place in sex-education classes? As the schools have hidden the curriculum from prodding parents, as they have tried to make grades look better by inflating them, as they clean up their presentations when they are pushing for the programs, so apparently did the teacher (whose classroom was filmed for the TV program I appeared on) modify her presentation.

Shortly after that television show, New York City exploded with protest when a teacher showed what the *New York Daily News* headlined as "disgusting, grossly offensive, explicit and perverted" film strips to an all-girls class at a Bronx high school. I felt a hollow victory when District Attorney Mario Merola said something like this had never happened before. Just how many times it continues to happen, we will never know. What smolders beneath the surface should be apparent now to everyone who views the behavior of our adolescents, teen-agers and those in college today. If not the material, then the philosophy of "choices" in sex education is the damaging element.

The film in the Bronx school depicted sexual intercourse and oral-genital sex, both common topics of discussion in schools today. The filmstrip was one of six in a package called "Love-making."

The teacher contended to the end that he did nothing wrong. Since he, along with the students, has been trained to see nothing wrong with such a presentation, he was justified in the way he saw his actions.

The bottom line once again was that while this type of movie would be forbidden to minors in a movie house, under the banner of "education" nothing could legally be done about it.

The school officials, like someone caught with his hand in the till, claimed the film had been blacklisted. It is an old tactic. And it works! Nevertheless it had still been purchased and shown. This, dear parents, is called "Academic Freedom."

Parents did fight back in Bergen County, N.J., when their high school required that students complete a course in sex education that included birth control, abortion and other aspects of sex for graduation. State Education Commissioner Fred G. Burke ruled that local boards of education could continue teaching sex education. In fact, New Jersey, Pennsylvania, and several other states are now getting ready to issue uniform guidelines on the subject and New Jersey, following the lead of other states, is entertaining the idea of making sex education mandatory.

But mandatory or not, the child faces it squarely every day, in every single subject, including the basic ones.

Dr. Margaret Gregory, supervisor of Maternal and Child Health Services, told the N.J. State Board of Education that increased pregnancies and abortions have urged the board to make sex education mandatory. "We can't ignore these thousands of babies just because a few old-fashioned parents try to stop their local school boards from offering some down-to-earth information on family planning."

The parent put-down is always present. As I stated before, the answer for the proponents of this damaging program is to give the students more, and more, and more, and to eventually call a halt to this battle by deeming sex-education necessary in all fifty states.

As part of the Carter administration's plan to curb soaring rates of teen-age pregnancy, the United States Department of Health, Education and Welfare has been funding programs focusing on teen-age boys. It is merely an extension of what is taking place in public schools all across the country.

On one such weekend in Rochester, N.Y., more than two hundred teen-age boys gathered at the University of Rochester. The session was called "Man '78." Part of the funding—$102,000 of it—came in the form of a federal grant to Rochester and Monroe County Planned Parenthood. Dr. Sol Gordon of comic-book fame was a guest speaker. Topics to be covered were: Am I Ready for Sex? Am I Parent Material? VD, Dating and Relating, Sex in the Media, Male Lib, Who Am I?

"The message seems to be that everyone is active," said spokeswoman Dorothy Wardell, a well-known advocate of sex education who has been active in the movement. "As for the sexually active teen-age male, we want him to know that now he's made that choice he should accept the consequences and act responsibly."

Again we hear the words of the sex educators: "choice," "responsible." We all know what Dr. Wardell and the sex education teachers mean. The teen-ager should use a contraceptive. That is being "responsible" in their eyes. If that fails, there is always abortion for the girl involved. Nobody, but nobody, puts as much if any emphasis on refraining from sexual self-indulgence.

"The federal money," wrote Patricia McCormack, UPI Health Editor, is part of $60 million to be used in [former] Secretary of Health, Education and Welfare Joseph Califano's adolescent health initiative. More federal intervention. Enter again the permissive "relative" Uncle Sam, again digging into your pocket to the detriment of your child and your family and your happiness.

The teen-age boys who were to take part in this weekend were told they have a need to protect themselves against venereal disease—and paternity suits.

Some of the statements on which they were quizzed were:

• It's not right to use birth control.
• Sex education is nothing but a waste of time.
• A guy should use birth control whenever possible.

The program to reach males over 25 proved unsuccessful, despite such inducements as beer, sandwiches, free condoms and even stag movies. So Uncle Sam decided to concentrate on males 15 to 24.

Where, I ask myself, are the parents of the minors who are going on this kind of a weekend?

Charlotte A. Teel of Cinnaminson, N.J., was right there expressing her feelings about sex education in her school by way of a letter to the editor. She reported twenty-eight "swinging sex ads" were shown to the class. Then the teacher instructed students to tell which ad "intrigued" them the most and asked the students to write an ad of their own. She called this type of teaching, "perverted sex."

One school-board member, speaking on behalf of the teachers, said he would uphold the right of teachers to use whatever source materials they wish. He did not want to "inhibit" his teachers by checking their reference materials.

A member of the faculty, said Mrs. Teel, said he intended to insure that the kids get their sex education. They were entitled to it.

"Do parents have a right to teach their children that some sexual behavior is sinful? Forcing students to decide between school authority and parental authority with respect to moral values," said Mrs. Teel, "can seriously harm both the family and the school." It continues to do just that—and the parents' protestations be damned.

Another school-board member, Lillian Fox, took the side of the parents. "According to state law, parents in New Jersey do not have options for religious or moral grounds. My position is parents should have that right." She confirmed that some students who work from assignments in a book called *Search for Values* have had to read and write advertisements for contraceptives.

Shortly after the Cinnaminson scuffle over sex education, Education Commissioner Fred G. Burke wrote that to excuse children from a portion of the program dealing with sex education "would give to a parent the authority which the Legislature has already vested in local boards of education." Schools clearly have more legal power over your children than you do.

These children have been taught from kindergarten up in some cases to "do your own thing." As they grow, many become even more obnoxious. In California a 10-year-old college where coeds roam bare-breasted and take courses in prostitution and how to have an hour-long orgasm came under the watchful eye of the Associated Press.

Called "More University," the AP release said students have sex and urinate outdoors. Blackie Burak, one of the twenty full-time residents of More and its legal counsel, said: "Some colleges are known for their English program [where?] or their history school.

Our goal is to become the foremost center of instruction on sensuality. I think we're the best, and I don't think we should be persecuted for it."

Dr. David Reuben, known for his book, *Everything You Always Wanted To Know About Sex and Were Afraid To Ask*, has come down hard on sex education. He said early-on that while human beings can become accustomed to having some aspects of their lives exposed to public scrutiny, "every well-adjusted (mark that, sex counsellors and teachers) person draws the line at sex."

In his book *Bayonets and Roses*, author Robert Marshall discusses some of the federal intervention in sex education. On page 15 of the OEO (Office of Economic Opportunity) report it says:

(A) It is time for the Federal Government to take responsible action on the issue of sex education. It should assist in curriculum development in the public schools and support demonstration projects aimed specifically at making information and services available to the sexually active teenager.

While masturbation is taught with abandon and no moralizing in the public schools, Dr. William H. Masters pointed out that masturbation is a crime in some thirty-six states. So no matter how you feel about the subject, the fact is that our children are, in many cases, being taught in the classroom to break still another law.

Mitch Leon, a spokesman for the N.J. State Department of Health, in citing the growing teen-age pregnancies in the country, said a mouthful when he stated that schools' sex-education programs "do not appear to be overwhelmingly successful" in alleviating this problem.

In May of 1978 the N.J. Senate Education Committee released a bill that would make New Jersey the first state in the nation to set up systematic rape prevention classes in public schools. The bill was approved by the Senate unanimously without debate.

The bill would cover pupils from kindergarten through twelfth grade. Children may, says the bill, be exempted if parents object. That is precisely the way sex education started out. You can bet that this program too will eventually become mandatory.

Pity the children! Now kids can really fear not only their father, brothers, uncles, cousins, but even the friendly retired man who lives next door. How many little children will wake up screaming from a nightmare after these classes? We are, indeed, a world of education gone mad.

The first and only poll I saw on the issue gave 82.9 percent approval—just as sex education was originally given the green light. I cringe to think of what these rape classes will do to further damage family relationships and the psyche of the child.

23.

More Child-Changer Programs

There was a time when the public schools basked in the approval of contented parents. Those were the days when the basics were paramount and the schools stressed discipline, supported the parents and family life, fostered art and music appreciation, and encouraged children in honesty, integrity and moral conduct.

But in the last fifteen to twenty years the public schools slowly, and then with great force, began to meddle in the very minds of their captive audiences, as they became what knowledgeable experts in the field have called "agents of social change."

Not only was sex education introduced, but shortly thereafter came a plethora of other social and psychological programs under the titles of sensitivity training, values clarification, situation ethics, and a program that the educational establishment had the affrontery to call morals education. Morals education is simply an umbrella phrase to cover all of the programs of social change that are already in existence.

Since everyone is screaming that the public schools do not teach morals, obviously a good public-relations person picked the title "morals education." The parents want morals to be taught? No problem. But in the end, it is just a new lid to cover the old garbage can.

The end results of all of these programs has been a severe dip in literate high-school graduates, a sexual revolution, a parent-child revolution, a drug culture, and a narcissistic child who thinks the world should revolve around his wants and desires.

The programs are subversive—100 percent subversive. When the average person thinks of the word "subversion" he usually conjures up someone ready to overthrow a government. However no term other than subversion suffices when you examine what has been done to our children and family life in the name of education. To subvert means to overthrow or destroy something established—to corrupt, to undermine, as in character or morals. What has been more undermined, corrupted, or has had their moral character besmirched than our youth?

Educators often refer to these programs as "innovative" or the "humanization of education." What they are teaching is, in fact, the disregarding of parental and religious influences by teaching secular humanism. Put simply: If it feels good, do it!

There is probably no one more knowledgeable on the subject of these new programs than Barbara Morris, who lives in the state of Maryland. She has studied and written countless articles on all of the programs that have successfully penetrated the public school systems in the last two decades. All of these programs gear the child to be autonomous. He is told he need look to no authority but himself for all of his wants, needs and gratifications in life. Such autonomy "canonizes adolescent rebellion," wrote Joseph J. Schwab in his book, *Theory of Knowledge and Problems of Education.*

"Your children are being alienated from you, from their American heritage and from their religious beliefs; and it's being accomplished through a process called values education," said Barbara Morris. "Everything your child values, believes in or thinks about is up for grabs: religion, sex, family, friends, hair styles, death, war, authority, et cetera."

One method that is widely used in the public schools to achieve these goals comes in the form of a diary. There, if the teacher assigns the diary-keeper to religion as a topic, the child records his or her thoughts, conversations and actions involving the chosen subject. They are then discussed and scrutinized in class.

In one English class, the final exam on what the teacher called "Seminar in Ideas" contained the following questions:

1. Discuss how Seminar in Ideas has helped you to examine your life.
2. Why do you believe in God? or Why do you not believe in God?
3. Trace the development of religion from the time of primitive Man and his reasons for "creating" God and discuss religion's place today.
4. Schools are closed. What, where, and how would children learn?
5. A common action by man since time began is protest. Why is

protest necessary? Does it work? If so, what kind of protest works?
6. Define Situation Ethics. Create a situation that you would normally consider immoral but due to circumstances would become either amoral or moral.

The English test ends with this signed message from the teacher:

Dear Students,
It has been a personal pleasure to work with this class. NOW, GO FORTH AND SING. CELEBRATE LIFE.

In another English test that fell into my hands, the student is asked to match the key words in one column with the best antonyms in another column. I found it interesting that the correct match for the word "defy" was "parent."

One parent group fighting these measures in the public schools wrote: "Language arts and reading books at the elementary level are being rewritten to draw children into self-confession, self-criticism, and the solution of moral dilemmas through situation ethics as determined by the classroom group."

One of the most popular fifth-grade social-studies courses is called: "Man: A Course of Study." It is known more commonly under the acronym MACOS. In an article written by Mel Gabler, who pointed out that MACOS was being used in forty-three states, he wrote: "In MACOS, wife-swapping is taught as a necessity; men practice cannibalism; baby girls are killed. The 11-year-old students 'role play' leaving their grandmothers to die. The MACOS booklets are filled with cruelty, violence and death."

Dr. Onalee McGraw has served as coordinator for the National Coalition for Children, an association dedicated to the preservation of the family and the defense of parental rights in education. In one of her many writings on the dilemma of the public educational system, she talked about the "new" morals education. She asks her reader to consider the following moral dilemma taken from "Hypothetical Dilemmas for Use in Moral Discussions," which has been prepared by the Education and Research Foundation at Harvard:

Sex as a Need: The Johnson family (with four children) was a very happy and close one. Mr. and Mrs. Johnson were in their '30s. One day Mr. Johnson fell from a third-story building where he was working. He broke his back in this accident and was totally paralyzed from his waist down. The accident did not result in economic hardship because of workmen's compensation. Three months after the accident, when Mr. Johnson came home, the problem began. Ms. (sic) Johnson, who was a young person, realized that she would have to give up sexual intercourse with her husband. If she did not want to give up her sex life, she had the following choices: either to get a divorce, or to have extramarital affairs.

1. Is it possible to separate sex from affection? What do you think she should do? Give reasons.

2. Do you think this woman should remain married to the husband? Why or why not?

3. What do you think would happen to the family if she had an affair?

4. If she decides to have an affair, should she tell her husband or keep it a secret? Why?

Along the same lines, the following are some of the types of questions widely employed in public schools under values clarifications:

Which do you think is the most religious thing to do on a Sunday morning?
• Go to church to hear a very good preacher.
• Listen to some classical music on the radio.
• Have a big breakfast with the family.

Critics of this particular exercise say it implies that whatever the student thinks is religious *is* religious.

A minority school-board member who is opposed to these new programs in the public schools sent me the teacher's hygiene outline for her pupils. Among the things the teacher was required to discuss was a debate titled "Marriage is a necessary evil" and a discussion in which "the student will be able to analyze, judge [for himself] and discern orally or in writing the personal, moral and religious aspects of the use of contraceptives."

The instructions tell the teacher she is obligated to discuss under birth control: oral contraceptives, sterilization, and abortion as various means of birth control.

If you are still deluded by the new name for these mind-changing programs in the public schools, and you still believe morals are being taught, let Sidney B. Simon, author of one of the most widely used books in this new type of education, put the matter to rest once and for all. Simon told an interviewer that teachers must be alert to keep "moralizing crap" out of their work with values.

Even *Better Homes and Gardens,* in their September '78 issue, warned parents that like all of its predecessors, this so-called values or moral education is again diluting every course: social studies, literature, science, health and even driver-training classes. Morals education, said the article, should not be confused with "formalized religious principles, or rigid moral codes."

"The emphasis," said the article, "is on moral reasoning and examining one's own values, rather than on inculcating specific virtues, such as honesty." There is, said *Better Homes and Gardens*, "a neutrality; any choice is right as long as the student can explain why he holds the value."

Another widely used form of the new teaching that is wreaking destruction and disobedience among our youth is one originally called "The Living Process Curriculum" or the "Magic Circle." Sitting in a circle, the children, led by the teacher, are encouraged to explore and share their private thoughts. The manual for the teacher suggests over a hundred fifty lead-ins to get the project underway. Some of the suggestions are noted here:

• Something about my physical self that makes me feel 'OK'— Not OK.

• A time that having a feeling (good or bad) got me in trouble.

• Something I used to believe and believe no longer.

• How I use my power with younger-older people.

No matter what the child talks about, the teacher is warned against "moralizing," "chastising" or "preaching." Once again there is no right or wrong.

The National Congress for Educational Excellence, a parent group that opposes these "innovative" programs, also reviews many of the films put out for children. Some of those reviews are reprinted here:

MOM, WHY WON'T YOU LISTEN? At the end one role-playing girl screams at her play mother: "You go around with that sick smile on your face all the time. You look like you are slobbering . . . I wish you were in pain . . . Oh, God, if I ever grew up to be like you, I would rather kill myself!"

I OWE YOU NOTHING. The role-playing teen-agers agree that since they "didn't ask to be born," the parents have an obligation to feed, clothe, house and respect them without any responsibility on the part of the child to conform to any house rules.

GUIDANCE FOR THE '70s—SELF ESTEEM. The teen-agers are given Playdough and told to make images of who they are. The viewer sees the kids making strange free-form models and each one tells what his means. They are asked, "What could you do to feel better about yourself?" "Who do you think you are?" In a sarcastic manner the therapist tells the children that they are always getting "advice from mommy and daddy and other experts."

Barbara Morris is forever digging to awaken decent parents who are unaware of how and why the finished product of a child whom they have put so much love into is turning out so badly. She calls the public schools "change agents."

To justify the accusation, she wrote in one article about guidelines for change-agent educators, which was published in "Social Change," Vol. 7 No. 2, a newsletter from the NTL Institute for Applied Behavioral Science. "It is of interest to know," wrote Barbara, "that a phone call to the NTL Institute for a copy of this 'inside' publication was promptly met with a flat denial that the publication ever existed! That should give a pretty good idea about how carefully the term 'change agent' is protected and kept from the general public," she noted.

"If there is still any doubt that schools do in fact function as change agents," she continued, "the reality can be seen in the March 22, 1974 newsletter of the Prince Georges County (Maryland) Educators' Association. In this issue, teachers were warned to oppose legislation that would have given parents access to their children's textbooks. Teachers were told 'OPPOSE SB 196 the PARENTAL RIGHTS FOR PUBLIC SCHOOL CHILDREN. Tell legislators that this legislation is not needed. May render schools ineffective as change agents since it would place all curriculum in the hands of parents.'"

Discussing the way values are taught in the public schools of America, Barbara Morris says, "The values you have passed on to your child—the values he comes to school with—must be clarified. They are not acceptable 'as is' because you did the unforgivable—you decided for your child, because it is your God-given responsibility and right—what values you want him to hold. Those imposed values which he did not choose freely must be clarified. He must decide, immature and unwise though he may be, whether or not he wishes to keep, modify, or discard what you have taught him."

24.

The Comptroller General Does a Whitewash

So hostile have informed parents been to the new programs that are being pressed on their children in the public schools, that two U.S. congressmen asked Elmer B. Staats, Comptroller General of the United States, to look into the matter.

In his letter, Congressman Daniel J. Flood told Staats that parents across the country "have protested that the books are subversive, irreligious, immoral, racist, sexist and just plain filthy." He called for an "in-depth inquiry" into the federal involvement in the matter.

Congressman Albert H. Quie said that incidents involving charges made that the federal government "is funding activities aimed at modifying the behavior of school children" had come to his attention. The charges, he said, have been both numerous and persistent, the most serious of which centered "around activities in the classroom directed at modifying traditional or accepted views of society."

Quie asked also that a study to determine to what extent there is federal funding for programs of "behavior modification" be done. "I would like to know under what authority and where it is being carried out."

Approximately two years after each congressman had sent in his separate requests, the study was completed. Released in April of 1977, it was, for the most part, ignored by the media. Titled, "Questions Persist About Federal Support For Development Of Curriculum Materials And Behavior Modification Techniques Used In Local Schools," it ran to eighty-three pages, and like the waste often associated with our government, a blank and unnumbered page was stamped in big, black block letters: BLANK.

In my opinion the report was a whitewash. Incomplete, it did not cover the specifics asked for and was riddled with excuses, evasions and omissions. If I were grading it as a thesis, I would have handed it back marked: Incomplete.

Throughout the report evasions such as these cropped up:

- Information about the capabilities and activities of participants engaged in educational dissemination is inadequate.
- An initial difficulty in identifying Federal funding in this area was the lack of precise definitions.
- Information on these activities at the Federal level is usually limited or nonexistent.
- Could not determine the amount of Federal funds supporting such activities.

The report did make some admissions, as in the digest portion:

Much concern has been expressed about

—curriculum materials, such as textbooks, teacher guides, or films teachers and students use in a classroom, and

—behavior modification, a professional term that refers to a family of techniques that teachers can use to bring about changes in students' academic and social skills.

This report put to rest any doubts that the public schools have played a major role in changing the behavior of every child they have touched . . . using the taxpayers' money to do it.

Commenting on curriculum materials, the report states: "Curriculum development might also be no more than an individual teacher's decision to develop and introduce supplementary material into the classroom." The report makes it all sound so innocuous with the wording "no more than" in referring to teachers doing "their own thing."

Acknowledging parental concern over these programs, the report read: "The complaint is more often a concern about a child's behavior (such as beliefs, attitudes, or actions) possibly being modified or changed. Many materials, activities, or techniques," the report admits, "could modify a child's behavior without technically being behavior modification."

While obviously talking about the parents' point of view, the report says, "The major cause for concern about materials and techniques appears to be disagreements as to the purpose of public education. One view is that public education is to teach children basic cognitive skills—reading, writing, and arithmetic—without attempting to alter personalities, standards, and values. Another view"—obviously that of the educational establishment and those pushing these programs—"holds that mastery of only cognitive skills does not fully equip children to deal with various life situations and that the public school system has the obligation to produce mature adults by going beyond instruction in cognitive skills. This additional instruction could include"—and may I add *does* include—"exposing children to and having them examine different value systems. These opposing views of what constitute desirable educational goals, particularly with regard to values, are an underlying reason for complaints."

The report also gives recognition to the fact that many citizens' beliefs are threatened by curriculum materials chosen to meet "value-oriented education goals." Critics see such materials as symbols of the drift of public education away from basic education toward personality development, life adjustment and excessive emphasis on what children think and feel, said the report.

"Also," the report says, "concerns have been expressed because a philosophy called secular humanism has been incorporated into programs dealing with values." Critics say, the report continues, "this philosophy, which espouses a person as a determiner of his or her own fate and the relativity of moral values, threatens the role of the family unit and opposes traditional precepts such as belief in God. Materials and techniques used for clarifying values and modifying behavior are viewed by critics as tools of secular humanism for altering children's attitudes, standards, and values."

Under Disapproval of Methods, the report said that concerns have been registered on the basis that "use of life-death games, diary keeping, classroom observation, and other methods for revealing the child's attitudes, opinions, and home-life conditions is seen as threatening the right to privacy.

"Citizens who disagree with the educational goals or methods of a curriculum also believe they have little influence in procedures and processes used to evaluate and select materials. Many believe that the school system neither wants nor values their opinion before selection occurs and that pressing a complaint about materials or techniques involves a time-consuming and expensive review process."

Parents also told those making up this report that they felt there was a loss of local control over public education, and that control has passed from local citizens to professional educators, "with teachers no longer recognizing that parents and other community members are their employers."

And finally—although with no definite figures or any of the

specific areas or materials that either of the congressmen had requested and the various groups had submitted—the report said, "The Federal role in funding the development of materials and techniques for use in local schools has increased notably in the past decade. A number of Federal programs support and control, in varying degrees, projects for development of curriculum materials and behavior modification techniques.

"Available data shows that large amounts of Federal funds go for curriculum development and dissemination and for other educational techniques, such as behavior modification."

"Overall data needed to determine the total amount of Federal funding for these activities and the impact of such funding does not exist."

The programs they did look into and reported on, after the specifics that were requested in Congressmen Flood's and Quie's letters, were pure pap compared to the concerns facing parents with children in the public-school system.

They covered such programs as the "Bilingual Education Program," "Education of the Handicapped," and "Indian Education." Under Health—and everyone who has been involved with a child in school over the last ten to fifteen years knows full well that Health is sex education—they completely whitewashed the issue by giving the following topics covered in class: "grooming, sleep, and skin care." The federal government has been extensively involved in providing funds for sex education since its inception, giving various school districts funds to set up model programs for the rest of the country.

Are you still wondering why your child's behavior is so different from what you have taught him?

25.

A Step in the Right Direction

There are few heroes today, especially in government. But one has emerged to take the first positive step to turn things around in the public schools. His name is Senator Orrin Hatch (R-Utah). Through timing, bluffing and compromise, he was able to bring an education amendment to the floor that would be subsequently signed into law by President Carter on Nov. 1, 1978. It is called the Hatch Amendment, or the Parental Consent Amendment. In part, it reads as follows:

> (b) No Student shall be required, as part of any applicable program, to submit to psychiatric examination, testing, or treatment, or psychological examination, testing, or treatment, in which the primary purpose is to reveal information concerning:
> (1) political affiliations;
> (2) mental or psychological problems potentially embarrassing to the student or his family;
> (3) sex behavior and attitudes;
> (4) illegal, anti-social, self-incriminating and demeaning behavior;
> (5) critical appraisals of other individuals with whom respondents have close family relationships;
> (6) income (other than that required by law determine eligibility for participation in a program or for receiving financial assistance under such a program), without prior consent of the student (if the student is an adult or emancipated minor) or in

168

the case of unemancipated minor, without the prior written consent of the parent.

Columnist James Kilpatrick, writing of the amendment, said, "Here and there, we may suppose, a few ultra-sophisticated parents will agree to putting their children through a sexual inquisition. In such an event, the parents and the inquisitors will deserve each other."

Citing a typical example of what is happening in our schools today, Senator Hatch talked of a sex education program in Wisconsin, which starts at the kindergarten level, where children as young as 10 are told how to get an abortion.

Senator Hatch was supported in the amendment by the colorful Senator S. I. Hayakawa, who said, "To inquire into the sexual attitudes and beliefs of eight-year-olds, to probe into their psychic and emotional problems, real or imagined, rather than into the level of their intellectual achievements—these are serious invasions of privacy.

"And messing around with the psyches of young people does not stop with testing and inquiries," he went on. "There are exercises in psychodrama, role-playing, touch therapy, encounter groups and other psychological games that have no academic significance whatsoever."

I called Senator Hatch's Washington office and spoke with Ronald Docksai, legislative counsel to Senator Hatch, who had worked closely with the senator on the amendment.

"It is binding," said Docksai of the amendment. The Office of Education of HEW is currently drawing up administrative guidelines, he said, that will be ready for the '79 fall school term. Docksai said it will be up to each individual state department of education to act on the amendment. The penalty for not complying, he said, will be that "federal funds will be withdrawn or withheld from the respective school districts which fail to adhere to the Hatch Amendment."

There has, he said, already been some flak from the National Education Association. "Representatives of the NEA called," he noted. "They were originally opposed to the amendment prior to its enactment and now the verb they choose to use is 'concern.' Basically, much of their concern is predicated on the effects the new legislation would have on the content of textbooks and other curriculum materials.

"What this does is to require written and informed parental consent for any form of academic testing on the elementary or secondary school level which is not achievement or scholastic-achievement oriented. The operative adjective is 'informed'—that they have to be given notice the student is being tested," said Docksai. This also applies to oral testing, he said. "For example, a skit play-acted in front of the class could come under testing if the teacher is monitoring the reaction of students.

"The way we got this accepted on the floor was to introduce three amendments: first, the parental consent; second, the cognitive skills amendment that would require congressional oversight over any money spent for curriculum materials; and third, one that would block all the grant money in the Elementary and Secondary Act. That would have meant that all fifty-two billion dollars would go directly to the states rather than going through the Department of HEW," said Docksai.

"Because this was a piece of legislation that would be considered prior to a congressional recess, we were able to convince the more liberal senators that we had the votes for at least two of our three amendments. We made the proposal to Senator Javits' staff that we would withdraw two of our amendments on the condition that we get the third passed," he said.

"Senators Javits and Pell were floor mangers for the ESA. We asked if they would agree to support our parental-rights amendment and to vow to fight for it in the pending conference committee. They agreed," said Docksai. In that way, the amendment was brought to the floor.

Unfortunately, Docksai said the amendment stops short of ordering specific programs—i.e. sex education, values clarification, etc.—out of the public schools.

The one major flaw in the amendment is that the parents will not get to see the test beforehand unless they ask for it. Even if they do get to see the test, how many will know the philosophy behind such testing? How many parents will simply sign the form brought home by their children with no questions asked? As Superintendent of Schools K. KiKi Konstantinos said, "Very, very few" parents look deeply into the well of education.

In a similar situation, one that involved the testing of school students in Pennsylvania to try to determine whether or not they were potential drug users, District Judge John Morgan Davis handed down a decision that aborted the testing. What he had to say in part of his decision certainly applies to the Hatch Amendment and parental permission for such testing.

"The parents are not aware of the consequences and there is no substitute for candor and honesty in fact," said Judge Davis in his

September 28, 1973 ruling, "particularly by the school board who, as the ultimate decision maker as far as the education of our children is concerned, should give our citizenry a more forthright approach. The attempt to make the letter requesting consent similar to a promotional inducement to buy, lacks the necessary substance to give a parent the opportunity to give knowing, intelligent and aware consent.

"The average American parent has a great and naive faith in 'scientifically' constructed tests. This faith is reinforced by the unconscious desire of the more insecure parents to avoid involvement and to depend on 'professionals' to make the difficult decisions in the education and maturation of their children."

26.

What You Sow

Our young people, hell-bent on setting records in areas where the youth of this country fortunately failed to do so in previous generations, seem to do nothing in moderation, but everything in epidemic or pandemic proportions.

In the buildings that were built to teach them, which have miserably failed, they are setting records for violence, vandalism and terrorism. "It is not isolated," said Stephen H. Edward, Jr., president of the California Teachers' Association. "It is general and it is epidemic. We see it happening in farm communities, in suburbs, in wealthy city neighborhoods as well as poor ones."

Vandalism alone, in public schools, is costing taxpayers $594 million a year, according to the U.S. Senate Judiciary Committee's Subcommittee on Juvenile Delinquency.

Dallas: After a teacher turned in a student who tried to rape another teacher, he was hit over the head and knocked unconscious by three friends of the student.

New Jersey: School buses and schoolrooms were damaged. When the juveniles who allegedly committed the crimes were apprehended, some of their parents could not believe that their children were involved.

Cleveland: A concert for school children was cancelled because students threw paper clips and hairpins at the Cleveland Orchestra musicians on stage.

Pennsylvania: The wife of a teacher said that her husband stopped a pupil in the school hall and said, "Son, you'd better put that cigarette out and get to class." The student then proceeded to give the teacher four full punches in the face, breaking his nose and causing fifteen stitches to his forehead.

In a report on the state of violence in the nation's schools that was headlined MURDERS, ROBBERIES AND ASSAULTS ROCK AMERICA'S SCHOOLS, a government study gave the following monthly break-down of some of the atrocities that are happening in our schools:

- 5,200 teachers are physically attacked.
- 2.4 million students and 128,000 teachers have something stolen from them.
- 25 percent of all schools are vandalized, while 10 percent are burglarized.

Countless stories abound and filter almost daily into the nation's press. They involve everything from pupil extortion rings to setting a teacher's hair on fire because the pupils did not like the marks the teacher gave them on their report card.

However alarming the statistics, a federal study said that only one-third of all incidents of school violence nationwide are ever reported to the police. Instead of being epidemic, this problem is probably pandemic.

For almost two decades concerned and informed parents warned the educators of the consequences of teaching along permissive lines—of telling each child his responsibility in life was first to himself and that to fulfill his wants and desires was paramount. And now that the narcissistic child has emerged, teachers and school administrators are running scared. What the educators have sown, they are now reaping.

In many of our nation's schools, if the kids didn't like regular English classes, they could choose from a host of other subjects and read or take courses in science fiction instead of the classics. If they didn't like a teacher, zap! Transfer out of her class. If they didn't like a subject, zap! Transfer out of it. Instead of learning perseverance, how to cope with adversity, how to get along with others, the educators told them they could have a "choice" in everything from English courses to intercourse.

We all remember the teacher in school who addressed her new students with steely eyes and told them forthright that she would "wipe the floor up with any troublemakers." If the class bully thought he would see if she was as good as her word, well, he only got one shot at it. Maybe the teacher was small and frail, and maybe she didn't exactly wipe the floor up with him, but she did collar him, throw him against the blackboard, and march him down to the principal's office. And the principal stood behind her 100 percent. It was an example you never forgot. She ruled supreme. And you learned. We all had teachers like that, and they were legends in their own times.

And we all had the teacher who was soft-spoken, who smelled of expensive perfume that your mother couldn't afford. She was gentle, and she prized every student in the room as if he or she were her very own. She, along with the "monster" that threatened to "wipe the floor up with you," stayed after school if you needed extra help. You loved her dearly. And you learned.

Today, with the soaring crimes in schools, the teachers—many of them poor examples of decent human beings, eager to be a "pal" to the students—seem unable to cope with anything successfully, be it English or discipline. When the going gets rough, they call for the school psychiatrist, the psychologist, paid disciplinarians, and sometimes even police protection.

As long as parents and children were suffering the effects of this new order of teaching, the educators didn't seem to care—they looked upon it as someone else's problem. Now that they are feeling the repercussions, it is a different story.

Commenting on the lack of discipline, one young teacher, whose "dream" it was to teach, resigned primarily over the lack of discipline in the high school where he had taught for two years. Robert J. Donahue, Jr., simply threw in the towel, he was so disgusted.

He put the issue into perspective when he said, "First of all, [in] any system where discipline is lacking . . . the students can't get a proper education . . . [and] students get away with murder. You can send a student down to the office for telling you to 'Go to hell,' but if the suspension list is too long, he won't be suspended because they (the administrators) don't want the list to get too long. So they give the student some detentions, but he just cuts them."

Donahue, a 27-year-old married father of two, said, "A teacher must have the respect of his students when he teaches. When a student looks at a teacher he should say, 'There's authority and I should have respect.' He doesn't. The students know what they can get away with and they do it."

A University of Miami English professor filed a petition in circuit court asking that Dade (Miami) County's "violence ridden school system be declared a public nuisance."

The action was brought by Associate Professor Robert Hosmon, who said, "It is my urgent hope that the result will be immediate institution of common sense measures in a school system unsafe for students, unteachable for teachers and—with its half billion budget—a bad investment for taxpayers."

In spite of all the violence in Hosmon's school, he charged that there had not been a single expulsion in the school in two years.

"Like Topsy," said Hosmon, "the problem of violence in our schools has just grown. When a hurled eraser was the problem, the offender was sent to the principal's office."

In a statement issued by the teachers' union, teachers confessed that they have "too often [been] caught up by outside social forces which have whittled down traditional academic and disciplinary standards." New Jersey Education Association officials said the result was "a relaxation of traditional academic and disciplinary standards . . ."

The NJEA pointed to pressure groups, politicians and the courts as an influence on school policies over the past twenty years. The results, they said, were making the school's power to make children learn decline "significantly in key areas."

They never once pointed the finger at themselves. Who was it that advocated, agitated, pressed and conspired against the parents to teach this new permissiveness and all of its accompanying social programs? The teachers, the administrators, and local school boards. If their public confession was worth anything, it only amounted to diarrhea of the mouth in a time of stress that was directly affecting the teachers, because they have not changed their teaching methods or materials one iota since making that statement in 1976. Teacher and pupil alike are still being encouraged to do their own thing, and the subjects taught under the umbrella of academia grow more deplorable.

"A number of concerned groups believe a large share of the responsibility must be laid to the moral values, or lack of them, that wittingly or unwittingly are imparted in the nation's public schools," asserted Elmer Von Feldt.

"One such newly formed organization," he wrote, "the Christian Civil Liberties Union, charged that the desires of parents are being mocked because their tax money is being used in many cases for the 'teaching of violence, obscenities, and disrespect for authority.'" The organization also noted "sexual perversions are being taught under the name of sex education, and corruptive textbooks that would shock any adult are being assigned by 'educators' for our children's consumption."

In an apparent effort to take the onus off the educational establishment, parents again took it on the chin when NEA president John Ryor blamed, with carefully chosen words, parental drinking, child abuse and TV for the discipline problems and poor performance of students. Mr. Ryor assumes that every parent has a drinking problem, abuses his child, and just sits and watches TV all day long. In no other building on such a massive scale (other than the abortion mills) are our kids more abused, Mr. Ryor, than in the rooms of today's public schools.

Florida's director of youth services, Joseph Rowan, said of the situation: "I used to blame delinquency on parents and schools about fifty-fifty. Now I blame the schools for 85 percent of it."

Those parents who have diligently warned, campaigned and fought this uphill battle for years against the "new" public school welcome you to the club, Mr. Rowan.

27.

My Mother, My Teacher

In 1642 Massachusetts became the first state to require compulsory education. It "enjoined to compel parents to teach their child themselves or procure teaching for them."

Some 210 years later the first law demanding compulsory attendance was passed. It required children 8 to 14 years of age to attend twelve weeks of school a year, with six of those weeks running consecutively.

Some 337 years later, in what would be signified ironically enough as The Year of the Child, parents would once again, in ever increasing numbers, feel compelled to either teach their children themselves or procure teaching for them, spurning the burnt offerings of the public schools.

The powerful 1.8 million member NEA, the teachers' union, would react in what was called "reverse McCarthyism" by one critic, when it gathered together several hundred teachers in our nation's capital recently to map out their next strategy against the growing dissension against the nation's public schools, the teachers and the new methods of teaching.

The theme for the NEA's conference was "The New Right: Human and Civil Rights in Jeopardy." While NEA president John Ryor tried to whitewash the real issue by saying conservative groups were trying to undo social gains made for women and minorities, he really got to the core of the reason these teachers were being given a crash course that would enable them to identify members of the New Right and their connections, by saying the hand of conservatives was evident in the back-to-basics movement, the increase in book censorship and threats made to what he called affirmative-action programs. If, in fact, this is true, then the rest of the country owes the conservative faction a debt of gratitude.

Recently I visited a school where the learning day began at 8:45 with a salute to the flag, then the singing of "The Star-Spangled Banner," followed by a prayer and Bible reading. This miniature classroom, with an enrollment of two, is inside of the home of Ken and Joan Briggs (not their real names). It stands in the shadows of a major city. The school itself exists because of the ominous shadows being cast on the children of our country by the public schools, which Ken Briggs refers to as "the government schools."

As I parked my car curbside in front of the Briggs' home, their daughters, Jeanine and Carla, are standing together on the front lawn. They are dressed in matching outfits their grandmother has sewn for them, itching to be off to a neighborhood birthday party for one of their playmates. These are the two students who occupy the desks in the miniature classroom.

The school these two girls attend is pro-morality, pro-American, and pro-God, says their father. It is located in an upstairs room of their home. Their mother is their teacher.

It is a pattern being repeated across the country. There is a steadily climbing number of parents who are taking their children out of the government's clutches by setting up their own schools in garages, basements, or funneling their children into private religious schools. These are the parents who charge the public schools with being antireligious, amoral, values-changing agents.

It has not been an easy road for all of them. The problem lies not in the teaching of children outside the bounds of the public school, but with those who are out to break the backs of parents who defy the pedagogues who rule public education and the government that supports them.

In 1975 a group of parents in Greenville, Ohio, were indicted, brought to trial, found guilty, fined and put under injunction because they sent their children to a Christian school that failed to comply to the Minimum Standards for Ohio Elementary Schools.

It surely must anger the educators to find out that great numbers of these children are surpassing their counterparts in public schools in various academic achievements.

In Yacolt, Wash., Patricia Smith is fighting an impending school board action aimed at returning her daughters to the classroom after she had taught them for four years in her converted garage. "I believe in a Supreme Being," she said. "And the religion I was teaching at home was being aborted in the classroom."

Mary Royer of Portland, Ore., head of an organization called the National Parents League, helps parents to set up schools for their own children and others.

Behind this growing movement she sees the "determination of parents who refuse to be further intimidated and who are protecting their children from the incredibly immoral incursion persistently thrust into the family structure and into the minds of the innocents."

Spotty as they are, there have been victories for parents. In Grand Rapids, Mich., Mr. and Mrs. Joseph Palmer, who maintained that the public schools were a corrupting influence on children, had the courts rule that Mrs. Palmer, who teaches the couple's children in their basement, did not violate the state's mandatory school-attendance law and that she was capable of teaching their two children.

Because the Briggses, whose one-room school I visited, do not wish to stir up any animosity, they have asked for anonymity. They do not, they told me, want to be cast in the role of "antagonists." The Briggses know all too well the histories of families that have been dragged before judges and even jailed because they have gone against the public school systems.

Joan Briggs tells me that to avoid the pitfalls of having to conform to a host of rules and regulations, they decided against becoming an incorporated school and decided their school would be strictly for their own children. "They have no guidelines for me," she said of the officials. "They just don't know what to do with me."

The Briggses said they have had newspaper and magazine requests to publicize what they are doing, but have refused them all. "I had to make the decision that my primary responsibility was to my family," said Joan. The public school that the Briggs' girls could have attended has likewise shunned any publicity on the matter.

The Briggses first thought about teaching their children at home when Ken was a U.S. military officer stationed overseas. Ken said he encountered many high school graduates in the service who had trouble reading comic books let alone military manuals. "I also had college graduates and lieutenants who worked for me who couldn't write—and one was an English major," he said.

Besides the failing academic level of public school children, the Briggses are deeply concerned with the amoral position of schools today. "We're watching a family maybe lose their kid because they can't bring themselves to take him out of school," said Ken. Rebelliousness and drug use, he said, were only two of the major problems the parents were confronting with their son. "He's being taught the things about how stupid your parents are. He's also gifted and he's flunking all of his courses," said Joan.

"Public schools are trying to keep the standards down because that way if there's less disparity between the bottom and the top it makes the bottom look brighter. But all they've done is keep the top lower," said Ken.

"I think that to say anything about the general public school system," said Joan, "I'd have to say that the public school system is like so many ideas that come into our society—a basically good idea, which sounded as though it would really work and had great potential, that has not worked.

"It has in fact become something really dangerous to our society because it can be controlled," she said. Even the compulsory education laws that were probably passed with good intentions, she said, are now imposed for other purposes. "They're used to control what your child is taught by forcing them to go to school."

By taking the action to teach their children at home, said Ken, they are not in the position of trying, like so many other parents, to undo what has been done to their children. "It's a lot easier to do than to undo," he said. "And already," he said in reference to teachers in the public schools, "we have one generation of poorly educated teachers—totally indoctrinated teachers. It only took one generation for Hitler to completely transform Germany," he pointed out.

"The irony of the whole system," he said of the public schools, "is you don't know you have a problem, because they keep giving the kids good grades. You really don't know you have a problem until they graduate and they can't read and write when they're eighteen."

"Or they come home on drugs," said Joan. "Of course, the basic objections would be the lack of morality taught in school, the lowered academic standards, and certainly there's no Christian orientation any more."

"State schools will always be around," Ken predicted, "because there are always people who can't wait to get their kids out of the house."

And so it was through observation and the experience of parents around them that the Briggses finally decided to act on their plans to have Joan teach their children at home.

"Once I had the idea," said Joan, "we started reading about things going on in education and from there we decided maybe it was not as impractical as it might seem."

They began by making inquiries from knowledgeable people in their state. Everyone told them they would never get away with it. Determined, Joan went to the law library and read and dug until she found a state statute with a loophole in it.

When Joan told her parents what she and her husband were planning to do, her father was not happy. "But," she said, "as he watched what was going on and saw how successful we were and saw how other children and their parents were having problems, he came along." It was the same with their friends at the outset— absolutely no one was enthused about their decision.

Once convinced that his daughter was going ahead with plans to teach his grandchildren at home, Joan's father became instrumental in helping her to plan the maneuvers she felt she would have to employ when she faced the public school authorities with her plan. "By the time she went into the principal's office," said Ken, "we had war-gamed this thing so many ways Joan was pretty well prepared."

Joan made her initial contact with the local school by phone. "They were very surprised," she said. "They didn't know what to do." They told her they would have to go to the state board of education. The state level passed the issue back to the local authorities. In the meantime, Joan stressed the idea that she would be happy to come into the school to talk. Eventually the principal of the local school set up a meeting with her, suggesting she might be interested in seeing what his school had to offer before she made any final decision.

Joan was noncommittal on the tour of the school, asking the principal if she could see the textbooks used in the grade schools. While he did not outright refuse her access to the texts, Joan said he told her they did not have enough textbooks to lend out. Joan said she already knew that parents were getting little or no cooperation in this area unless or until they forced the issue. Since her mind was already made up, she did not push the matter any further.

"I let him know first of all that I was very concerned about situation ethics, about the academic standards, about sex education—all sorts of things that he wasn't ready to debate me on at all," said Joan. "He couldn't say that he didn't teach these things, he couldn't say the academic standards haven't gone down. But I didn't fight with him about it. I felt it was very important not to."

What she did let the principal know, as a cool matter of strategy, was that she had already contacted national groups who would be interested in parents being denied the right to teach their children at home. "I just wanted them to know right away that they could have a real problem if they didn't want to cooperate; because I think that they'll step on you if you don't indicate that you could be a little bit of a problem. And I was prepared," she said laughingly, "to be at least a little bit of a problem."

After the visit to the public school, Joan contacted the school again by mail and told them she would be happy to have her children tested or even seen by a psychologist. ("Not that I really wanted that to happen," she added, but it was all a part of the war-gaming.) To this day, they have not requested that her children go through either procedure.

It took the school's attorneys some four to five months to study the state statute she had given the school officials. "That was a long time to research this simple question," she said.

Joan's next step was to submit a detailed sample plan of what she would be doing each day of the week in her at-home schoolroom. Weeks lapsed and there was no reply. Joan called them on the telephone.

She was told that their lawyers would go over it, then a child-study team, then the superintendent and finally the board of education would have to review her school program.

While the school officials had originally told Joan she might have to meet with their lawyer, she had responded by saying it would be fine, and should she bring her lawyer? That meeting never transpired. "I never met with them. I actually wanted to," she said. "I was *so* ready!"

Eventually she received a letter giving her permission for only one year to teach her oldest daughter. The following year she enrolled their younger daughter into the home-study classroom where she was "teacher." The local schools told her she need only submit the same type of plan detailing the school day and curriculum as she had done the previous year.

Joan is now into her fifth year of teaching her own children at home. I asked her if she believes the school authorities are hoping she will eventually give up on her venture. "Oh, I think they hope I will tomorrow!" she said emphatically.

For the oldest child, Jean has used the Calvert School's at-home program. They supply everything, she said, right down to the pencils. The Baltimore, Md., based organization has been functioning for seventy years supplying missionaries and those Americans in the foreign service with school materials and curriculum for kindergarten to the eighth grade. They have only recently begun extending their programs to parents in the States. "Their only stipulation," said Joan, "is that you have permission for your child's home instruction from the local school."

However, their youngest daughter is enrolled in the Christian Liberty Academy (CLA) located in Prospect Heights, Ill. CLA's stance is totally different. "The Christian Liberty Academy advises you not to even tell the authorities—it's not any of their business—

you have the right to teach your children at home, so don't get embroiled with them," said Joan.

I have since contacted the Rev. Paul Lindstrom, headmaster and founder of the Christian Liberty Academy. He not only confirmed what Joan told me, but added that while it is not legal in every state to teach your children at home yourself, the academy believes that the requirements of certified teachers and state approval are unconstitutional stands. "We have helped numerous families," he said, if they run into a legal squeeze. However he added, "Most do not encounter problems."

"We give free legal advice, send telegrams to school principals, write letters, contact congressmen, provide legal documentation to lawyers, and appear in court anywhere in the world at our expense," said Rev. Lindstrom.

Rev. Lindstrom also confirmed that it is his stand that school authorities need not be told (if a child is entering school for the first time) that the child will be taught at home. If parents already have children in the public schools and would like to take them out, he said it is not a difficult task. "Parents tell the school authorities that they are enrolling their children in a private school. We send for their school records," he said.

Parents are turning away from the public schools, Rev. Lindstrom said, "because of the anti-Christ, humanistic and regressive government school system." He feels it is definitely a trend that will continue to grow.

The Christian Liberty Academy's home-study school program was developed in 1971. After years of planning and working with students from different backgrounds, grade levels, abilities, states, etc., it was decided in 1976 that they would try to enlarge the program "in that we now had a viable alternative to inferior education," said Rev. Lindstrom. "We expected that we might double our enrollment." In two years, he said, "we have grown from twenty-five to about fourteen hundred students as of October, 1978." The students, he said, are from all fifty states, South America and Canada. They are growing each year and the expected enrollment by the end of this year is five thousand.

Both Calvert and the Christian Liberty Academy, said Joan, send all of the academic material to the parent for the year. While the parent is the tutor, the overseeing teacher is at the private school's headquarters, where official transcripts of each student are kept.

The Briggs' children do not have to spend as many hours in school as their public school counterparts. Their formal school day ends at noon, with an hour of art or music after the lunch break concluding the school day. "When you only have two children and one teacher," said Joan, "you simply do not require all this time." Actually, she said, she could complete the required schooling in less time if she chose. "My children really have more time for creativity, which is one of the public school's favorite words," she said.

All of the children's papers are sent to school headquarters. Report cards are issued from that center, sent to the parents to sign, and are returned.

"We use the old books," said Ken, "when it was good to be an American and the stories had morals."

"That's one of the things we found—there are thousands of parents doing this," said Joan.

The Briggs' girls take an hour of ballet a week and an hour of gymnastics at their local "Y," plus other gymnastics. "There are no chinks in her armor," said Joan's husband with obvious pride.

Joan and Ken impress on their children that Abraham Lincoln, George Washington, Thomas Jefferson and Thomas Edison also were taught at home.

How has this at-home study affected their children's social life? Well, they are far from social outcasts. The day I was visiting the Briggses, the girls returned from their friend's birthday party loaded with all the usual party paraphernalia and a passel of playmates in tow. "The people who have children the ages of our children appreciate the fact that our children are nice children. They like to have their children play with our children. And I hope this will continue," said Joan.

There are still those who are astonished when they learn what the Briggses are doing. A common remark, said Ken, is: "That's a tremendous responsibility you're taking upon yourselves—to teach your children at home." But Ken is ready with a reply: "We're responsible if we send our children to the schools, too. We're culpable if we just turn 'em loose and let those people do what they wish—let the teachers do what they're told to do. How is my responsibility changed at all?" It is an answer, he says, that causes the questioner to pause and think.

According to the latest figures available in the Standard Education Almanac, the price of educating one child in the public schools per year ranges from $732.05 in Kentucky to $2,098.49 in New York. For the Briggses, the cost per child per year for either the Calvert or the Christian Liberty Academy at-home courses is under $250.

Urging other mothers to go forth and multiply the at-home study course, Joan said, "A mother has to remember one of the primary things all people should know—that educators, teachers, don't have any particular Divine knowledge on how to teach or what to teach. A lot of them don't even have a gift to teach anymore. So a mother doesn't have to have a great inspiration or a great intellect or anything. Just by her own interest and her own natural ability, she certainly, if she has completed high school, can teach."

In fact, Joan said she has learned along with her children. As the children progress into the upper levels of education, Joan said if a parent ran into difficulty on a particular subject she could always hire a private tutor. But she also said the mother should not rule out the help a father might lend when he comes home in the evening.

It is unfortunate, said Joan, that the public has become conditioned to accepting the myth that a mother cannot teach her children. "The most natural form of teacher in the world is the child's mother. There isn't a big dichotomy. I don't have to go to their schoolroom and put on a black dress and put a bun on my head to be a teacher. It's really a natural thing. You do it when your child is born and it's just continued," she said with the confidence born of five years of successful teaching at home behind her.

"They actually call Joan 'teacher' in school, not mommy," said Ken of his daughters.

Joan said it is important for at-home parent-teachers to have the school day fairly structured. "I won't say I'm completely inflexible," she said. But, she added, it would be difficult for her children to be taught at home if they didn't feel they were going to school. "The school days are pretty consistent," she said, other than Wednesday, when they attend chapel.

"They like their schoolroom," said Ken of his children. "And their friends come to do projects with them."

Last year Ken and Joan took their daughters to a psychologist for testing. "We really wanted to make sure from an outside source that they were really doing all right socially, emotionally and intellectually," said Joan. The girls tested out as bright and extremely bright. The older is two years ahead of where she would have been grade-wise in the public school.

"One of the things I thought might be a problem was working on their own," said Joan. "So when I have, on occasion, not been able to be here myself for a period of time, it is interesting to note that my children can take care of themselves."

"They have a very positive attitude about school," said Ken. "They literally, on rainy days, go to their schoolroom and read, or copy assignments out of a book, or whatever. They just have a good feeling about it. And they will work on their own. It's such a basic need in a child to please her parents. It's there," he said, "unless it's taken away."

Joan's father is now an integral part of his granddaughter's at-home schooling. He now serves as the substitute teacher if emergencies or doctor's appointments have to be met. Ken refers to him as "the guest lecturer."

Looking back on it all, Ken says of his wife's accomplishments with their children: "Obviously, I'm very proud of her."

"So many problems that I foresaw," said Joan, "particularly their own personal, emotional development, and the problems that other people told me would arise, simply have not. They don't cling to my apron strings as most people said they would. 'Your children will be dependent on you,' they warned me. It's not true. They're secure and they can go out and they can walk into a room full of other children, other people, and they feel good about themselves."

"We send them to library programs, to the "Y" for dancing, whatever, to make sure they're with their peers. We have no intention of raising our children in the closet, in their house, with no contact with the real world. They would turn out to be weird," said Joan.

"But parents can, primarily fulfilling all the functions them-selves, raise a normal, well-balanced child. And even a better child," said Joan. "The parents have to regain their role and realize that they can render it positive."

28.

Et Tu, Catholic Schools?

By 1976 John Cardinal Krol of Philadelphia was criticizing the "secularistic values" being taught to public-school children. Those values, the Cardinal said, "exclude references to the religious and seek their basis in beliefs about human nature and destiny limited to this world alone."

Krol, along with twenty other bishops (both current and retired), urged public schools to "readily exempt" pupils from programs to which they or their parents objected to on "religious or moral grounds."

Those statements border on being hypocritical when one looks at the condition of the Catholic schools of today. They are being challenged from within by parents not only for their departure from traditional religious teachings, but for their highly touted "Becoming a Person" program which is the equivalent of the public school's sex education.

"There is a wall in the Catholic schools between the parents and the bishops, and it seems to be the educators," said a Catholic friend of mine who is part of the parent-battle being waged with the Catholic schools.

John Reid has withdrawn his four school-age children from St. James Grammar School due to the "Becoming a Person" program. His wife, Maureen, said she had asked permission when parents went to the first meeting to discuss the topic and to present speakers who had opposing views on the program. Among the names she presented was that of a Catholic priest. Each name she submitted was branded "unacceptable." Reid said he objected to many things, among them 10-year-olds knowing about sexual intercourse. "They don't need to understand exactly how things work at that age," he said.

I found the answer of "unacceptable," given to Mrs. Reid on her list of submitted names, interesting. I had been called by a mother who asked if I would come to her parish to present my point of view, along with Father Edward Atzert, a Catholic priest; James Likoudis, a staunch anti-sex-education advocate; and Professor William Marra of Fordham University.

She told me that Mr. and Mrs. Charles Comito, who had been appointed by Bishop George W. Ahr to serve as assistant directors for the Trenton (N.J.) Diocesan Family Life (sex education) Bureau, had already presented their favorable side and she wanted the parents in her parish to also hear the opposing view. I said I would be happy to go.

The woman then took the list of four names to her pastor. She called me the following day to tell me that he had checked off each of the names she had submitted and commented after each one of them: "Unacceptable."

I told her what her next step must be if she was to succeed in letting parents in her parish hear the dark side of the sex-education controversy. But she, like so many other parents, chose flight instead of fight. She removed her children from the Catholic school and put them into the local public school. Even though her children would be getting sex education there also, at least she would not be paying double the cost for an amoral education.

Pickets protesting the introduction of a sex-education course at St. Joseph's Elementary School showed up. Father Lawrence Donovan, pastor of St. Joseph's Church, said no teaching manuals for the "Becoming a Person" program were in the school. But a father, Robert Babiak, said he saw a manual in the school the night of a Parent-Teacher Association meeting. When Babiak and his group distributed fliers on the subject after Mass, the priest had them removed from the windshields of the cars.

And so, sadly, we must include priests among those who will not give parents a voice—even in a private, religious school.

Only one cardinal to my knowledge—John J. Cardinal Carberry of St. Louis—withdrew the "Becoming a Person" program, calling the series "theologically deficient."

Our Sunday Visitor, a Catholic newspaper, solicited the pro and con opinions of its readers on the issue. For five successive weeks it printed the letters from parents that ran five to one against the "Becoming a Person" program.

The one organization that has probably done more to inform the Catholic parent of what is taking place, in what can now only be termed the formerly Catholic schools, is Catholics United for the Faith (CUF). CUF's president, Kenneth D. Whitehead, in an article entitled "It's the Parent's Job," told of a woman from Spokane, Washington, who withdrew her daughter from the Catholic school because of sex education. The woman said she would no longer support the Catholic schools until "Roman Catholic moral teachings are returned to the classroom."

Another Catholic parent, who also objected to sex education, wrote to CUF and said, "We find it easier to send our children to a pagan school, and tell them it is pagan and what to expect, [rather] than send them to a pagan school calling itself 'Catholic' and have them choose between us and the faculty as to who is right when it comes to faith and morals."

Father Edward Atzert also writes for CUF in its monthly newsletter. He is not above calling down those who espouse untruths to push the new morality and sex education being thrust upon Catholic children.

Taking to task Msgr. James McHugh, Director of the Family Life Division, U.S. Catholic Conference, who favors the program and who wrote that the "Becoming a Person" program is "in accord with Catholic teaching and is based on Christian belief and values," Father Atzert responded, "The BAP course is quite at odds with the official teaching of the church and contains little of faith or of values that are essentially Christian.

"Moreover," he continued, "it is not altogether fair of Monsignor [McHugh] to refer to many dioceses that have adopted these programs and many bishops who have issued favorable pastoral letters, when he ought to know that many more dioceses have no such program and some bishops have written pastoral letters in opposition. We have a right to suspect a program that needs propaganda of that sort for its support."

Just as the textbooks of the public schools have changed, so have the religious texts from which the Catholic student learns. Even the Ten Commandments have become a matter of "values." Thou shalt not steal has become: Though shalt not steal—sometimes.

Out of this all will come the same product the public schools are turning out if the battle is lost. The saddest part of it all is that those who will have led and taught them call themselves God's chosen ones.

29.

Another Religious War?

In putting this book together, I kept finding bits and pieces of information that did not seem to fit into any particular outlined chapter. Filed temporarily under miscellaneous, they fit together like the pieces of a jigsaw puzzle to form this chapter. The subject is perhaps the most formidable enemy of those who are determined that the new order of things be carried out to completion. For a total victory, it must be eliminated, or at best be pushed to the back of young minds. Its name: Religion.

Religion and morals have been compatible companions. If we are to raise children without morals, it stands to reason that the importance of a Supreme Being must be eradicated from young minds. How successful has this incursion been by those who want it emptied out of our lives?

A recent Gallup poll taken at the direction of the National Council of Churches in America concluded that some of the results "were ominous for the future of organized religion."

The poll found that Americans place less importance on religion in their lives than they did in the two previous decades, which is just about the time all of the social programs began coming into the nation's schools. Those who go to churches and those who do not, generally find that the churches and synagogues fail to give spiritual direction, according to the poll. The majority agreed that "most churches and synagogues have lost the real spiritual part of religion."

Gallup said that such results represent "a severe indictment of organized religion."

Well over eight years have elapsed since I traveled to a hall where sex-education movies were being shown to dissenting parents who wanted the programs halted. I had gone for one reason alone: to listen for one statement purportedly made in a sex-education movie. I had heard that movie would be shown at this particular place. The one statement I went to hear had been reported to me second-hand; it was so incredible as to cast a definite doubt in my mind as to its existence. I was to hear that sentence in that movie that night, and it has haunted me for almost a decade now.

It was this: "By the year 2000 there will be no more organized religion and fathers will no longer have any authority in the home." As I look back, it is apparent that those who were trying to change our children's behavior early-on knew what they were about—and their goals were set.

Just looking at the vast majority of actions of today's teen-agers, it is easy to conclude that they feel no responsibility to anyone but themselves. It's not that our government is threatening us with prison if we worship in the synagogue or church of our choice; and no one is kicking in our front door to collar us if we are caught worshipping God in our home. It is much more subtle than that. It is the teacher who seems irritated when the student brings up religion. It is the psychologist who says religion puts one in chains. It is the diaries of religion that school children are asked to keep and then discuss openly in a classroom setting. It is religion and its value being threatened, undermined and diminished on a daily basis by those who think it will thwart and stunt the "social growth" of the young.

Jews say today they are persecuted for their religion. Christians claim the same. Catholics say they are singled out in the antiabortion fight. Jehovah's Witnesses also claim persecution. They are all correct in their charges. Religion is being spat upon and diminished in every way possible today. If proabortion agitator Bill Baird had his way, he would pit Christian against Christian. Of the Protestant role in the future, Baird said, "I'd like to see them go after the Catholic Church."

When the parents of Kanawha County, W. Va., eventually reviewed all of the controversial books and presented their final report, it began with very telling words concerning the educational systems of today and the damage done to religion in the name of education.

"If you induce a community to doubt the genuineness and authenticity of the Scriptures; to question the reality and obligations of religion; to hesitate in deciding whether or not there be any such thing as virtue or vice"—it read—"whether there be an external state of retribution beyond the grave; or whether there exists any such being as God, you have broken down the barriers of moral virtue, and hoisted the floodgates of immorality and crime."

The movement to eradicate religion is so widespread today, it prompted the launching in 1979 of a new transdenominational organization of U.S. Christians called "Freedom of Faith: A Christian Committee for Religious Rights." In their initial statement to the press, leaders of the Protestant, Roman Catholic and Eastern Orthodox religions joined in declaring: "Most ominously today, religious repression is the policy and practice of many governments. Some of these regimes are officially atheistic; others claim to be religious or even Christian in character.

"In our culture and others the virtues of justice, tolerance, compassion and charity are often and openly despised; spirituality and belief in God frequently are held in contempt." This new committee's aim is to fight for religious freedoms, which it sees as being increasingly suppressed in the world.

Where can we point the finger for the decline in religious beliefs in the United States? To a multitude of areas, not the least of them our government-supported public schools.

In fact, when one looks at the structure of the public school's curriculum and its philosophy in all of the social programs that have been introduced (that there are no right or wrong answers—only the individual's values are to be honored), I believe the public schools are the biggest antireligious "cult" operative in the country.

By the droves, our children have been attracted to various religious cults in our country. But nowhere, no matter how large the numbers, can they top the mandated attendance of some 44 million youths that are forced daily to the exposure of a philosophy that is antitheistic.

While parents whose children have joined religious cults claim their children are "brainwashed," so can it equally be claimed that every year, and year after year, the children of the public schools are coerced in the same manner. Only the language of the mind change is different. In the public schools it is called behavior modification and values clarification—morals education or sex education.

In the end, it does change the child, and like the religious cults that are infesting our country, it alienates the child from the parent.

Children in outside religious cults are physically removed from their parents. Children of the public-school anti-God "cult" are removed from their parents psychologically and morally. Where else is a child, often ridiculed by teachers and/or classmates, made to feel unsure of the religious beliefs he was previously taught? In the religious cults and in the public-school "cults."

Education used to pride itself on individualism. Instead the child today must conform and be a follower if he is to escape ridicule and be accepted into this new society.

Education today, concerning the matters of morals, claims the child is permitted "free choice," but as with the nine hundred dead people from the People's Temple cult in Guyana, they too suffer a certain death—not of a physical nature, but a death of morals and religion.

What other "cult" in recent history has changed so many young minds and successfully turned them against the values that were set down by their parents? By sheer numbers the captive audience of the public schools is the single and most potent of all "cults" operating.

Wilhelm von Humboldt, a nineteenth-century scientist and explorer, who described himself as "liberal" and a "humanist," said, "Whatever we wish to see introduced into a life or a nation must first be introduced into its schools." The quote deserves a lot of serious thought.

In 1978 in South Dakota, while every Christian was gearing up for the holidays, the ACLU filed suit in federal court against the Sioux Falls School District, the five members of its board of education and its superintendent, challenging the constitutionality of religious and Christmas assemblies held in the city school system.

About the same time, the ACLU went to court to stop the singing of Christmas carols with religious overtones in classrooms in Baytown, Texas.

How long will we have to wait before "In God We Trust" is removed from our coins? When will we be forced to scrap A.D. [Anno Domini—The Year of Our Lord] and B.C. [Before Christ] from our calendar of time? How long before a clergyman will be denied permission to give an invocation at high school graduation exercises?

In the waning days of 1978 the Internal Revenue Service began applying unparalleled tactics to private schools, many of them religiously oriented. The crux of the matter is that the IRS is trying to break the tax-exempt status of these public schools on the basis of discrimination.

There are an estimated eighteen thousand private schools in the country. For many parents it has been an answer to the inferior education and the amoral teachings of the public schools. If private schools do not have a sufficient number of "minorities" in their enrollment, they will lose their tax-exempt status.

The move infuriated many members of Congress and officials of private schools, who protested to the IRS saying such a move would ruin private schools financially, since so many of them are run on a shoestring.

"The purpose of the IRS is to collect the taxes . . . not to enforce social policy," said Sen. Strom Thurmond, (R., S.D.) to the IRS panel as it began four days of scheduled hearings into the matter. Rep. Barry Goldwater, Jr. (R., Calif.) called the proposal an "outrage." But a representative of the ACLU said it was a measure that should have been imposed twenty years ago.

William B. Ball, prominent attorney from Harrisburg, Pa., who has been called "the most successful defender at law of church-related schools anywhere in the land," also testified at the hearings. "I do not represent any racist schools, but I am very much concerned about religious liberty," he told the IRS panel.

Challenging the definition of "community" as used in the IRS proposal, Ball said the schools he represents do not represent the common definition of "community" but instead serve "their own faith communities." Such measures as proposed by the IRS, he said, would "attempt to force the schools of the faith communities to be related to population patterns of public school districts."

Under the Proposed Revenue Procedure, Ball continued, "The church school is forced either to bear the very significant consequences of being government-classified as discriminatory or else it must accept the hitherto unheard of intrusion upon its liberties of having the government say whom it shall enroll as a student. This violates due process, but—worse—it violates religious liberty."

So we see again the arm of government in action against religion. They are storming the last bastion in this fight of determined parents who have shunned the public school in an effort to raise moral and religious children.

So complete has the job been on our children that the students defended a biology teacher in Winslow Township, N.J., who told a joke in class that reportedly made references to nuns and to one nun having intercourse. He was fired, but the children held a protest, asking that he be reinstated. Why should our children be expected to be aghast at such religious jokes in the classroom or to abhor such a teacher? It is not in the nature of their learning today.

For atheists to get their message across loud and clear, they have broken another barrier. In November of 1978, in Madison, Wis., an advertisement, believed to be the first atheist commercial produced in the nation, began its three-times-a-week appearance on TV.

For religious freedom are we to found a new country every two hundred years?

Eager to cater to the young and to keep their numbers solvent, many churches have turned God's word around to accommodate youth. Concessions are made on every front for our children. Many parents have therefore stopped going to church, because they find this pandering to the young a blasphemy of their beliefs.

But the churches need only be patient. One, at the most two, generations of Americans will only have to die off, and they will have free sailing with the new generations. Meanwhile, they need only frustrate and hold strong against the remaining wall of parents who are trying to push this element out of their religions.

It seems the important drive of religion is to increase their numbers, no matter what Biblical or traditional beliefs must be stomped to death in the process. Patience is the word. Eventually, they hope, all will be well when the parents and grandparents are gone from this earth.

Infiltrating many of the religions is the new breed of clergy that is the counterpart of the new breed of teacher. Hand in glove, and with the help of the U.S. government, they walk lockstep to stifle the parent who still believes there is a right and wrong to living—to crush this giant called Religion.

30.

Cults and Our Children

Religion is stubborn. It refuses to die. It lives anew in our children who flock by the thousands to join religious cults. Most of these children are beyond the legal age for parental intervention, but parents do battle for the release of their children anyway.

There was a knock on our front door one evening. When I opened the door at 8:20 P.M. on a dark and brisk fall evening, there stood a young girl who looked no older than our own 18-year-old daughter. Her hair was short, shiny and dark; her rosy cheeks reflected the nip in the air. Her eyes looked as clear as those of a trusting 4-year old. She was a Moonie (the nickname given to the followers of Korean-born Rev. Sun Myung Moon) of the controversial Unification Church, which boasts more than 2 million followers in 120 nations. I asked her in.

She was selling trinkets and candies. It was as if fate had brought her to my door. But I had barely ten minutes to talk with her. She kept glancing furtively at the clock on the mantel, telling me over and over that she had to rendezvous with the others in ten minutes or she would miss her ride.

She told my husband and me that she was 23, had majored in psychology at a major American university, was raised a Catholic and was from North Dakota. She claimed that when she joined the Unification Church, there was not as much media controversy over the organization.

When I asked her if she received any pay, she answered, "No. They give you everything you need—food, a place to stay and clothing." I asked her if they bought her clothing. "No. They give you the money to buy it yourself."

How, I asked her, do people receive her as she goes door-to-door? "Some people scream at me," she said, an ever present smile on her face. "Others ask a lot of questions."

In the beginning, she told me, her mother was very upset about her decision to join the Unification Church. But her father, she said, was not that involved in his own religion and was happy, "because I live with such high moral standards."

"I owed two thousand dollars for my education, and they [the Unification Church] paid that debt for me when they knew I was going to stay with them," she said.

After being in the cult for several years, she said her parents' feelings have reversed. Her mother is now happy she joined, but her father is not. "Whatever the media say bad about the Unification Church," she said, "my father thinks of even worse things to say . . . but," she added like a stuck record, "he's happy that I'm leading such a good and moral life."

She said she had worked for a short time with prostitutes in New York City, trying to help them change their lifestyles. She found the metropolitan area "too frightening," so the church moved her to headquarters in New Jersey.

She found a "joy," she said, in working with young people who were "doing so much good in the world."

When I pressed her for more time, she withdrew a four-page pamphlet from inside her nylon ski jacket and gave it to me. It was pure public relations work put out by the Unification Church.

As she left, we warned her that there were no sidewalks and deep drainage ditches along the main roads. Putting on her mittens, she said: "God will bless you for being so trusting." To myself I thought: I hope you have not misplaced your trust.

I had found her irresistibly innocent-looking, mannerly, and with a sunny disposition that many parents yearn for today in their own youths.

While I had no desire to give financial support to the Unification Church, I bought a box of candy for $3 from her in the hopes of tracking down the manufacturers and talking with them.

I thought about this young woman for a long time after she had left. Here she was, a psychology major out begging for money for her church—her wares were cheap jewelry and candy. If parents asked their children to go door-to-door selling candy and trinkets to help support the family, how many would gladly do it? If parents of today gave their children a limited clothing allowance, how many would sulk and rebel? If parents asked their children to hand over all their earnings, how many would?

These children choose discipline, religious guidelines, morality. These children have been run through the same mills of society that told them they could do whatever they wanted with no consequences, and yet they chose this path. The "brainwashing" notwithstanding, they at first go willingly. What were they telling us?

It seemed to me that they had scratched their way up and out of a society that they could no longer bear to live in. On the way up they were recruited by a cult member—and they were ripe for picking. Here would be a haven for them. Here someone would set down rules, and they could be free to worship again without ridicule.

These, I believe, are the human beings who deep down know that life needs restriction to be happy and successful. The schools, their parents, their religions, society, had given them too much of a free rein, and its was too much for them to cope with.

But they are "brainwashed," you say. I will not argue that point with you. But haven't our children also been brainwashed? Neither way is the right way, in my opinion. It is unfair to any child to "brainwash" him. And many are still children who are in their 20s today—we have perpetuated adolescence in so many ways.

Is not religion all a process of "brainwashing"? I would prefer to call it a teaching. A following of God's rules. Put simply, a division of good from evil. Few parents raised "religious fanatics" prior to the cult era. And some twenty years ago few parents raised the type of child that is breaking records in destruction, either.

The morning following the Moonie visitor, I called and spoke with an executive of Madison Enterprises, Inc., of Conshohocken, Pa. He would speak to me about the Unification Church and his corporation if I would refer to him simply as a "spokesman." That agreed to, he said there was no connection with his company and the Unification Church other than the selling of the candies to them. "We sell to them because we're required to sell to them by law," he said.

The box of fifteen green-covered mints that I had purchased for $3 he told me his company sells to the Unification Church for $14.40 a dozen.

"The few [Moonies] I've met," said the spokesman of the candy corporation, "are really super kids. They're not really brainwashed," he tried to assure me. He said he has visited their Washington headquarters and been in their houses. "One is cooking, the other is cleaning, and another one goes out and does fundraising," he said. "When you look at Moon—you have to wonder," he said with reservation in his voice.

Three years ago, he said, he spent a good amount of time trying to establish a relationship with the Moonies. "They are not secretive," he said. And that, he said, was all he wished to say on the matter.

From the various exposé pieces written about all of the cults, all is not as rosy as the picture presented to me by the young Moonie who visited my home.

"Many groups discourage children from contacting parents," wrote David Black in his article, "The Secrets of the Innocents: Why Kids Join Cults," which appeared in *Woman's Day* magazine.

Dr. Joyce Brothers shares my feelings about children who run away to join far-out religious cults. Many, she said, are not running away from strict authoritarian homes, but there is some evidence that youngsters want less rather than more freedom.

Psychoanalyst Ira Mintz's observation is that many youngsters seem to want sexual restraints and are seeking a strict, ascetic society with built-in controls. She also pointed out that victims of "destructive cultism" often lose their capacity to grow independent and become physically ill, developing pathological thought patterns.

The estimate is that there are at least 150 and possibly 2,500 cults operative in the United States today.

What bothers me not a little is that numerous national politicians, including Sen. Edward Kennedy, Joan Mondale, Rosalynn Carter and former Treasury Secretary William Simon, have been photographed with members of these cults.

31.

Cohabitation

"Cohabitation" . . . another word popularized by our youth . . . another spin-off of their "choices." In the last eight years the Census Bureau said that the number of unmarried men and women living together has more than doubled.

One-third of the students surveyed at Cornell University admitted sharing a bedroom with a student of the opposite sex. Only 7 percent of the students in the survey said that they would not live with someone of the opposite sex.

It is becoming a commonplace enough practice that our liberated youth think nothing of standing before television cameras to evangelize this lifestyle.

College campuses across the country have scrapped any rules or regulations that formerly banned this practice. Should a college, such as Brigham Young University's Mormon school, try to hold the line, it will find opposition. The Justice Department has threatened to sue Brigham Young unless it changes its off-campus housing policy aimed at keeping male and female students apart. They claim this policy is violating the Fair Housing Act of 1968 by permitting sexual discrimination.

Interviewing the mother of six children for a magazine article I was putting together on a medical problem, the conversation turned, over a cup of coffee, to coed college dormitories.

This mother told me the following true story: It took place at a prestigious Eastern junior college that her daughter, whom I shall call Amy, attended.

"When we went down in the spring to see the college, we went to see the rooms. They said to my husband, 'I hope you don't mind, but you have to stay in the lounge because there may be girls in the hall downstairs.' So I went down with Amy," she said, "and we saw the room, and indeed there were girls in the halls. It never occurred to us that the only type of housing available was coed dorms."

In September Amy's parents drove her again to the junior college to begin her freshman year. "There were a lot of young men . . . you know, roaming around with suitcases," she said. "We thought they were brothers, boyfriends, or the young men who were on the other side of the dorm. We still didn't give it any thought—that it was a coed dorm. We were sure there were certain rules and regulations. There were no rules and regulations, and if there were, they were never, never enforced."

"Everybody," she continued, "says that when there are coed dorms like that, well, there is no sexuality connected with it—the girls look on the boys as brothers. This couldn't be farther from the truth.

"My daughter woke up one morning and her roommate was in bed with a guy." Next door to Amy's room, she said, were four girls who slept, indiscriminantly, with any and every male. The housemother would come in the morning and pull the sheets off the beds to get the young males out of bed.

"The drug problem is dreadful, They [school authorities] turn their heads the other way," she said.

"What finally upset Amy so much that she had to call home for help was that her roommate had a guy in the room who was not even a student there and he'd been mainlining. He was completely freaked out, and she was frightened. She was afraid to go into her room to go to bed that night.

"So my husband went down that night loaded for bear, to take Amy out and to get our money back." In the end, Amy stayed on and her roommate was removed.

"Do you know what the big problem is?" she asked. "Our junior schools especially are going bankrupt because people are sending their children to community colleges. So they're closing their eyes to all of it. This is not just at the college our daughter was attending, but it's at a number of schools—our big universities that have coed dorms.

"Here again, the parents won't demand it [separate sleeping quarters and regulations]. And why? Part of the problem," she said, "is they are loaded with girls whose parents have a lot of money. Those parents often don't care what their kids do as long as they stop doing it in the community and being a source of embarrassment.

Amy said the girls are on the telephone saying, 'Mom, can't I come home this weekend?' and mother has all kinds of excuses. A check for one hundred dollars arrives on Monday or Tuesday.

"In other words, 'We went through hell while you were here in high school'—maybe they were on drugs, maybe they had the wrong kind of boyfriends. Whatever it is, the parents pay anything to get the girl out of the community, just hoping she'll grow up a little bit, get married, maybe. This is a truism. This is what's happening. And this is why our colleges are closing their eyes to the sexuality, the drugs and everything else," she said.

"Sex," she continued, "has become so commonplace it has lost its impact as far as being right or wrong. Our daughter didn't want to be in the coed dorm. She said, 'Mother, it's terrible. You have no privacy. If you have to go to the bathroom in the middle of the night, you have to be all bundled up.' In fact," she said, "Amy became quite a heroine in her own right at school, because there were other girls who felt just like Amy, but they were afraid to say anything."

While the junior college removed Amy's roommate to placate her father, their policy did not change. Amy's parents decided to let her finish out the balance of the year.

But still another incident was to take place. When Amy stepped out of the shower one day, she discovered a strange man showering in the next shower stall. It was not a face she knew from the campus. Calling home again for help, Amy's mother immediately contacted the school authorities. "I was treated like an hysterical mother," she said.

At the conclusion of her first year, Amy was withdrawn from the school.

Apparently there was enough cohabitating at Michigan State University to cause two of the university's students to set up a business that would conspire to keep the parents from knowing about their son's or daughter's sexual partners. For $20 a month, they rented out their campus mailing address and phone number to cohabitating students who could give this address to their parents as a ruse, while they bedded down with their partners elsewhere. This enterprising duo also allowed their student clients to move into this location temporarily when their parents came for a weekend visit.

While I would agree with Amy's mother that there are parents who will buy off their children just to keep them from embarrassing the parents in their home locale, there is another group of parents who react differently to cohabitating offspring.

These are the parents whose son or daughter is living with

someone of the opposite sex, but when they come to visit the parents, the parents say: "They may sleep together at their place, but under our roof they have to abide by our rules. They must sleep in separate beds." It is but another compromise by the parents. Afraid of losing their son or daughter, they take no moral stand.

On leaving college, many will continue this destructive lifestyle. Some will call it a "trial marriage." Dr. Nancy Clatworthy, an associate professor of sociology at Ohio State University, once thought living together before marriage was a pretty good idea. "But to my amazement, I found that this was not the case," she said.

Dr. Clatworthy began her ten-year study on cohabitation in 1968. What she found was that those couples who had not lived together were more content with their marriages, had greater respect for each other and agreed more on day-to-day matters. Even in the area of sex, she said, couples who had lived together before marriage disagreed about it more often.

"Overall, cohabitators are appreciably more violent than marrieds," was the conclusion of another recent study done by Kersti A. Yllo and Murray Straus, of the University of New Hampshire's sociology department. Their findings disputed researchers who believed that more violence was found in legal marriages.

Yllo and Straus were also surprised by what their study had turned up—they had expected the opposite results. Instead, they found that cohabitating women are almost four times more likely than married women to suffer severe violence.

Richard Gelles, a sociologist at the University of Rhode Island, was commissioned by the National Institute of Mental Health to do a study on child abuse. What Gelles' study revealed was that nearly 2 million children are abused each year by the parents.

Parents under 30 years of age, he found, are 62 percent more likely to beat a child than older parents. "It is quite possible that our study has uncovered a violent generation under 30 years of age," said Gelles.

The account I read of Gelles' study did not categorize the marital status of the parents involved—i.e., single, divorced, living with a member of the opposite sex who is not the natural parent.

I have no statistical evidence to back up my observation, but I have noticed over a long period of time that the "new morality" often enters into the picture of child abuse. It is a proven fact that teen-age mothers often abuse their children, but time after time when I read of these heinous cases where a child has been beaten or murdered, it is the "boyfriend" living with the natural mother who is the guilty party.

In former, more rational, times a mother who was cohabiting would have been declared "unfit" as a mother. If that measure of fitness were reinstated, it just might save a lot of lives of the innocent by-products of our times—the infants and toddlers of a cohabiting parent.

32

Wartime Babies

There is usually a baby boom following a major military war. This confrontation between parent, child and bureaucracy is no different. Today, the United States is the world leader in teen-age pregnancies.

A fertility report issued in August of 1978, released by the Census Bureau's population division, shows that the annual number of illegitimate births in the United States has more than quintupled between 1940 and 1975.

The figures showed that the annual number of births occurring outside of marriage went from 3.6 percent of all births in 1940 to 14.3 percent of all births in 1975.

The illegitimacy rate for teen-agers increased by 50 percent just from 1962 to 1975. From 1971 to 1976 the percent of unmarried 17-year-olds who had had sexual intercourse increased 54 percent, according to two nationwide surveys conducted by researcher Mary Grace Kovar. By 1979, in a study released by three population experts at the Johns Hopkins School of Hygiene and Public Health, almost two of every three females had had sexual intercourse by age 19, nearly all of it premarital.

All studies point to the fact that teen-age pregnancies are yet another record-breaker among our youth that defies all social, economic and ethnic categorization.

President Carter's plan is to give more money to contraceptive clinics. The national mentality of those in a position to turn these horrendous statistics around marches on with the same rhetoric that put our children there in the first place: Give them more information, more contraceptives, more abortions.

Today, only 6 percent of babies born are put up for adoption. Teenage mothers add to the welfare roles at approximately $2,250 per year for each mother and child.

Syndicated columnist and author Jimmy Breslin wrote of a mother who overheard her teen-age daughter and her girl friends saying they would opt for pregnancy, have a baby, and go on welfare. Breslin puts the issue down to living in a project, but statistics and studies prove otherwise. When the mother asked her daughter who was going to pay for the baby, she responded, "I'll get on welfare when I have the baby and get my own pad."

Of all children born out of wedlock, almost 50 percent end up on welfare, said Joseph Califano, former secretary of HEW.

A man who asked that he not be identified because of the responsible position he holds in his community, told me this story concerning a young member of his family:

The young, unmarried girl had become pregnant by a young man who was a drug addict. "She decided, after a period of turmoil, that she was not going to abort his baby. She had the baby, and there was no question she was going to keep the baby. She went immediately on welfare, which," he continued, "I understand. She's not married, she has no physical means of support."

What did irk him and other family members was what she did with her welfare money. "She saved her welfare money to fly to the state of Washington from her home state to visit a friend for a month. Now that money is being given to her to support her child. She happens to live with her mother" (good old mom, again keeping the child from responsibility) "who is taking care of her child and her.

"She saved that money just to fly up and fly back to see a girl friend. It happened to be a friend of the boy who made her pregnant in the first place. And *that* girl was on welfare in Washington and had a baby out of wedlock also.

"She felt that was justified—that this money should come to her. She deserves it and she's in need of it and they have to give it to her . . . as though she had done something that they had to give it to her. And that's it.

"To me, I went bananas. I just . . . I didn't say anything to her, because I'm not her parent. I don't think I should. That's just inconceivable to me that someone would think that she deserves that money and for that reason," he concluded.

So widespread is the pregnant teen-age epidemic that group-health plans and union contracts are now supplying maternity benefits for workers' unmarried, pregnant daughters.

The dangers of teen-age pregnancies are multiple. Dr. G. C. Thosteson has cited their physical immaturity, poor nutrition and lack of early medical attention as some of the problems. The infant mortality rate for children of mothers under 15 is more than double the rate for those of mothers in the 20 to 34 age group. Young mothers, according to one study, are more subject to toxemia, postpregnancy infection, high blood pressure and anemia.

About 30 percent of the illegitimate births today are to mothers 17 and younger.

Along with the steep rise in teen-age pregnancies in the United States has been a parallel rise in teen cervical cancer. "Cervical tissues in teen-agers appear to be less resistant to the effects of possible harmful substances, including those in the male ejaculate," said San Diego gynecologist Dr. Thomas Slate.

Dr. William Creasman of Duke University's Comprehensive Cancer Center concurs, noting that in girls 15 to 17 years of age, the cervix is especially vulnerable to cancer-causing agents.

Sexually active girls are twice as likely to get cervical cancer as are those who do not engage in sexual activity until later in life, reported a study titled, "Adolescent Coitus and Cervical Cancer."

Because of sexual promiscuity, some teen-agers will never be mothers, either. Abortion can make motherhood impossible and so can gonorrhea. Dr. Paul J. Weisner, director of the Venereal Disease Division of the Center for Disease Control in the United States, said, "We estimate that between fifty thousand and eighty thousand young girls and young women are made sterile by gonorrhea every year." At times it also causes male infertility.

Dr. Julius Richmond, citing that one million teen-age girls become pregnant every year and six hundred thousand become mothers, said, "If these trends continue, more than 10 percent of AFDC [Aid to Families with Dependent Children] families will be headed by a woman nineteen or younger at a cost of more than three hundred million federal dollars in welfare aid.

"Perhaps mentally the girls are capable of parenting," said Lois White, principal of the Edgar Allen Poe school in Baltimore, an institution for young mothers and pregnant teens, "but realistically, not at all.

"Adolescence is an unrealistic age, and this has nothing to do with being a parent. These girls see themselves as being able to be very competent parents," she continued. "After reality hits, they become abusive parents because they feel they've lost out on their teen years. They just don't believe they can't handle a young baby and go to school at the same time."

A case in point was 17-year-old Barbara Avery of Chicago. The young mother told the police that she wanted to attend a birthday party being given for her, but she could not find a baby-sitter for her infant. Consequently she threw her infant daughter down a garbage chute on the second floor of a South Side housing project in Chicago and went to the party.

A ring of truth came out of the mouth of one 16-year-old pregnant girl when she said, "All of us are spoiled. I don't want my daughter to be spoiled."

In 1975 a press release from *Seventeen* magazine came across my desk at the newspaper where I was working, for editing and a headline. It cited "ignorance," not availability and encouragement from every corner of the country, for the skyrocketing rates of teen-age pregnancies and venereal disease among teen-agers.

The solution: Recruit teen-agers and turn them into sex counsellors under the sponsorship of schools, clinics, Planned Parenthood offices and government agencies.

"Applicants who want to be counselors usually must furnish references from teachers and others who can assess their maturity, emotional health and responsibility," read the release. "They are then interviewed and tested by adult professionals, drilled in sex facts by qualified authorities."

There is no mention of parent involvement at all—of course. The teen-age recruits, said the article, will learn not to pass moral judgments on their peers, not to give advice, to maintain confidentiality and where to refer their peers for help.

"Peer counselors are at work in high schools from San Francisco to New York, colleges throughout the country, Hot Lines where callers can get information over the phone 24 hours a day, and clinics that specialize in birth control and gynecological services for young people," the article pointed out.

The parents are skirted once again. They will train the young in their ways and bring forth more of their own to add to their army.

The Ford Report, authored in 1978 by James H. Ford, M.D., a member of the AMA and the California Medical Association, supports what parents were saying who had their fingers on the pulse of public schools back when the social programs were first introduced. In his report, Ford lists some of the reasons we are living in such a tumultuous teen-age world:

- Adolescents need the protection of the law to protect them from sexual exploitation by predatory adults, sexually sophisticated peers, and commercial sex interests including so-called "family-planning" centers and drug firms.

• Current federal policies which promote birth control services to minors without parental knowledge or consent increase teen-age promiscuity, VD, abortions, and out-of-wedlock pregnancies among the young.

• Public policies in the area of human sexuality must reflect traditional familial relationships and civilized values to counter the effects of the new barbarism known as "the sexual revolution." This means the promotion by public and private authorities of the sexual norm of abstinence for unmarried persons and fidelity and continence for married couples.

Parents were saying the same thing in the mid-'60s when the big wheels of the schools were pushing sex education, only nobody paid any attention to the belled cat.

33.

Kids and Contraceptives

I have listened to all of the arguments concerning the minor child and contraceptives, both from parents and from doctors who favor the joining of these two volatile elements. They are all the same: "They are going to do it [have intercourse] anyway, so why not protect them?" is a favorite. Another is: "If they are going to have a sexual relationship, then let it be a responsible one." Still another: "It's their body; let them decide what they want to do with it. The choice is theirs."

Another argument given is the availability of the Pill. But we must back up. Every statistic compiled points to the fact that prior to public schools taking on social programs and the relaxation of laws concerning minors, we were raising moral children.

In 1978 the Supreme Court ruled seven to two to strike down a New York law that had banned all advertising of contraceptives, made it a crime to distribute any contraceptives to a person under 16, and permitted only licensed pharmacists to distribute them to those over 16. This statute, ruled the Supreme Court, infringed on the privacy of minors.

But state laws governing minor children had already been tumbling. In 1974 only twenty-two states still maintained that a young person must reach the age of 18 before he could obtain contraceptives without parental knowledge or consent.

Shortly before the Supreme Court's decision pertaining to minors and contraceptives, a Michigan federal court's ruling that required family-planning clinics to notify parents before giving contraceptives to minors was vacated by the sixth U.S. Circuit Court of

Appeals. It left the Michigan clinics free to continue to issue birth-control devices to teens without parental knowledge.

Along with these new measures has come a tremendous profit in contraceptives. It is estimated that the sale of condoms alone, in 1978, climbed to $150 million a year—doubling the figures of five years ago.

Dr. Julius Richmond, assistant HEW secretary, told a House subcommittee that 11 million of the 21 million adolescents in the 15 to 19 age group have had sexual relations. That's over half of our teen-agers. "The statistics are staggering," he said.

It continually amazes me that our officials are constantly talking in exclamation points concerning the behavior of our young people and yet are, or appear to be, too dumb or too politically involved to realize that it is the government and its laws, working in concert with the government's teachings in the public schools, that have brought about these staggering statistics.

Their solutions are always more of the same poisonous medicine for our children.

By 1971 it was apparent that our young people would be breaking still another record, this time with another spin-off from sexual promiscuity—venereal disease.

In a 1979 article on VD, Patricia McCormack wrote of authorities who say the "VD capital of America" may be more an age group than a place. They put the spotlight on sexually active teen-agers, especially in the 15 to 19 age group, calling VD in that group pandemic—more severe than an epidemic.

"Venereal disease among the 21 million adolescents—both sexes—aged 15-to-19, is estimated to total more than 2.5 million cases annually," Samuel Knox, program director of the American Social Health Association, told the United States Senate Committee on Human Resources.

Our youth are being hit with herpes simplex virus type 2, a sexually transmitted disease that has infected 5 million and is spreading. Each year 300,000 of those suffering with genital herpes suffer excruciatingly painful outbreaks that last from two to five weeks. There is no known cure. Herpes is highly contagious and those who have it are advised not to have sexual relations—not now, or in the future, as long as it is active. It has wrecked many young lives. For their promiscuity, there will be those among our youth who, unless a cure is found, may never marry or know the private and intimate joy of consummating that marriage.

What part do the public schools play in this scheme of things? I think Dr. William A. Block, a doctor who is entrusted to teach sex education to children at the Cherry Hill public schools in New Jersey, gives a good indication. I have twice debated Dr. Block on radio on the issue of public school sex education. We do not see eye-to-eye on any aspect of it.

In the early 1970s, Dr. Block had a three-hour sex-education session with four boys and three girls of high school age. He was so proud of this meeting, he put it into print.

The meeting had been set by Andrew, a student whom Dr. Block referred to as his confidant. Before the students arrived, Dr. Block asked himself these questions: "What is their sexuality? And what right do we have even to probe?"

In my opinion, I don't believe he had the right to probe, but probe he did. He asked the group such questions as, "What would you do, girls, if you found yourself pregnant?" "What does love mean to you, Kathy? You said before you don't have to love to ball." "Will you live together—change partners—what about marriage?" "What about 'fuck'? Do you ever say that?"

Immediately following the session, Dr. Block felt compelled to send an open letter to those seven students as their father figure. He threw out the window any and all reference to abstention, morality and religion and parental involvement in one fell swoop when, in his concluding remarks, he wrote, "I go on record now: I do not disagree with premarital sex, but it must be an honorable and responsible affair." To the girls he wrote, "I give you the Pill—with love and respect."

Contrasting Dr. Block's stand is a five-year study conducted by Dr. Seymour Fisher with 300 women volunteers, most of whom were in the 20-to-30 age bracket. Dr. Fisher's study showed that high-orgasm women tended to recall their fathers as having a definite set of values, being demanding and holding high expectations for them. Most low-orgasm women remembered their fathers as being casual, overly permissive and short on definite values.

Dr. Block certainly falls in line with the latter group of fathers. He is not unique in his approach. Daily, our children in the public schools are being told much the same thing. It is also the mentality of many population groups, where our children go legally, without our knowledge or consent, and receive much the same information.

Dr. Block and his ilk are popular figures in today's youth-oriented society. It is the parent who wants to deny these things to his child that is the unpopular figure. We are indeed a world turned upside down.

Would you like to forewarn your daughter about the pitfalls of becoming a teen-age mother? Then don't send for the booklet, "The

Hassles of Becoming a Teenage Parent." This free pamphlet (we are all paying for the writing, printing, offices and distribution of this trash) is put out by the U.S. Department of HEW, Public Health Service, out of Rockville, Md.

The title itself is misleading. If you think the government is publishing this booklet to tell your teen-age daughter the care, the love, the time, the responsibility, the dangers and the cost of becoming a teen-age mother, guess again. It is purely a book on contraceptives: where to get them, how no one will tell your parents, etc. This is more of your tax money at work once again—against the parent, morality, and ultimately against the unsuspecting and inexperienced teen-ager. But read for yourself some of the material.

Under the heading, "Getting to know you, yourself," is the following:

> In many communities, family planning centers and those who work in them are trying to set up special programs to reach teenagers, and better than that, they know that to reach you they must offer something worthwhile. Not a lot of warnings of 'don't do it,'—but an open door where you can find honest talk, interested young staff people and a place to work out your own solutions to almost everything that's on your mind: sex, relationships with people, how to talk to your parents, VD, and almost anything else.
>
> Many family planning agencies do this confidentially. Some have 'rap' sessions, some do private one-to-one counseling, some have special telephone information services for teens, some will refer you to other community agencies for advice and help, and some will help set up sex education programs in schools and colleges.

Under "Staying unpregnant":

> In sex, as in everything else, the basic obligation for people of any age is to determine what is responsible behavior. That certainly includes taking steps to avoid unintended pregnancy. The usual way to keep an egg and sperm from meeting is to use birth control (contraception) during sex. Before marriage, whether or not to be sexually active is the considered decision of the persons involved.

Under "Information, advice or supplies":

As society's attitudes change about teenage sexual behavior,
information, medical and personal advice, and contraceptive
supplies are becoming more accessible to young people. In most
states, teenagers can buy condoms and other nonprescription
contraceptives in pharmacies. In some communities, private
physicians can help you. Confidential VD treatment is available in nearly every state. College health departments often are
good places to turn to—so is the local health department of
Planned Parenthood Center. Look in the Yellow Pages under
"family planning."

What did "The Hassles of Becoming a Teenage Parent" tell you
about? Contraceptives.

Writing on the subject of contraceptives being doled out to minors
without parental involvement, Robert A. Destro, general counsel
for the Catholic League, said, "What most parents do not realize is
that the government and Planned Parenthood consider parental
involvement in this area to be unwise, improper and unconstitutional. In short, they see parents as a threat to the 'success' of their
programs. Thus, steps are taken [legal, regulatory and procedural]
actively to exclude parents from the process."

In 1978 Mrs. Edward T. Garrity, Jr., of Narberth, Pa., wrote a
scourging letter in reply to the *Philadelphia Bulletin*'s editorial
condoning a contraceptive action involving minors.

"I was absolutely appalled at the recent decision by the
Department of Health, Education and Welfare to give $80,000 to
teen-agers to bring their peers into Planned Parenthood for
contraceptives," she wrote. Mrs. Garrity went on to further state
that she was equally appalled that the newspaper's editorial
condoned such action. "Where will it end?" she asked.

It will end, Mrs. Garrity, in more suffering for the teen-ager and
parent alike, or it will end in a victory for parent and child alike, if
only enough parents, like youself, Mrs. Garrity, are sufficiently
appalled to see to it that these damaging practices are stopped! But
then I am hoping for miracles.

The program Mrs. Garrity wrote of was being agitated for back in
April of 1972. A national population commission had gathered in
Washington to urge special programs of birth-control services for
teen-agers (requiring adoption of state laws permitting minors to
receive contraceptive and prophylactic information and services)
and a repeal against laws forbidding advertising, store display and
vending-machine distribution of contraceptives.

Five years later the matter was before the Supreme Court. It is interesting to note that the test case was New York—the headquarters of Planned Parenthood.

Shortly after the Pennsylvania legislators lowered the age of consent for medical care from 21 to 18, the University of Pennsylvania opened a birth-control clinic for all of its students, be they married or single. The services would provide students with contraceptive pills and devices at a nominal charge. It was sponsored by Planned Parenthood.

Three months before the university opened its new facility, it was already gearing up for business. A 58-page book had been written for its students by Dr. Elaine C. Pierson, M.D., who also lectures on sex education. She said what she wrote was simply the "Puritan ethic."

Written on the book's cover were the words: "Pap test," "syphilis," "rhythm," and "abortion." "What I'm saying is that I can't tell you what to do about sex, but whatever you do, do it well and knowledgeably, which is just the Puritan ethic," she said.

At an international symposium held in St. Louis, Mo., the growing epidemic of venereal disease was attributed to the Pill, among other things. Dr. R. R. Willcox, consultant venereologist at St. Mary's Hospital in London, said physicians "should make the point that the population cannot have their cake and eat it." A study that was released at the symposium revealed that more than 500,000 persons in the U.S. suffered from undetected syphilis.

A story written by a 15-year-old girl for her school paper (many similar themes have been written in school newspapers) entitled, "Birth Control: Enjoying Sex Without Fear," caused a lot of static. It was not the first such publication, nor will it be the last that will reflect the teachings of the public schools.

The last paragraph was the center of the storm: "With the knowledge of modern medicine, unwanted pregnancy will no longer have to be a problem and youth can enjoy premarital sex without fear."

It is apparent that Uncle Sam will protect his "little girl" in every way. He must be proud of such literature. It is what he has permitted his teachers to teach her and she has apparently learned her lesson well.

For those students who do not know what lengths they can go to in their school newspapers, the ACLU and Planned Parenthood are now holding classes to teach those students.

No one tells our children as fervently of the side effects of these contraceptives, as they diligently press for their use. And the ill effects are multiple. Blindness, the risk of liver tumors, blood poisoning, painful intercourse, brain damage—the list is long.

Dr. Carlton Fredericks, Ph.D., writing in his Hotline to Health column in *Prevention* magazine, cited a British study that showed the death rate from diseases of the circulatory system in women using oral contraceptives was five times that of women who had never used the Pill; the death rate in those who took the Pill continually for five years or more was ten times higher than women who did not take the pill.

"Often it is pointed out by proponents of the Pill that pregnancy itself has risks, the argument being that the scale balances, and is favorably weighted by the virtual elimination of unwanted motherhood," wrote Dr. Fredericks. "That argument is demolished by this study, which showed far more deaths from the Pill than were caused in another similar group of women by the complications of pregnancy."

Dr. Robert Kistner of Harvard Medical School, one of the original clinical researchers who, in 1955, aided in the development of the Pill, now has second thoughts about the sexual freedom that he aided.

"For years, I felt the Pill would not lead to promiscuity," he said. "But I have changed my mind. I think it probably has—and so has the IUD [intrauterine device]."

Dr. Kistner also expressed concern over the fact that among young women, gonorrhea was pandemic. He called it "the number-one communicable disease in the United States, more common than the cold," and said that when women stop taking the Pill and want to become pregnant, they are sometimes sterile, and the greater chance and risk of developing cancer of the cervix is also there. "There is evidence that changes in the cervix preceding cancer are more common in young girls who have frequent intercourse and multiple partners prior to age 18," he added.

All of this, and the fact that morality plays no part in the lives of our youth, is what sends the parents to war against Uncle Sam, once the symbol of patriotism in our country.

Schools get into the issue in other ways too. At one school, students from age 14 to 18, boys and girls alike, were encouraged to squirt contraceptive foam into their hands. It is a scene repeated, and repeated, and repeated in our schools.

In another school an instructor, to show its qualities, took a condom and blew it up for the students. Although the Philadelphia School Board has prohibited teaching birth-control methods in their schools at this point, some teachers, working with Planned Parenthood, go ahead and arrogantly teach it anyway.

One of the teachers said that blowing up a condom was a means of making people comfortable, to "take off the pressure." "You're talking about some things that were taboos," said the teacher.

Another teacher commented: "One of the boys said he was glad he took the course [on contraceptives] because he now feels comfortable asking a girl, 'Are you covered?'"

In March of 1979 the Philadelphia School Board approved the teaching of contraceptives in the schools. One man, who was quoted widely on TV, radio, and in the newspapers, said we would be turning out Pill-popping whores, and the next thing that would happen would be that schools would become abortion referral services.

It just goes to show how ignorant parents are. Sex education has been in the Philadelphia schools since the mid-'60s, and Planned Parenthood has been going in with their contraceptive campaigns even before the Philadelphia School Board voted for it. Schools already are abortion referral services. Once again, the answer is more of the same—only this time they were making it official and public. What really irks me is that the press didn't do its homework and treated it as if it were something new.

Philadelphia Board of Education member Felice Stack, an opponent of sex education (but a minority member), put her finger on it all when she said, "I find it upsetting, because every time I look at an article about teen-age sexuality, it talks about how complicated their lives are, and the big cry always seems to be teach them birth-control methods. The big question is, why don't we tell them that it is not a good practice for a teen-ager to engage in sexual behavior? It is not the time of their lives for it. Why don't we tell the truth, that teen-agers can avoid all of these complications by not engaging in sexual intercourse?"

Why, Felice? Because it would destroy Uncle Sam's experiment.

34.

The Changing Profile of Today's Doctor

Whether this is an era of fallen professions is yet to be calculated. But there is a sure sign that not only the teaching profession, but the medical profession as well, is slipping in public esteem.

Those who have contributed to the slide of doctors' esteem are those who have replaced the family doctor with a doctor who helps to destroy the family. He now dispenses drugs to known drug users, has become involved in Medicare and Medicaid fraud, and has further violated the family by dispensing contraceptives, VD treatment and arranging for and performing abortions for minor children without parental knowledge or consent, or even a "tsk, tsk."

Today's "damaged" doctor also writes books encouraging teen-age promiscuity and, like Dr. William A. Block of Cherry Hill's schools, preaches the same.

Writing in the *American Journal of Obstetrics and Gynecology*, a doctor recently proposed that the United States adopt a system of two-year "paramarriages" for the young, saying it would allow teen-agers to vent their sexual energies in a socially acceptable manner, thereby reducing tensions between parents and teens. Just what type of parent would find this suggestion to be "socially acceptable," this disgrace to his profession does not name.

I first met Dr. Daniel H. Williams at a convention I was attending in the hopes of finding some material for a column I was writing. Dr. Williams, at that time, was the medical director of two drug clinics. His topic at the convention, where he was one of the guest speakers, was drugs.

When a member of the audience asked him what a parent should do if he found his child was smoking marijuana, he drew laughter, some of it tinged with nervousness, when he replied that after talking to the child, maybe the parent ought to try it himself.

I would later interview Dr. Williams for my column. He would tell me that he was really a fence-sitter on the subject of marijuana use and that he knew doctors who grew their own marijuana at home. It worries me not a little to think that a doctor doing a diagnosis, writing out a prescription, or scrubbing for surgery might be high on drugs.

I subsequently interviewed Dr. Williams for this book, to discuss with him the changing profile of today's doctor. In private practice, Dr. Williams is a pediatrician. He sees a lot of teen-agers.

Married and the father of three children aged 7, 12, and 18, Dr. Williams spoke candidly from two points of view: that of the physician in today's society and that of a father. I found all that he told me to be a microcosm of the conflicts and concerns facing all parents, and the changing attitude of many of today's doctors.

On the issue of drug treatment, Dr. Williams, who spent most of the interview batting at flies with a swatter, said he thought he could legally treat a minor child on drugs without parental intervention or knowledge if the child was ill enough. As to whether or not he would inform the child's parents of the problem of drugs, he said it would depend on his judgment of the child's maturity. Citing the 16-year-old, he said: "Some of them are mature enough to accept the responsibility of their own problems and others aren't."

He would not necessarily inform the parents, he went on, "because sometimes it's more complicated than that and you lose the trust of the patient. He won't come back to you.

"Let's say a 16-year-old comes in and wants birth-control pills. Should you call her parents and say: Hey, little Suzie is out here doing her thing, or should you say: Suzie, if you're going to do your thing: one, you should talk it over with your parents; two, I'll give you birth control, but these are the complications of birth-control pills; three, these are the complications of NOT taking some kind of contraceptive: pregnancy, venereal disease, blah, blah, blah? If they're old enough to engage in frequent sexual activity, I think they're old enough to accept the responsibility."

I cite Dr. Williams statistics that indicate overwhelmingly that these kids are far from "responsible." "Well," he counters, "they're capable of having sexual relations."

The rise in sexual promiscuity among the young, he says, occurred when the family clan fell apart. He also lays the blame at the feet of television and lends some truth to the statement that parents do a lot more compromising with their children today.

"There's a little joke that I tell my patients now," he said in reference to all the conflicts our youth are causing their parents . . . "that I'm forming a new program here. It's called the Parent Abuse Center. What you do is you call in if your children are abusing you. We come out, we arrest the children, and we put you and your husband in a foster home for a year." There is no question, he says in a more serious vein, that children today abuse their parents—even physically. "The question is," he asks, "why do we let them do that?"

I ask him if doctors are not doing an awful lot of assuming when a minor comes in and asks for contraceptives. Isn't there the possibility that if the doctor does not give him contraceptives he will not engage in intercourse?

"Oh, sure," he admits. But then he cites the rising statistics of teen-age pregnancies to me to justify the doctor's action. Pregnancy, he said, can ruin a young life and severely affect the child's parents' lives and that of the entire family. "We can say no," he said to dispensing contraceptives to minors, "but it's the parents' responsibility to say this is not socially acceptable."

How, I ask him, does he know the child asking for contraceptives does not have parents who find such conduct socially unacceptable.

"This is 1978, it's not 1958," he told me by way of an answer.

Dr. Williams says that every time he does a physical for a young woman going off to college, he asks her if she would like birth-control information. He justifies that by saying that he knows that "once they hit college they're PROBABLY—maybe 80 percent of 'em—going to have some kind of sexual relationship."

Some parents are present when he asks that question; others, he said, he knows would object. These are the parents, he said, who "won't accept the fact that there are people out there having relationships like that who are not married, who are teen-agers. And what am I gonna do if they won't accept that? If I ask that, they'll be horrified! What'll happen then? OK. The parents will rebel against me for even bringing it up. OK. I not only lose their confidence, but I lose the patient. It's OK, but I don't want that to happen."

Dr. Williams is never nasty to me, no matter what questions I ask him. He is more than willing to discuss whatever it is I toss at him and at least give me his honest feelings on the subject.

For today's youth, he thinks the ideal relationship would run something like this: "If you're going to have sex relations, if you're going to masturbate, if you're going to explore your sexual feelings, why not do it with your parents being aware that that's what you're doing? At least be honest with yourself and your parents. Great! But admittedly, most people can't do that," he says. "Or if they do it, they do it with this: Is that the right thing to do? I even have these feelings, you know. I'm a parent, too.

"For example: My daughter, when she had her menstrual period, came down and told me at dinner. We were having dinner with a couple that we hadn't even seen before—never met! She had enough understanding of what was happening and enough confidence in me to come down and say, 'Dad, I'm having a period, and isn't it great!' and go back upstairs. I was flabbergasted, number one, that she told me during dinner with people that I don't even know."

He said he thought about the episode for a while and concluded that it "was great!"

When I commented that it was certainly a departure from what we call modesty, he replied, "Yeah. But the kids ARE that way."

I grow quiet and he senses my mood. "We're not talking morality, are we?" he asks. "If we're talking morality it's a different story. What we're talking is the normal body, the normal developing teen-ager who is certainly having sexual feelings at 16, 17, 14 years, and some younger. And if there are feelings and we're in a society where we want awarenesses becoming much more important, why not be aware that you have sexual feelings and gratification is part of them? And why not let them do that?" Morality aside, he says that instead of society being beset with young mothers and illegitimate children, we have to give out advice on contraceptives.

In the future, Dr. Williams said he sees "people who are going to live together before they get married; because of living together they're going to have to be sexually active. And personally, morality-wise, I don't think that's so bad."

When I ask if this is not further alienating the family concept, he replies in the affirmative and the old standby: "We have to change with the times.

"I'm not a physician where I have to justify the rapid changes of the world to people," he says to me. "All I can do is lead my own life. And the way I lead my own life with my kids is that I want my children to come to talk to me about their problems. Admittedly I come home late at night and they haven't had time to talk to me and I'm probably in the position of many busy fathers. I try to make time for them. It's very difficult," he confesses.

Talking about his own children, he seems to change course. "I'm not suggesting that everybody go out and go to sleep with everybody in the world. I think that's wrong. Morally I think it's wrong.

Physically it's not such a good idea for [the] spread of venereal disease, et cetera. BUT, I think if they [teenagers] are going to have very heavy petting or sexual relations, they should be prepared."

Again returning to the minor seeking a contraceptive from the doctor, he says, "What I would tell her is I'd like her to talk this over with her parents and I think I have to leave that all to her. I can't make those decisions for people. But I don't think I have a moral obligation to tell them this girl has come to me for contraceptive advice.

"Let's put it this way: A couple of generations ago a doctor would never have given them contraceptive advice, no matter what. Period. Because they weren't married."

Citing the rise of venereal disease in the young, he concludes, "The only way we can get it down is to give them advice about how not to get it, or if they get it, where to get the proper treatment without their parents' consent. If you wait for the parents' consent, you ain't never gonna get it. Just getting sex education in the schools has been murder."

I tell him I place much of the blame on sex education for the changing morals of our youth.

He almost goes into cardiac arrest. "Oh, no, no, no, no, no. No, no. Oh, come on! Don't give me that bullshit! That's absolute bullshit," he says, swatting at another bug. "What you're saying is stick your head in a hole when there's a problem, but don't teach anybody the rights and wrongs of it and let the problem go on."

The problem, I tell him, is that in sex education no one says there is a right or a wrong. And like himself, they tell the child if he is "responsible" it is OK to go ahead with sexual activity.

"No, they're not saying that. They're NOT saying that!" he says with great emphasis.

I cite him various examples. He says, with genuine incredulity, "You mean they're saying it's OK if you want to go out and do it?"

"Yes," I answer.

"I don't believe it," he says. I give him more examples. He becomes more receptive. "Why didn't we know about that? If you know where that literature is, you ought to bring it to the public. Haven't you told them it's in the school system? Haven't you written to the school system and said this is the literature you're putting out for these kids?"

I tell him I did better than that . . . I wrote an entire book on the subject.

"And nothing happened? Did you write to the school board of that township? Well, I can't believe most school boards would let something like that go through. Do you know more than one [school where this is happening]?" he asks quietly and with growing concern in his voice.

I tell him I wrote about the entire country and its involvement in sex education.

As I try to move to another question, Dr. Williams returns once again to the issue of sex education. "I haven't done any research on it, but it seems astounding to me that school boards would tell children how to have sex without anybody around—let's put it that way," he says pensively, referring back to literature that was in one school's bibliography for sex education that I have told him about.

"Well, unless one talks about a problem, how are you going to get a solution?" he asks. I respond by saying sex education was the program that created the monster by saying it's OK, you're sexually active—just be sure to use a contraceptive. God forbid, you should get pregnant. But that's OK too, you can have an abortion.

Dr. Williams is digesting the topic. "MMM, HMMM," he said, growing concerned-looking.

Sounding like so many of today's parents, he says, "I had a hard time when I was a kid and I don't want them to have a hard time," he says of his own children. "Well, I think that we overdo it," he admits.

We talk of the demands made by today's teen-agers, and I say that whatever it is they want, they seem to have the same cry as the colorful Reverend Ike who says, "I want it right here! Right now!"

"You're absolutely right," says Dr. Williams. It is something, he says, that has also crept into the parents. "We're becoming an individualized society. I agree a hundred percent. And it's part of the problem, if not THE problem . . . that we don't have responsibilities for other people. We don't have respect for them, either."

We expand on the selfish attitude of today's youth—into their refusal to curb any sexual feelings, even knowing it is morally wrong and that their parents would not approve, knowing that the girls will even risk pregnancy. "Oh, I don't disagree with that. Sure I agree that they want it now, and that's for sure. It's a 'Me' attitude for sure."

Mothers, unable to cope with all the teen-age problems, he says, are taking drugs and alcohol; but fathers become workaholics. "Hey, I see it," he says. "And that's their out. Don't bother me with that, because I have something to do at the office. See ya! Boom! They're gone. So they don't have to worry about teen-age pregnancy, the girl out sleeping with other people, the boy who's breaking windows in the local school or vandalizing, or whatever it's going to be," he says. He hopes, he says, that his own children will toe a moral line.

Dr. Williams says he came from a home with a working mother.

He recalled the thoughts that ran through his mind as a youngster: "Why is she working when everyone else's mother is home? There's nothing to do in this house." He tells me he peeled potatoes and even set the table for his mother. How many children today, he muses, would voluntarily do those things. From his reminiscing he talks about the working mothers of today—the ones that must work and the ones who are working just to indulge in materialistic things. When his young mothers ask him if he thinks it will hurt their children if they work, he said he answers, without hesitation, by saying: "Absolutely, a hundred percent, for sure."

Expressing his feelings for the rough-going of parenting in today's world, he says, with pain, "Uh! Unbelievable!"

How, I ask him, is the parent who provides a good home, whose kids have a religious upbringing, who monitor their TV programs, who spend a lot of time with their kids, who truly communicate with them, and suddenly, boom!—they find their kids engaged in some fashion or another in this whole mess of today . . . how then do parent and child live together?

"With a lot of difficulty," he says.

I am glad that Dr. Williams and I have talked for so long. He tells me I have given him a lot to think about. Is Dr. Williams (as other doctors who think and act the way he does) really the parents' enemy, or is he just being swept along with so many others who are uninformed and think what they are doing is the best they can do under the circumstances?

And who was it in the end who buried his head in a hole—Dr. Williams or I?

There is a footnote to this chapter that is put in days before this manuscript is sent to Arlington House:

I call Dr. Williams on the phone to check on a detail that we covered in the interview. He is excited, telling me he is so glad I called. He has been trying to reach me, but did not know how.

He has been called, he tells me, to be a guest speaker on sex education for a school. "Isn't it ironic?" he asks me. He would like to read a copy of the book I wrote on sex education. He will drive to my home to get it. I tell him I will have someone deliver it to him.

Dr. Williams tells me that he has told the woman who called him to speak on behalf of sex education: "You've got to have Gloria Lentz, too. This woman really knows all about it." I ask him the name of the school where he is being asked to speak. He tells me, and I cannot stop laughing. He is puzzled. I tell him I will bet him one of his new horses in his stables that they will never permit me to speak. I know the district well, wrote about it, and had them lash out at me in public for the exposé I wrote on their sex education program. As he didn't believe what was going on in sex education classes, this too seems improbable to him.

As of this moment, the day he was to speak has come and gone on the calendar. I am expecting a new horse any day now.

35.

Are Some Doctors Just Doing Their Own Thing?

As of 1974, according to the appendix of the ACLU handbook, *The Rights of Young People,* 1977 edition, approximately two-fifths of the states, including New Jersey, still listed 18 as the age when children could obtain contraceptives without parental knowledge or consent.

What, I began to wonder, gave doctors such as Dr. William A. Block and other doctors in private practice license to be dispensing contraceptives to minors in the state of New Jersey, if in fact the ACLU handbook was correct.

I knew that married minors, emancipated minors, minors with a Medicaid card, or minors with a venereal disease could obtain contraceptives, but what about Mr. and Mrs. Average American's child who was getting contraceptives from their family doctor?

The big question was: Were doctors in private practice in the state of New Jersey acting within the bounds of the law when they dispensed contraceptives to minors without parental knowledge or consent from as far back as 1970 to today? If not, how many, I wondered, had been flirting with a potential legal time bomb? I began digging.

I first called the ACLU offices in Camden, N.J. The woman with whom I spoke did not have any answers. However, she told me I was in luck. There was to be an ACLU meeting that evening, and all the "legal brains" of the ACLU would be there. They were sure to have an answer for me. Would I call back? I did. They did not have an answer, she said.

She in turn referred me to the Newark, N.J., offices of the ACLU.

They did not have an answer either. They referred me to Nadine Taub of the Women's Rights Clinic at Rutgers University. Her offices said they did not have an answer.

Next I called the law offices of N.J. State Senator Barry Parker. Parker's office had no answer to the question.

Next I contacted Congressman Edwin B. Forsythe's office in Washington. Forsythe's administrative assistant, Brian Kelly, said he would look into the matter and get back to me.

In the meantime I called the Medical Society of New Jersey. I spoke with June O'Hare. Several days later she called me back to say that the society had checked everywhere, including the law library at the State House in Trenton. "They have nothing," she said.

After another week or two had elapsed, Martin E. Johnson, director of public affairs and medical education for the Medical Society of New Jersey, called me. "According to my sources, it is illegal if they [doctors] are doing that—if they are giving contraceptives to the sexually promiscuous minor child without parental knowledge or consent," he said. It was, he said, the official stand of the society as of the day he called me, which was Feb. 9, 1979. Doctors, he said, could be getting around the issue by saying they were prescribing the Pill to stabilize the minor girl's menstrual cycle. "That may be their out," he said.

I continued to check. Richard Knight of the Governor's Commission on Children and Youth in the state of New Jersey said he would check my question out and call back. He called back and said: "We don't know."

Next I called the Department of Community Affairs, the Health Department of New Jersey's family planning section. Anne Okubo called me back. She said clinics could make their own policies. "The department," she said, "does not have any rules or regulations governing dispensing of contraceptives to minors. However, they have a policy that says no one is denied services regardless of race, sex or age—and that would include minors."

Concerning doctors in private practice, she said the law is unclear, but indicates it is not permissible for them to be dispensing contraceptives to minors without parental consent. The matter, she said, was in litigation.

Brian Kelly of Congressman Forsythe's office was to call me back several times on the matter. "I'm having as much trouble as you are finding any answers," he told me.

Kelly said he had lucked out at the national headquarters of Planned Parenthood, the Department of Justice, and the Attorney General's office. The Assistant General Counsel of Health Care

Financing in the Department of HEW told him point-blank that there was "no federal law" governing this issue.

Kelly then forwarded to me a 1972 opinion by the then Attorney General of New Jersey.

Some states, said the Attorney General's opinion, took into account the maturity and mental capacity of the minor and the unavailability of a parent or guardian. "Whether New Jersey courts would follow this principle is questionable enough to advise against its advocation by the State Department of Health."

"Since the dispensing of birth-control devices," read his opinion, "along with the clinical diagnoses and advice necessary thereto, may only be characterized as a 'method of treatment of human physical condition,' (according to N.J.S.A. 45:9-5.1) surely parental or other appropriate consent must be given before such services are rendered to an unmarried minor."

So there it was. The Medical Society of New Jersey called the practice "illegal," and the former Attorney General of the state of New Jersey advised that parental or other appropriate consent must be granted before giving the minor contraceptives.

How many other states, I wonder, have doctors in private practice that have licensed themselves to be the judge of whether or not they will give the minor contraceptives and are perhaps running afoul of the law?

36.

A Visit to Planned Parenthood

I turned into Sansom Street that sunny September afternoon to keep an appointment I had made with Douglas Jackson, Executive Director of the Philadelphia Chapter of Planned Parenthood. I had told Jackson I was writing a book on the rights of teen-agers and wanted to talk about Planned Parenthood's involvement. He had been receptive.

I had no trouble in locating Planned Parenthood's headquarters. Outside of the building hung a huge royal-blue banner with Planned Parenthood lettered in gigantic silver letters on it.

I had purposely arrived early, to look everything over. As I stood outside for a while, the din of trucks loading on the narrow Philadelphia street blended with the other metropolitan noises. As I watched from across the street, two young girls exited the building at different times. Each was wearing the blue-jean badges of her era.

I finally stepped across the ribbon-like street, walked up a flight of outside stairs, and went into the building. To my immediate right was Planned Parenthood's library. In it were two round tables and a scattering of chairs. The books were for perusing or buying. I glanced over some of the titles: I saw only two books on babies—one dealing with prenatal care, the other with infant care. For the most part, the book titles spat out the new morality: *The Right to Abortion, Sex Without Shame, The Children's Rights Movement, Values Clarification, Woman's Body—Woman's Right* (on its cover were two women, each with a raised arm and a clenched fist), *Practical Guide for the Unmarried Couple, Our Right to Love,* some of Sol

Gordon's tasteless comic books, and *Abortion Is a Blessing*, whose author, Anne N. Gaylor, guested on Larry King's coast-to-coast popular radio program as the president of a group called Freedom From Religion. On King's show, Gaylor had three times referred to Christ as "flaky."

Glancing at my watch, I moved to the elevator and went to meet Mr. Jackson on the fourth floor.

I was ushered into his offices only to be told that he was sorry, he had tried to get in touch with me, but I had left no number at which to be contacted, and he had a meeting to attend. Would I mind if I instead interviewed Planned Parenthood's Associate Executive Director, Patricia Burks? I told him that would be fine.

For a short period of time, both Jackson and Burks were with me as I set up my tape recorder and drank the coffee they offered me. They were, said Jackson, on the brink of celebrating this chapter's fiftieth anniversary.

Jackson began talking about the Supreme Court's ruling in 1976 that he said simplified abortion for minors by knocking out parental consent. However, he said, concerning contraceptives, there was a piece of legislation that spelled out the circumstances under which a minor could receive contraceptives in the state of Pennsylvania without parental involvement.

"There may be exceptions under the law, but I think you'd be very hard-pressed to find one in terms of the clinics," he said.

"We see anyone regardless of their [sic] age or marital status or ability to pay," said Burks.

Since I was primarily interested in the teen-ager and the minor, I said, could they tell me how Planned Parenthood sees its role in society pertaining to this aspect?

"Well," said Jackson, "I think that our basic premise is that teen-agers are sexually active; at least a large percentage of teen-agers are sexually active. The premise that we operate under is that it is obviously better for that teen-ager to prevent that pregnancy than to have to deal with the pregnancy after the fact. So we are very supportive of teen services—offer teen services—are pro sex education."

Expanding on their activities with teen-agers, Jackson continued: "We are developing a Teen Conference; we're doing a program with the National Organization for Nonparents on rights of student reporters, because we've had so much trouble in terms of trying to have some newspapers publish articles around sex education and human sexuality. We have a training institute that works with professionals who work with teen-agers, teachers. We train teachers, we train nurses, we train social workers, we train case workers, we train youth workers of all descriptions. And we provide medical services."

Are they presenting their programs to schools? "I think we get into most schools," said Burks. "What's that unit on . . . contraception?" she asks Jackson, who is gathering papers together to leave for his meeting.

"It's on sex education, fertility and contraception," he answers.

When I ask about funding, Burks tells me they have many sources, including government, fund-raising, contributions, foundations, mailings and fees charged those who can afford it or are not on Medicaid.

"Government money that is available to us is to provide contraceptive services. The sources are Title Ten of the Public Health Services Act," says Burks. Another source is the social-service equivalent of Medicaid. "Under that funding we are required to see teen-agers without charge," she says.

Title Twenty, she tells me, was implemented July 1, 1978. "Now, with the Title Twenty funding, we do not charge teen-agers." It will, she says, cover treatment for VD and birth control for teen-agers.

Altogether there are 190 Planned Parenthood affiliates in the U.S. and 650 clinics. The yearly budget is $90 million. Planned Parenthood has a staff of 3,000, plus 20,000 volunteers.

Former U.S. Treasury Secretary William E. Simon, talking about the tax situation of today, commented: "Politicians use the tax system to redistribute the wealth to benefit special interests in order to get reelected, to perpetuate themselves in Washington." For fiscal years 1975-1978, under Title Ten Funds, $91,626,156 dollars of your tax money went to Planned Parenthood. That does not include the funds they receive from Titles Fourteen and Twenty.

How much does it cost to get an abortion at Planned Parenthood? "We charge $150 for an abortion," Burks said. What if the teen-ager doesn't have $150?

"That's a problem," she says. "Right now Medicaid is reimbursing for persons who have medical assistance cards." In order to accommodate other teen-agers, she said, "we and most of the other societies have made some arrangements to defer payments. Either we'll charge a reduced fee, set up a financing plan for the person— but we have very few abortions to provide at no cost . . . for us to go out of business. Some of the other clinics are able," she says, "and we are able to see a limited number of people without charge, but it has to be very, very limited.

"Right now thirty-five percent of our patients either pay or give us a medical card, or we charge them a reduced fee. Thirty-five percent of our patients, and a large number of abortion patients are very young," she tells me.

What happens when they go into a school? "It depends on what the topic is. The topic can be anything from reproductive anatomy, where you just go in and talk about plumbing. Sometimes the schools may require that students have parental permission. That," she says emphatically, "would be their requirement, not ours."

Some students, she said, "are looking for approval, someone to say it's OK for me to make up my mind to do whatever—whether that is to remain a virgin, to remain celibate or to have intercourse.

"A big thrust of our program is to talk about values clarification, to allow the individual to use his experience to arrive at decisions. That your decision about sex, whether that's homosexuality, masturbation, whatever it is—the decision is based on your life's experience. And what we want to do is to facilitate people to come into those decisions. We don't make those decisions for other people. We might talk to them about—you know, if you become sexually active, what does that mean? What does it mean for the relationship? What happens if you become sexually active without contraception?"

When I ask Burks to better define values clarification for me, she says, "It just allows the person to explore what their [sic] options are.

"We have kids coming into the clinic who are 12 years old," she said. And then, switching back again to going into the schools, she said, "You know, we're not going to go in there with the 'Thou Shalt Not' but if that's the way you've always made your decisions, then you should consider that when you make your decision about sex."

I ask Burks to take me step-by-step through what happens to a teen-ager who comes to Planned Parenthood. "First of all," she said, "you'd make an appointment. We have an active patient load of about 25,000 [a year]."

Suddenly, we are interrupted by the voice of a young girl. She sounds distressed and it sounds as if she is saying, "I'm 15 and I'm pregnant!" The interview grinds to a halt. And then, like the extra volume associated with TV commercials, a man's soothing voice says, "Planned Parenthood . . ." There is more talk from the young girl, but it is muffled. Intermittently, the commercial aspect comes through loud and clear and we hear again: "Planned Parenthood . . ."

"A movie?" I ask. "Yeah," answers Burks. We resume the interview. She tells me that the majority, 70 to 75 percent, of their patients are under 25. I ask if they are seeing more preteens and teen-agers than they did ten years ago. "Yes. Most definitely," she confirms.

Burks returns to the topic of teen-agers who come for the first time to Planned Parenthood. She assures me that they receive a physical, and a medical history will be taken into account when a contraceptive is being considered. Again, she stresses, "For a seventeen and under, income does not matter. We're going to see her without charge."

The "patient," as she constantly calls the young teen-ager, is then sent to an "education session." "We explain to them, first of all, our services." This is done in groups. Different contraceptives are discussed and depending on the population, she said, they might also talk about sterilization.

From there, the young person is given a pelvic or urine examination if she thinks she is pregnant, or a blood test. The entire process, she said, usually takes from two to four hours. "We use licensed physicians, usually OBY-GYN [obstetricians-gynecologists]. We occasionally use nurse practitioners," she said of the examinations, but when that happens, she assured me a physician is also on the premises. "We'll give her an emergency number if there is a problem. And we will give her information on what to look out for. Any potential problems. If you're using the IUD and you bleed heavily," she says by way of example.

Do youngsters comprehend and absorb all of this? "Oh, sure!" Burks reassures me. "We talk to teen-agers especially, about what they like about Planned Parenthood. There are several things: One: Our staff is young and they're very understanding. Two: We're approachable. And three: They know they've gotten a full examination.

"The other thing that's usually very important and would probably interest you," she says, "is that our services are entirely confidential."

If teen-agers either want an examination because they think they might have VD, if they want contraceptives, or if a young girl opts for abortion, how can they be sure that nobody will know? I ask.

"It's a condition of employment that every Planned Parenthood employee respects . . . confidentiality."

"It's something that is just understood?" I ask. "Well, it's not just understood," she says impatiently. "It's a condition that's stated very clearly in the personnel policies.

"And we will not release information to anyone about who receives services. I won't take you down to the clinic to show you around for exactly that reason," she says firmly.

When teen-agers make their initial visit, Burks said they are told: "We will not give any information about you—about whether you were seen here, or about the services, to anyone. The only way that someone can get into our records is by patient consent or by a court order. You have to take us to court," she says adamantly.

Has that ever happened? "Yes, it has," she says. "Of course it has. I guess a typical scenario is a daughter comes in, gets pills. You know, most of our teen-age patients opt for pills, then go home. Mom goes through the purse and finds the Pill and finds Planned Parenthood's name on it, and calls you mad as hell. 'What the hell are you doing serving my daughter!' And the person who answers the phone will say: 'I cannot tell you whether or not we saw your daughter.'"

Planned Parenthood then encourages the mother to talk to her daughter, said Burks. "It is extremely, extremely rare for a parent to proceed beyond that," she says. "One of the reasons is not that . . ." and here she breaks into a laugh, "everything works out hunky-dory, but what it means is that if you find that your 14-year-old daughter has been here, it means going to an open courtroom and saying: 'Here. We have medical records.' We can say: 'Your daughter came here with venereal disease' or 'Your daughter came here because she was sexually active.'" Burks laughs heartily again. "You know, most parents don't want to go that way.

"No one in the country has ever successfully sued a Family Planning Clinic," she said with pride.

Of the angry parents, she said, "We talk to them: 'You know, your child has made a very responsible decision. You should think about that. Maybe you should approach your child. You know: I know you're going to Planned Parenthood. Let's talk about it. If you accept that, you're not going to alienate your child.'"

How, I ask, can Planned Parenthood deny the child has been there if the parent sees its name on the Pill box? "We do not deny it. We will not discuss it," she says flatly. "If you came in here and came in as a patient, and your husband wanted to know whether you were here, we would not even page you over the intercom. We will not do anything. To say that a Planned Parenthood employee would breach confidentiality would be to tell me that the Pope or a priest told somebody to turn Jewish."

To maintain confidentiality, she says, if a child cannot be called at home, she must leave a number where she can be reached at another location.

How do they take a youngster through abortion? Pat says an examination is done first to confirm the pregnancy and then a counselor will talk to the girl about options. Defensively, she says, "It's called option, options—not abortion options."

I am not stretching my imagination, she assures me, when I ask if a 16-year-old could be on her third abortion. But abortion, she says, is only a small percentage of Planned Parenthood's involvement.

Why aren't Planned Parenthood's programs working? I ask, citing the astronomical escalation of pregnant teen-agers. "We're not going to take the weight of that on our shoulders!" she says with exasperation.

She tells me that she thought everybody from her generation was a virgin, and then laughing, says, "Well, as the truth comes out, that's not always the case."

I agree, but tell her statistics cannot be avoided—kids are more sexually active today, and this new surge is still climbing.

"Our society has two minds about sex. They say, 'Do it.' You know, everything around you says, 'Do it.' You look at the TV, you look at the clothes, the music. You look at everything else—and there's just been a lot of pressure to have sex. But basically people have sex because they enjoy it. Teen-agers are no different than 4- or 5-year-olds, or 8-year-olds. They enjoy it. I think teen-agers have more freedom now than they might have had a while ago," she says.

Going back to her own high school days again, Burks says that her hygiene lessons were basically, "Don't." "And we were terrified. I don't know about you, but I was terrified I would become pregnant. That kept me on the right side," she said laughing.

I ask her if that was so bad. "You know, I don't know whether it was bad or not. It was just what happened. And it happened to most of us. Teen-agers now, you know—they're no dummies. I think that what we need to teach them is not so much about sex, but about responsibility."

I ask her to define responsibility and she plays the same record as the other advocates: "I think we as a society have to say that if you don't use contraceptives and you don't plan to be pregnant, then you are acting irresponsibly."

I set up a hypothetical situation for Burks: A mother brings her young daughter in and says they both agree the pregnant girl wants an abortion. However, the child really does not want the abortion. How does Planned Parenthood ferret out the child's true feelings?

"We always talk to the child alone. By the time counselors have been here for a year or even when they first start out—they know how to interview. They know there's something not right."

When asked if a young girl could go to her health teacher or a school counselor to ask to be checked to see if she is pregnant, and if they will refer her to Planned Parenthood, Burks says there is no need for her to go through a third party. "She can call here herself," she says.

When I ask her how Planned Parenthood meets the opposition who say, "Abortion is killing a baby," she says they are a society guilty of fetus worship. "And I don't think that you can worship the fetus. And I think that's what they do."

I tell her about young people talking about the issue of abortion in my home. I tell her some of the kids say if an abortion takes place, the baby will surely die, but the girl who has committed her baby to death will not die.

It enrages Burks, and she becomes rabid on the subject. "Sometimes she will! And dammit, they will deny an abortion to a woman who will die . . ." she says, turning dramatic for the first time during the interview, ". . . to a woman who would die if she became pregnant.

"Now you talk to them. Talk to them!" she spits at me, obviously referring to prolife people.

I tell her that I don't think the prolife people are thinking about that aspect. I choose my words wrongly. Her sudden change in personality has thrown me. What I meant to say is that in such a case the prolife people would opt for the life of the mother, but Burks is already reacting to my poor choice of words.

"They don't actually think of a lot of things!" she rants. "They don't actually think of women who might be driven, as women have, to stick knitting needles up themselves. Did they ever think of the desperation of that woman—to stick a knitting needle up herself?" Burks is obviously relating to the much-publicized case of a young woman who did abort her baby by using knitting needles, because her boyfriend didn't want the child after he had impregnated her. I point out that the young woman did not have to resort to that method, since abortion is now available.

But Burks is on her soapbox and becomes very upset. "Abortion was not available to her. She didn't have the money, you know, or she may have seen it . . . I don't know what her situation was," she rambles on. "She was very late.

"There are women who could not live with the prospect of bringing . . . there are women who are doing everything possible for them to prevent a pregnancy short of abstinence, and they become pregnant. Every single method will fail. And I will tell you that the minute you walk into Planned Parenthood.

"There are women who want other things for themselves than to have a child right now. It may be selfish," she offers, "but it's their butt. I just don't think you can, you know, worship the fetus."

I tell her she has hit on a key word, "selfish." We have, I say, evolved into a very narcissistic society. "Yes, it is," she agrees.

"What I'm saying is that because I'm a woman, don't tell me that I have this type of job and that I have to live this type of life. I want to make that decision," she says, once again climbing onto her soapbox.

"Because I'm black doesn't mean I want to do this. Because I'm fat doesn't mean I want to do this. Because I'm skinny doesn't mean I want to live this way. But I have to be able to make those decisions for myself. And I think to force a woman to become a mother really, really degrades motherhood—to force it on somebody. Anybody can be a mother if they [sic] just want to," she says with fire in her voice.

I am tempted to argue with her, to remind her of the hundreds of teen-agers who will never be mothers because of abortions or a venereal disease, but I am already sick of her not coming up for air on the subject.

She rattles on still more, repeating again the convictions she has learned from God knows where. I look at her. She is a pretty woman. She is flesh and blood, the same as I. I see before me a person I might have liked in another time and another place—back in high school, when our philosophies were more of a match.

I shut off my tape recorder and begin to gather up my things. I feel sorry for Patricia Burks; but I feel sorrier for all the children who will come in contact with the likes of her.

37.

Children Killing Babies

In 1973 nearly 12,000 legal abortions were performed on girls under 15; for girls under 20 the figure shot up to 244,000.

In 1975 judges ruled in New Orleans and Colorado that laws formerly requiring parental permission prior to a minor receiving an abortion were no longer valid. It was called "a serious blow delivered to parental rights" by Colorado's Right-to-Life committee president.

On July 1, 1976, the Supreme Court took away the last vestiges of parental authority governing abortion. Justice Harry Blackmun said that states did not have the authority to give parents "an absolute and possibly arbitrary veto" over a minor's right to an abortion.

"Constitutional rights do not mature and come into being magically only when one attains the state-defined age of majority . . ." he said.

Those who were following the issues involving the dissolution of one parental right after another knew this area had been just a matter of time in falling too.

After all, hadn't that meddling old fool of a "relative," Uncle Sam, already given the public schools the money and license to teach their children that abortion was an alternative to pregnancy?

It was clear that he wanted his children (and they were, step-by-step, becoming *his* children) to frolic in love-making. As a highly permissive "relative," wielding tons of power, he did not want his children to suffer any consequences. He had already helped to fund the abortion clinics. Now he would further indulge his children by keeping their meddling parents out of their hair on abortion.

If only he could have enough sperm banks and the ability to produce a baby that could mature for nine months in a test tube . . . if only. Then he could do away with parents forever. In the meantime, he would just have to continue to batter them down.

He would win, eventually. He could buy his own army. Best of all, the parents would pay for whatever his children wanted. Let's see: There were the schools, the teachers' unions, Planned Parenthood and various other population experts, the sexologists, the courts . . . and then there was always jail for the parents if they got too out of line. He could relax. He didn't want to be a distant "relative" anymore. He longed for fatherhood. And it would be his! His children would love him. He would indulge their every whim and never chastise them. Surely he knew the way to a child's heart.

Even before it was legal, there is evidence that abortions on minors were being performed anyway.

In 1973 Parents Who Care (PWC), a citizens' group protesting curriculum materials and methods employed by the Montgomery County Public Schools, wrote to County Executive James P. Gleason concerning a "purported procedure for secretive abortions for minors, involving public school personnel, Montgomery County public officials, the Planned Parenthood Association, and various abortion clinics."

In a letter from Malcolm Lawrence, director of public relations for PWC, Lawrence stated: "The Parents Who Care organization has just been informed by a ranking official of the Montgomery County Public Schools system that an average of 10 minor girls per week are given pregnancy tests in Montgomery County high schools by a representative of the County Health Department, who is called into the schools by either the school nurse or a counselor. Those girls determined by the test to be pregnant are then referred by the County Health Department employee to the Planned Parenthood Association, which in turn arranges for the girls to be sent to clinics in Baltimore and elsewhere for abortions.

"All of the steps in the procedure reportedly take place without notification whatsoever to the parents of the girls involved. We were told that in one recent case a girl receiving a saline injection aborted her baby prematurely and became infected; at that point—and only at that point—were her parents notified.

"Our interest in this procedure is obvious. We are parents and taxpayers. If minor children of this County are being channeled into abortions by public school and County Government employees without notification to the parents, the implications are appalling from both the moral and legal standpoints."

In 1974, Mrs. Randy Engel, executive director of the U.S. Coalition for Life, testified before the Committee on Interstate and Foreign Commerce Subcommittee on Public Health and Environment. Part of that testimony is given here:

"Teen Scene is operated by Planned Parenthood of Chicago. The program began in 1971 with an HEW-funded grant totalling $259,000.

"In the spring of 1972, an 18-year-old resident of Chicago made a prearranged call to Teen Scene to 'arrange for an abortion for his 15-year-old girlfriend.' He was told that he must make his own plane reservations on a flight which would be pinpointed by Teen Scene and he must bring in a signed notarized statement of responsibility by anyone twenty-one years or older. He was then told that Teen Scene would arrange for a limousine to meet the girl at the airport in New York, take her directly to the clinic where an abortion would be performed and she would then be transported to the airport to return to Chicago the same day." It was what Mrs. Engel called "Teen Scene's abortion package for minors."

Ellen McCormack, the unsuccessful antiabortion candidate for the Democratic Presidential nomination, said she was "horrified" by the Supreme Court's 1976 decision that a minor could get an abortion without parental consent.

She sounded the warning to parents by saying, "They would deny minors protection of the parents and say that the state has more power over the minors of this country [than their parents] and that's a frightening thing."

Of the four million in the U.S. who had abortions between 1973 and 1977, according to a report from the Alan Guttmacher Institute, 75 percent of those abortions were performed on unmarried women, and two-thirds of all the women were younger than 13.

No recent story has been as wrenching as that of Barbaralee Davis. Barbaralee, 18-years-old, had gone to the Hope Clinic for Women in Granite City, Ill., for a suction abortion at a clinic approved by the local board of health. Although she complained of weakness and pain following the abortion, Barbaralee was discharged and sent home. She required help getting into the car and lay on the back seat all the way home. She died less than twelve hours later.

An autopsy revealed a rip in her uterus and a severed artery. Two quarts of blood lay in her pelvis. Imbedded in the wall of her uterus was a face and part of a spine.

Dr. C. Everett Koop, internationally famous pediatric surgeon from Children's Hospital of Philadelphia, said during one of his prolife lectures: "We were told that thousands of women were dying each year at the hands of criminal abortionists. Some said ten thousand a year, some said five thousand. The facts from the United States Public Health Service showed that the deaths from all abortions, legal and illegal, never exceeded a hundred and ninety a year," he brought out in reference to those who said abortion laws needed liberalizing.

Today the estimated figures, with abortion legalized, reads that one out of every thousand women dies from legal abortions.

Is abortion profitable? No question about it. Back in 1974 a group of fifty women who staffed the Women's Medical Services, Inc., a Philadelphia abortion clinic, quit their jobs over what they called "medical profiteering." The disillusioned women were upset when they found out that three doctors, each of whom worked one day a week at the clinic, were splitting up approximately a quarter of a million dollars a year in profit, besides what they were making in their private practices.

In 1978, after a five-month investigation of abortion clinics, the *Chicago Sun-Times* found dozens of abortions performed on women who were not pregnant, an alarming number of cases of disorders caused by unsterile conditions and poor postabortion care. It was investigative reporting at its finest. The reporters also found incompetent doctors (some even unlicensed) who were paid by the abortion, and who worked so fast they even refused to wait for anesthetics to take effect. They also found that referral services were using hard-sell techniques to convince women by phone they need and should have abortions.

In January of 1977, at a meeting held at HEW—convened by the Health Subcommittee of the Secretary's Advisory Committee on the Rights and Responsibilities of Women, and represented by most of the Planned Parenthood and population groups—criticism of inadequate government funding and too much parental involvement was voiced.

"The state is the third party to the parent-child relationship," said Harriet Pilpel, legal counsel to Planned Parenthood. She urged that children be granted legal entitlement to contraception without parental consent through a "pediatric bill of rights."

A 15-year-old public school student by the name of Nancy also spoke at that meeting. She told of the Planned Parenthood-led program's attempt to inform small cells of youngsters on where to obtain services and to teach them techniques on contacting others.

"We can tell people everywhere, like my sixth grade sister's friends, that otherwise might not hear about it," she said with enthusiasm. "We have to let our friends know that abortion is okay, that it's not murder or anything." When she saw the uneasy looks on the faces of some panel members, Nancy added, "It's controversial."

But controversy has never stood in the way of giving our children what they now demand—and Nancy's fires of enthusiasm were fed anew when, the following year, HEW provided Planned Parenthood with $80,000 to keep Nancy and her friends happy. That money was just for one city. The total cost was never mentioned.

On March 19, 1978, Pennsylvania joined a nationwide movement to circumvent the U.S. Supreme Court's 1973 decision permitting abortions. Both legislatures of Pennsylvania and Kentucky have approved bills calling for a national constitutional convention to write an amendment to the U.S. Constitution that would ban most abortions. The movement began in April of 1975 when Missouri enacted the first resolution. Eleven states have now done the same.

Approval by thirty-four states is necessary before a convention can be convened. Any constitutional amendment approved by such a convention must then be ratified by at least thirty-eight states.

Just how much of an epidemic is teen-age abortion? At a fact-finding forum on teen-agers and sex that was held in New York, it was determined that more than half of all teen-age pregnancies in 1976 were terminated by abortion. The increasing number of teen-age abortions had surpassed that of adult abortions. The sharpest rise was among 13- and 14-year-olds.

In a subsequent study released two years later, sociologists from Johns Hopkins University showed that the first pregnancies terminated by abortion among black and white girls almost doubled from 1971 to 1976.

Uncle Sam is winning.

38.

Father Mike

I have heard from young and old alike that young girls contemplating or having had an abortion beat a path to the door of Father Michael T. Mannion, called Father Mike by the kids.

I have also heard that Father Mannion is usually dressed in lettered T-shirts and his approach to helping these kids is unorthodox.

The day I meet with him in his Camden, N.J., diocese offices, where he is with the Youth Ministry, he is wearing the Roman collar and a black suit. He is 33 years old, but looks 22.

Father Mannion talks in the language of the psychologist. He readily admits that to some factions of the Catholic church his approach to helping these kids in distress is sometimes thought of as one of the problems with the church. Traditionally, he says, people would expect a priest to tell the kids: This is right, and this is wrong—period. Father Mannion says he doesn't operate that way.

For instance, after a pregnant girl has "worked through" her feelings about abortion with Father Mannion, and then goes through with it anyway, he'll put his arms around her when he sees her again and will give her a big hug. If she wasn't hugged after each of the previous two abortions, he thinks maybe she won't have a fourth abortion if she knows somebody cares.

Father Mannion says his approach is to look for "processes of discussion where the kids are in a trusting, open, confidential setting; where they have the opportunities to totally disagree with the value I'm setting forth; but then, without rejecting them, the group process can then bring forth the Christian value, because of the sharing."

Father Mannion has also worked with and talked with a lot of parents. He says parents of today have "an insecurity syndrome," a desperation to be accepted and loved by their children. They say, "If I discipline my child and he rejects me, as a behavioral reaction to my discipline, I don't know if I can handle that rejection. Therefore, I need his acceptance. And I allow myself to be manipulated into—almost programmed into—disciplining him in the way I know he'll accept."

Father Mannion urges parents to feel free to reject an intolerable action of the child, but not to reject the child. Just because a child has perpetrated a major tragedy on the parents, he says it doesn't mean the final chapter's been written. He gives me an example: "If she gets pregnant, it'll really hurt. But I'm not going to reject her. I'm going to reject her action. I'm going to discipline her for it, but she's going to know that through it all I deeply love her."

I ask him if this is realistic in today's society where parents are beset with children who time and again fly in the face of any disciplinary measures, or any love that their parents have doled out?

"If the love is consistent and the parental security image and self-image is strong, and the kid still doesn't come around," he says, "they can't keep flogging themselves. They've done their best. This child has a free will and an open mind. This child has influences bombarding him seven days a week that are incredibly beyond the imagination of most parents to comprehend. Kids," he says, "will test their parents."

Father Mannion can see a kid being put out of his home, too. But the manner in which it is done, he feels, is important. Father Mannion said the action should be taken before the parents reach the boiling point. They should first enumerate for the child the reasons why he is being asked to leave. Parents should state that it is not being done out of hatred, but that the child is interfering with the unity of the family. Then, he said, the child should be given a date when the move must be completed. "We don't have to kill flies with sledgehammers," he said. "And then," he advised, "don't back off."

Father Mannion works primarily with girls 14, 15, 16 years of age. "Half the girls I work with aren't even Catholic," he said.

Parents are sometimes the reason kids abort, he says. "For example: A girl comes to me and says, 'I'm pregnant.' We work through a lot of feelings and she has the abortion sometimes. And I'll say, Honey, why? When we worked through so many feelings, *you* came to your conclusions—why did you have the abortion? 'My dad could have never handled it.' The dad," he said, "had conditioned her, since she was a child, to know: If you ever come home pregnant, I'll beat your head in. I'll run my car off a cliff. I could never handle it, and on, and on, and on. Perhaps with the best intentions in the world, the thing that programmed Suzie since she was 3 years of age," he says, "is to tell her what they could and could not handle."

I tell him his theory does not hold true with parents who have told their children from the start that whenever they are troubled or in trouble, they should feel free to come to them; who have told their children that while the Ten Commandments are a good set of rules to live by, they realize that everyone is human and does err.

He agrees that most parents will accept their daughter's pregnancy. He says he has been involved with pregnant girls breaking the news of their pregnancy to their parents countless times. "If the girl is going to go through with the baby and have the child, I always offer to go with them to tell the parents. I'd say 90 percent of the time the parent says, 'I kinda felt that was what it was.'

"Then, sometimes, there's still a little bit of an emotional outbreak. And there's still a lot of tears. There might even be a table pounding or a wall pounding. I encourage the kids to understand that the parents have to work that through."

Contrary to what is being programmed into today's kids, Father Mannion says, "In most of the cases, the parents stand right by the kids. And the parents are so grateful that the kids told them. It's a greater hurt when the kid doesn't tell."

Father Mannion recalled one family where the pregnant teen-ager waited seven months before telling her parents. Her reasoning was the longer she waited, the less time her parents would hurt. "They accepted it beautifully," he said of these parents. "She had the baby. She kept it. And the daughter's whole reason for not telling them was not fear—it was, 'I love 'em so much, I'm not gonna tell 'em until I have to.'"

On a much smaller scale, though a presence, are the parents who will threaten to throw the girl out if she doesn't get an abortion. They will manipulate their daughter into abortion, he said, by say-ing to her: "Well, you know, graduation's coming up and you wanted that car . . ." or "You want that dress . . ." These are the parents, he said, who, after the abortion is a fait accompli, will take their daughter to dinner or buy her a prom gown. "These parents are really disappointing," he said.

Of the girls who have had abortions that seek him out, he said he knows they are coming to him because they are sure he will not hand them prepackaged condemnation. But, he says, he is not doing them a favor saying the abortion really doesn't matter. "It does matter. A life was lost there. We have to face it and then heal it from there," he said.

The girls who have aborted, he said, tell him of waking up at night and wondering: "If I had the baby, would it be crying now? Would I be nursing the baby? Would I be buying clothes for it?" He tells me many young girls will become pregnant again in an attempt to make up for the abortion.

Often, he says, a girl riddled with guilt and regret will "crash" after the abortion. There are those, he said, who will blame society for programming those emotions into the teen-ager. He will argue that point. "It's a guilt because as long as she totally doubts that that was a human life, she can vindicate herself. Once a doubt slips into her mind that that was human life, her whole neatly tied package of conscience just gets exploded apart."

Many girls need psychiatric help after an abortion, he says, but few get it. Naming a local mental institution, Father Mannion says an entire section of it is devoted to young girls who have had abortions.

"Abortion isn't the problem," he said. "The problem is we don't value things unless our standards suggest they can be pragmatically used by us here and now.

"I think somewhere in our educational system we gear kids to believe to be different is disastrous. We've confused unity with uniformity."

It is good insight, he said, to say that government today does everything for the child.

Concerning the inking out of the parents' involvement in a minor's decision on abortion, Father Mannion says, "I would rather see that invoked as an exception rather than the way it is now. I would like to see the law on the side of the parents. They have a right to know."

Father Mannion deals with these young girls after the fact in many cases. I cannot help but think that if somewhere along the line somebody did tell these kids right from wrong, the path to his door might not be so worn.

39.

Parental Basic Training

Not only are parents teaching their children at home, forming parent unions, and protesting this all-out war on other fronts, but local groups of parents dissatisfied with their children and the educational environment that envelops them are finally getting street-wise. Like many minority and special interest groups, they are organizing.

As blacks have obtained their rights, as women have obtained their rights, now parents are demanding the same. They have finally picked up their wounded bodies from the battlefield and are using the words that spell success to any cause: assertiveness, aggressiveness, preparation, organization, infiltration.

A two hundred-member Parents' Union in one New Jersey county joined fifty other parent groups throughout the state to press for a lobbying voice in the state capital. "Our goal as a state organization is to have our own door in Trenton," said Karen Raulston, a spokesman for the county group. "That door will be marked NJACE (New Jersey Association of Citizens for Education), and it will cater to parents—the only group, organizers feel, that doesn't have a say in the education of children."

"Parents," continued Karen Raulston, "have traditionally been left out of the decision-making process, but it is the parents who foot the bills. The time has come to change that."

In 1978 a nonprofit organization calling itself Coalition for Educational Reform was started. Among their goals were quality education, decent textbooks and religious freedom. They plan to strive for state-by-state textbook evaluation and laws to enforce the action. They believe that education is the function of the family and not of the state.

The organization's aim is to establish parental rights as primary to the welfare of the child. Another goal is to remove all courses from public schools that in any way involve the religious beliefs, practices, moral training, sex training or cultural and spiritual heritage of the family. Also listed in their aims is a lobbying arm for credit-card education, where each school-age child's parents can select the school of their choice.

In the beginning, those who have now become part of a national organization were, for the most part, dedicated but ineffective when they stood alone or in small groups. Now that they have coalesced, they are a force to be reckoned with.

I flew to Massachusetts for the sole purpose of interviewing two mothers who had worked singly, then jointly, and then in concert with a national organization.

Their names are Janice (Jan) Niedzialkowski and Mary Mc-Carthy, both of Worcester, Mass. Jan is a product of the public schools. She and her husband, Fred, are the parents of four children, who range in age from 14 to 25, and the "parents" of a young Mongoloid child who lives with them and is under their care.

Mary attended parochial school until high school, when she transferred to the public schools. During the first eight-year marriage span to her husband, Mack, she lost three pregnancies. Mary and her husband eventually adopted two girls, now 16 and 11 years old.

Both Jan's and Mary's children have alternately attended both public and Catholic schools.

Neither woman ever expected in her lifetime to be doing battle with the educational system. "I did not feel personally that God put me on this earth to be a career woman," said the red-haired Mary. "I felt that I had another obligation, and that was to be a mother. I believe with all my heart and soul that it is one of the hardest jobs a woman has today—to try to raise a child to the honor and glory of Almighty God, because I believe that there are numerous forces outside the home that would lead a child to a way of life that might, on the surface, seem rewarding to a child, but ultimately would not prove to be beneficial or fulfilling to the child. The thing lacking most in children today is instilling in them their own self-worth and their own value in the eyes of their creator," she said.

Prior to their meeting, Mary and Jan had each been working separately and with others in the area of sex education in the schools. Mary had already aided in establishing a local organization to fight this intrusion. She first got her feet wet when she read a notice in the personals column in her local paper that said: "Parents. If you are interested in the books your children are learning from, come to a meeting . . ." Mary and her husband went. "We went primarily because we had children in the school system and, naturally, were interested."

When they got to the meeting on Plantation Street, approximately a hundred and fifty other people were there. The meeting centered on a book being used at Quinsigamond Community College in Worcester. It was, said Mary, "riddled with vulgar expressions and the underlying theme of this particular book was disrespect for this country, disrespect for the flag and more or less do your own thing and hold nobody accountable for anything other than yourself.

"Now I would say that I was just about as naive and just about as green as could be," she said. "This really shocked me to think that this was what children were learning from."

The upshoot was that another meeting would be held. Mary went. And here she and Anthony Hmura, the father who had placed the original ad in the paper, were to meet. It was his son who had brought the book home and shown it to his father. At the following meeting, attendance dropped. "By now we're beginning to weed out those who are deciding they're not going to get mixed up in any controversy," Mary said.

Mary took the book to David Lionett, a candidate for whom she was campaigning for the state legislature. "And here again, being naive, I figured, well, he's going to investigate this problem. Well, David did do some investigating to some extent. But the book was never removed or anything like that. And from here began the take-off of my education as to what was going on not only in the colleges, but I assumed and very quickly found out that this type of literature was used in our high schools and right on down the line." From what Mary calls "the filthy literature," she soon became self-educated in other programs being used in the schools, such as secular humanism and values clarification.

At the next meeting the small group decided on a name. They would call themselves Citizens Upholding Responsible Education. Mary would chair it.

The person most responsible for informing her of what was going on in the public schools, she said, was Dr. Carmen Reade, a high school science teacher from Norton, Mass., who traveled back and forth from his home to the meetings—a three-hour drive.

One weekend Mary and her husband, Mr. Reade and his wife, and a Mr. and Mrs. Ernest St. George (Mrs. St. George is treasurer of the organization to this day) went to Cape Cod to talk over the situation of the schools and to plot their strategy. "Carmen," said Mary, "suggested that we go before the Worcester School Committee and make Worcester the base. If we could break the back of these programs there, it would automatically spread out to other areas of the state."

Naively expecting cooperation, Mary wrote a letter to the Worcester School Committee asking for the release of reading lists and sex-education films. She got no response.

From there Mary went to a member of the Worcester City Council. He suggested she go unannounced, so no time would be permitted for an "alibi" to come down from the offices of the school superintendent. Mary, accompanied by several other parents, took his advice and went to the top—the superintendent's offices.

The superintendent took their names and addresses, said Mary, and "he let us know that he was a very busy man and that he didn't like our coming unannounced, and he didn't like our asking for reading lists, and he didn't like our asking for other materials. What we were asking for was impossible for them to gather together. The books we were objecting to were coming off of qualified reading lists; they had been approved by prominent individuals.

"At this point I informed our superintendent of schools, very respectfully, that I well realized that he was a very busy individual. Since we were paying him $35,000 a year, I thought that he could very well account to us a little bit. It was his custom that if a student objected to a program, the student could leave his classroom, march right down to the administration building and immediately be seen and pacified. Now," she said, barely pausing for a breath in her retelling of her initiation, "I informed him that we were busy mothers. We had waited one hour and a half, patiently, and we were going to have our say. And we stood our ground. I also informed him that he was not impressing me at all with his reading off of so-called approved reading lists. We were only interested in the God-given degree of human decency, and we credited ourselves with having the inborn intelligence to recognize whether or not something was indeed good or bad literature, filthy or appropriate reading. So we parted on a very sour note. He let us know he would not cooperate with us in any way. I informed him that that was to be my last visit to Twenty Irving Street—that he and I would meet very often in public and that he should come prepared for it."

No better up-front representative could be desired by any organization seeking a voice than that of Mary McCarthy, who must have kissed the Blarney Stone. I would bet my money that Mary could out-filibuster Senator Filibuster. She never minces words, never leaves an opponent wondering what she is all about. When Mary McCarthy speaks, you know where she stands.

The parent group's next step was to petition the Worcester School Committee. There, too, it was made clear that cooperation with the parents was not on their minds, said Mary. About three-quarters of the Committee, she said, went into a long line of rhetoric and defense about the materials in the school, using what she called the "same old verbosity" about pornography being in the eyes of the beholder, and parents were not qualified to make decisions in these matters.

"So with that, all during this time now, my education is unfolding before my eyes," Mary said. Her naiveté by now had not only faded, but it is unlikely she will ever again suffer from this deficiency.

At this juncture Jan and Mary met. With Jan, Mary found her persuasiveness was not a necessity. She did not have to convince Jan of fighting the good fight for the children. "Janice was already abreast of the situation and knew immediately what I was talking about and vice versa. And it still remains that way today," said Mary.

Mary has gone on to write newspaper columns and to make well over a hundred appearances on the condition of today's schools in the area of what she calls "gimmick education." Meanwhile, Jan does all of the leg work for her. "I would specifically wish to emphasize the fact that without an individual like Janice, it would be impossible for me to do what I do. Ninety percent of the credit most assuredly should go to Janice," she said in the charming Massachusetts dialect so often associated with President Kennedy, "for putting together research for me, for always being there to back me up. I can always count on Janice at the drop of a hat."

As Jan and Mary continued their fight on a local level, they began to get spotty newspaper coverage. Parents fighting the same battles began corresponding with their organization. In the mail one day came a letter to Mary from Mrs. Joanne McAuley, president of the National Congress for Educational Excellence based in Dallas, Texas. Mary wrote back. Mary's state organization had grown to some 5,000 parents. They decided to merge their state group with NCEE. "And let me tell you, it was the best thing we ever did," said Mary. NCEE became a national organization in 1975 with representation in thirty-five states.

When word leaked out of the groups' merger, Mary said Worcester's school superintendent, Dr. John Connor, labeled them the Pure Cure Group. "You realize when an individual cannot break your argument, he naturally resorts to personal ridicule," Mary said. "The favorite expression of our superintendent of schools was to refer to us as The Pure Cure Group UNTIL," she said emphatically, "one night on the radio I asked him if he were opposed to purity in young children. After that I never heard him make that reference again. For once, he became tongue-tied. There was no answer."

In 1978 the NCEE was invited to the National Schoolboard Convention to display the materials they were concerned with. It resulted in the NCEE's publication, *The School Bell*, almost tripling in subscriptions, as school board members signed up to receive it.

"They are beginning to realize," Mary said of the National Schoolboard Association, "that parents are coming alive, and parents are no longer going to be put off. They have got to begin to recognize parents and deal with parents." Mary said that among NCEE's membership are some teachers.

Joining a formidable national group of parents made the local parent organization's credibility skyrocket. "Now that we are the NCEE, nothing transpires that I do not receive a telephone call to have our opinion on," said Mary, who is now on the national board of directors of the NCEE and chairman of the Massachusetts branch.

Today Mary receives calls and mail from parents all over the country. They complain about teacher behavior, films being shown and programs that their children are being forced to participate in, which they feel have no bearing on the world of academia. And Mary advises them.

"The first thing I always tell parents is: Get your facts. Read up and study up on the issue as much as you can. The second thing I always tell them is to organize, but don't worry about numbers. Don't worry about going to a meeting and having five thousand people there, because you're never going to do it—so don't even think about it," she said of a group's beginnings. "In other words, Almighty God and one is the same as an army."

The problems facing newcomers to the fight are twofold said Mary: "First of all the majority of parents still don't have any idea as to the content of programs. Secondly, I tell them do not be put off. I would say that the best weapon that a parent has is exposure," said Mary. "They, the implementers of the programs which we are discussing, cannot stand exposure."

Exposing is the area in which Mary is exemplary. She never flinches nor wavers in her belief or her rights as a parent.

Of the national organizations of parents that are forming Mary said, "I think the most important thing is that they are drawing parents in from all walks of life, and they are making them more aware. They in turn are talking to others. It's just mushrooming."

"We're all there on common ground," said Jan, who has for the most part been listening. "We're all working for the same purpose—for the same good of the children."

The key to it all, said Mary, is to elect to local school boards and to state boards of education men and women who do know what is right for children. "The majority of people that are elected to office are backed by people that have money," said Jan, "and that can be a problem."

Eventually NCEE sees itself as a bloc vote that will be of sufficient importance to have legislators and decision-makers sit up and pay attention to the parents.

Once a year the NCEE holds a convention. Each state representative talks about what has transpired over the last year in his state, the progress made, how to progress step-by-step toward their goals. For the next day and a half workshops are held to aid parents in this fight.

Guest speakers come from all over the country to speak to the parents, as did Congressman Robert Dornan from California, himself a former national head of Citizens for Decency Through Law, the nation's oldest organization to fight pornography. It was Dornan who, as a freshman congressman, went to West Virginia to see for himself what the battle over the books was all about. Dornan has suggested, said Mary, slapping a lawsuit onto school teachers and administrators for invasion of privacy.

Another part of the NCEE convention is known as the "X-rated Film Festival." Here parents can view the vulgarity of what the school children of America are exposed to in the public schools. It alerts them and familiarizes them with new films that can be coming into the schools.

Many of the films and the questionnaires doled out to children in the public schools, said Jan and Mary, make assumptions about children. "In other words," they said, "the underlying theme is always the assumption that the child is engaging in sexual or drug activities.

"In a nutshell," said Mary, "the purpose of the NCEE is to protect local autonomy of schools, to defend and support parental and family rights and to promote the teaching of basic, academic skills."

NCEE members are also gaining school-board seats on the local levels, said Jan, which they feel is significant.

In the future will come lobbyists from the NCEE, lawsuits, the doing away with tenure for teachers, teacher accountability and the eradication of "gimmick education."

Jan said she sees clearly what has happened to our children. "The drug culture, the free love, the contraceptive that is served up with the breakfast cereal in colleges—the ability to have an abortion if you 'made a mistake'—children never having to think about 'the mistake' before it happens, because it can all be taken care of. No problem. Never have I heard anyone that is running one of these abortion mills ever refer to the scars that are left on so many of these young women who have had abortions. I believe there are many suicides because of the young women not being able to cope with what they have done. Instead, they're always promoting, 'We'll take care of any situation that comes along!'"

Touching on the movies, Mary said her entire family went to see *Grease*, which was given a PG rating. "I was very happy that our 16-year-old daughter didn't like the movie at all. Both my husband and I thought it was simply vulgar beyond words. There was a double meaning to just about every expression or term used throughout the movie. It was just uncouth in and of itself, I felt."

Returning once again to the issue of public schools, Mary said, "The good teachers are retiring early left and right because they are unable to bring themselves to buckle into the new school system's methods and materials for teaching. I had a principal tell me that he was opposed to introducing certain programs into the school, but he was told by the superintendent of schools, 'Look, the program is in. You use it and you shut your mouth,'" said Mary.

Discussing what is happening at state colleges, Mary told of a retired fireman who came to her because his young daughter, a student at Worcester State Teachers College, came home upset. "The current gimmick there is to blindfold all the students and they go around fondling each other." When the girl told her father about it, he went to the head of the college, who called in the professor responsible for the program and his assistant. "The father was told that he should mind his own business and let his daughter handle this course," said Mary.

"And he informed these two individuals that since he was paying for the course and thought it was morally degrading, they had best watch their step and curb their activities or he'd have their jobs." The father called Mary to ask if the NCEE would back him in any action he took. "I assured him we would," she said.

The public schools are in need of a complete overhauling, in Mary's estimation. "I think they are definitely lacking in competition. The public schools today have an almost complete monopoly, and this is very bad. But there are more and more private schools, at much financial sacrifice, coming into being. I think the more that do," she continued, "will be good for the public schools.

"I believe this country was founded on strong parents and this is what we need to get back to. I believe the children today are not lacking information, but the main thing they are lacking is formation of character. I think children must be introduced to a vocabulary of words such as purity, chastity, abstinence, decency—which is totally unheard of today. And I think we need to instill in these children that nothing in this life comes easy," said Mary.

I asked these two mothers if they ever thought, when their children were infants, that those same babies would grow up to be involved in one of education's and society's greatest battles. "Never!" said Jan without hesitation.

"And I never thought, in my wildest dreams that I would be engaged in the battle that I'm engaged in today," said Mary. "I think it's a very difficult time for parents—here again, because of the many outside influences.

"I guess through the ages parents have thought that theirs was the worst generation to raise children," said Jan, "but I do believe we have reached the ultimate."

40.

The ACLU "Talks" Conservative

Much blame has been placed at the feet of the American Civil Liberties Union (ACLU) in so many areas, not the least of which has concerned parents'-versus-child's rights. Controversial radio talk-show host Bob Grant has even gone so far as to call them the "American Criminal Liberties Union" on the air.

I thought it might be interesting to take the conservative point of view to the ACLU for discussion. I called the offices of the Philadelphia Branch of the ACLU, telling the person who answered the phone that I would like to come in and discuss certain areas from the conservative point of view.

After waiting on the line for a brief time, I was told that Spencer Coxe, president and executive director of this branch, had been told what I had in mind and she would now connect me to his phone.

After identifying myself to Coxe, for expediency's sake I asked: "Did your girl tell you my reasons for requesting an interview with you?" Coxe immediately crosses swords with me over semantics. "She's *not a girl!*" he said in a reprimanding tone. I had not used the word "girl" in a pejorative way (in fact, the voice had sounded like that of a young girl to me); nonetheless Coxe was touchy on the matter. It would not be the last issue we would come to blows over, though it was certainly the most minor, in my opinion.

Coxe agreed to the interview as set forth. Several days later I was taking the rickety elevator inside 260 S. Fifteenth Street to the offices of Coxe and the ACLU.

I found his office drab, with dust everywhere—from the dented old file cabinets and the manual typewriter, to the air conditioner, which was noisy and not operating well.

Coxe is a tall and lanky figure of a man, dressed in the fashion of the mid-'50s. His charcoal-gray summer suit sported thin lapels. On his plain white dress shirt hung a limp, thin necktie. It was apparent that Spencer Coxe was about more pressing business than keeping up with fashions.

I found Coxe to be a pleasant sort of man and an avid and ambitious talker. So much of the rhetoric that falls from the lips of the liberal implies that the stand he has taken is painful, and he prefaces statements with: "I don't like this myself, but . . ." Coxe was no exception. How one can devote a lifetime of work to actions one personally finds reprehensible—by choice—is more than I can fathom.

"We make no distinction as to whose First Amendment rights are involved," said Coxe of the ACLU. "Obviously it is the unpopular person who has his free speech rights infringed on rather than the popular person. So we're almost always in the posture of helping somebody unpopular because they're the ones that need help."

The ACLU, he said, is currently active in equal rights, women's rights and the rights of homosexuals.

Coxe had spent twenty-six years with the ACLU. He retired several months after this interview to teach at Antioch.

Where, I asked, does the collateral come from when the ACLU is defending a minor? "When we go to court," said Coxe, "our lawyers do not charge fees. The ACLU pays the out-of-pocket expenses where the client cannot do it."

We gently cross swords again (and I immediately see his keen ability for not giving a question more value than it deserves) when I ask Coxe if he thinks the conservatives are making a valid observation when they insist that the ACLU always jumps on the liberal bandwagon and does nothing for the conservative element. He replies by saying blandly that it is a valid observation that some people will make such statements. "I frankly don't know what the word liberal means," Coxe says. "I really don't know what the word means." That will be Coxe's only stab at living up to his media image of being witty. I will find him a skilled swordsman when it comes to verbal fencing. Skilled, confusing and contradictory. He appears to talk conservative and then liberal on the same subject.

Coxe also makes it clear in many areas that the ACLU is primarily concerned over the rights of the children—and not necessarily in conjunction with the parent.

Coxe mentions a column written by James Kilpatrick, a well-known conservative, supporting the Hatch Amendment and aimed at preventing schools from asking students personal and psychological questions. "I couldn't have agreed more with what he said," said Coxe. It was his branch of the ACLU, he says, that got the only court opinion that was ever handed down on this very issue.

The case involved an attempt to psychologically test eighth graders in order to predetermine drug users in three school districts. The complaint came to the Philadelphia office via a parent whose child was scheduled for this testing, and who had been denied access to the test prior to its implementation. The psychologist who was involved in the testing had claimed that if the test was made public, it would invalidate the findings.

The ACLU, said Coxe, obtained a copy of the test and found it to be riddled with such personal questions as "Did your parents cuddle you when you were little?" The psychologist who had been contracted by the schools to do the testing was confronted by the ACLU and the conclusions of experts who said its implementation would have "devastating" results. One school district then terminated the psychologist's contract, another waited for the legal outcome before making a decision, and the third school said it was going ahead with the testing.

Once in court, it became "a battle of experts. It was none of the school's business," said Coxe. Schools, he continued, are not experts in the area of drug problems. "They're not therapeutic experts and it's none of their business."

The judge rendered a decision that the test was a violation of the students' rights, said Coxe, "because it constituted an invasion of privacy which could not be justified by any important governmental purpose."

Coxe is not a man known for his brevity. "I love to talk," he admitted. In his retelling of this particular case, as with a long-winded professor, the student mind may wander. It was not until I transcribed the taped interview that I realized the involvement of the government implied in the judge's decision. How accurate, I wondered, was Coxe's memory?

I followed up by obtaining a written copy of the judge's decision. Coxe's memory was like a steel trap. The judge's opinion reads: "The Court, in balancing the right of an individual to privacy and the right of the Government to invade that privacy for the sake of public interest, strikes the balance in favor of the individual in the circumstances shown in this case."

It is significant. One can rightly assume, then, that the government has the right to invade one's privacy "for the sake of public interest," or, as Coxe has put it, to justify "any important governmental purpose."

During the interview I ask Coxe why the ACLU has not gotten

into the sex-education fray, since that and other elements of the public schools also pry into the personal lives of students and parents. If this is true, he says, it is highly objectionable. But, he continued, "As far as I know the ACLU does not object to informing children about sexual matters. Our concern is with the rights of children—not to have their privacy invaded by questions and by probing into matters through questions which are not the school's authority."

When I insist this is being done in the public schools via sex education and other programs, I am hard-pressed to accept Coxe's answer: "I have been here for twenty-six years and no parent has ever called me up and protested about a sex-education program in the school."

Coxe again "talks" conservative when he says, "I, for one, would take very seriously the conscientious objection of a parent to a course of instruction which offended that parent's moral values." I soon realize it is again his personal opinion as he continued, "Well, that's a very difficult issue as far as I'm concerned, and there's a lot of disagreement within the ACLU about teaching moral values in the schools."

Aligning the ACLU with the child, he says, "And you know there is also the possibility of a conflict between a child's desire to know something and a parent's desire not to have the child know something. Now, in that kind of conflict, I think the general tendency of the ACLU would be to favor the child's interests rather than the parent's interests.

"I personally am against compulsory education," he says, digging out a paper he has written on the subject and giving it to me. "I am not speaking for the ACLU, but I think it is a violation of freedom to force children to go to school at all. I have not convinced the ACLU that they should take that position, but I think that is relevant to the question you're asking, because if children did not have to go to school, then if they don't like what's taught, they can walk out!"

Earlier, having played games with me over the definition of the word "liberal," he speaks now bitterly about the conservative. "You see, I think conservatives are grossly hypocritical. They don't mind at all to make children give a pledge of allegiance to the flag, which the children may object to; they don't mind at all about propagandizing the children about the virtues of capitalism. The Right Wing wants to use the schools for its propaganda and they're against having the schools used for somebody else's propaganda." Coxe rants on about military recruiters coming into the schools and businessmen espousing the capitalist system.

"But suppose a school district made an agreement with the

Communist Party to talk about the glories of Soviet Russia? Why, all hell would break loose!" He goes on to lament the fact that a school in Lancaster County, Pa., still has prayers. The ACLU's hands are tied, he tells me, unless somebody is aggrieved and comes to them.

I tell him that is not always the ACLU's style—that they often will openly solicit, even in the press, a test case they would like to litigate.

Unabashed he says it is not their style in Philadelphia. The ACLU there is overburdened with work.

On the issue of obscene materials being shown and used in the schools, he says obscenity is a matter of judgment. "Our job is not to protect people from obscenity."

When I tell him parents have been denied curriculum materials, he says, "I think it is everybody's right to see the materials the public schools are using."

Religion, I say, is being undercut in the public schools today. Coxe claims the ACLU would immediately leap into action if my charges are true. "It would be highly objectionable for the school to be antireligious. I mean, we would object instantly if a teacher said—taught a class—don't waste your time going to church. Don't pay any attention to what your parents tell you. That would be a violation of the First Amendment and we would instantly act," he assures me.

I mention the undermining of the religious beliefs of students whose religion opposes abortion and tell him that abortion is taught in the public schools as an alternative to pregnancy.

"Well, it is!" he replies, as if he is talking to the village idiot. While I concede the reality of abortion as an alternative to pregnancy, I again point out the conflict with a child's religious upbringing. "I think the schools have to be very careful not to go the next step and say: So therefore, if you're pregnant, get an abortion. I agree with you there." However, he feels it is justifiable to teach it as an alternative to pregnancy without proselytizing.

I ask him if the ACLU has had any effect on Supreme Court decisions. "Oh, yeah!" he says with pride in his voice.

"The prayer case was a Pennsylvania case. That was where the U.S. Supreme Court held that religious observances could not be held in public schools. That case began in this office. And from that complaint that came in by telephone one day, the U.S. Supreme Court held that public schools may not conduct religious observances."

"I would like to see education fairly much restricted," said Coxe, sounding momentarily like a conservative, and then adding: "I think.

"I object very much to schools becoming social service agencies. I

can tell you and the readers of your book that we would welcome—
we would deal with and welcome—the opportunity to deal with a
complaint that any school in Pennsylvania is promoting abortion,
because I think this is a misuse of the school." Before you jump up to
reach for the phone to call the ACLU, I had better make it clear to
you that Coxe does not consider teaching abortion the same thing as
promoting. He was very clear on that issue.

While moments before Coxe said he thought schools should be
restricted in what they teach, he vacillates once again when he
says, "I think that everything should be discussed in public schools,
as long as they're not taking on a role beyond education."

I drop the subject, convinced he has gone from left to right and
crisscrossed too much already. Of one thing only am I sure. And that
is that the ACLU has at least been thinking about and watching
closely what is going on in the nation's public schools.

Would he agree that the power traditionally vested in parents to
guide their children in moral, sexual and social matters has eroded
over the last ten or fifteen years? "Yeah. I think it has," he says. Why,
I ask him, does he think this has happened? "Because children have
revolted against their parents," he says. They have always revolted,
I say. "No," says Coxe. "In sexual matters they have revolted more in
the last fifteen years than they ever have before."

Would he say the Supreme Court has played a major role in this?
"No," he says. I point out that in the mid '60s the Supreme Court
ruled that a person's constitutional rights begin at birth, not at the
age of majority; that in 1976 the Court again ruled that a minor
child could have an abortion without parental intervention that in
many states it has become legal for minor children to obtain
contraceptives and obtain treatment for social diseases—all of
which has cut the parent out of the picture. I also point out all the
various government agencies and government supported agencies
that step between parent and child.

He does not deny the rulings that have been handed down, but he
protests. "No. I don't think that's what's happened, really. In the
first place, I think that the Supreme Court is recognizing that there
has been a young people's revolution in this country and a sexual
revolution in this country. I think what the Supreme Court is saying
is, largely, the government is no longer automatically on the side of
the parents.

"A great many of the court's opinions," continued Coxe, "that
you're referring to, have simply prohibited government agencies
from, if you will, siding with the parents against the children, and
they've made the government neutral."

I say this so-called "neutral" ground has become a battleground. How can he say the government is neutral when it makes laws, and then to make sure they are carried out, gives agencies such as Planned Parenthood financial support to carry them out, and government schools are telling the children about these services? When the government supplies funds for contraceptives, VD clinics, abortions, and the supporting of the baby born to a minor child—how then is government neutral?

Coxe insists these laws have simply struck down the state laws and the power of the state to act in these areas.

"It also struck down the parents' involvement," I counter.

"Well, wait a minute," says Coxe. "Let's examine it. What it is doing—and this is very fundamental—what it is doing is preventing the parent from using the power of the state to enforce the parents' will upon the child. And I think this is a proper trend.

"You're perfectly right," he continues, "what the courts have done is to take children out of special categories and treated children more like adults. But it's simply by restricting the power of state government," he insists.

Will he not at least agree with me that it has, whether by design or not, thwarted the parents in areas where parents had traditionally intervened?

"That's . . . Yes. I would agree that the Supreme Court decisions and the court decisions in the field of abortion particularly have increased the capacity of a child to engage in sexual activity without interference of the parents. Yeah. But I don't want to let go quite yet, because I want to make this point. I wanna go back to what I said at the beginning of this section of our discussion, and that is, the Supreme Court is following and not leading." The Supreme Court, he insisted, didn't invent the sexual revolution.

I ask him who he thinks did. "People did!" he answers with obvious annoyance. I tell him the public schools did. "Well, the schools sure didn't begin the antiwar movement," he says, shifting the issue. And then: "Look, I am opposed to Planned Parenthood coming in and propagandizing in the schools," he says.

He bounces back and forth over Planned Parenthood coming into schools and pushing contraceptives and abortion. Perhaps they shouldn't be permitted in, he says, and then: If they are, then so should the Right-to-Life people. "I would not want anybody to come in, because I wouldn't want to make the school the battleground for an issue which has so many moral overtones," he says.

He bounces around again, saying that if a student should bring up these subjects, the teacher should have the right to answer the student. He winds up saying he thinks it's OK to discuss the pros and cons. He is spinning in a whirlwind at this point, jumping from one position to another.

I finally say never mind about his opinion—how would the ACLU stand on the matter? "I don't know. We've never discussed it here. And nobody's ever raised this question."

His final stand is that if the parents don't like it, they should send their children to a religious school. Suppose parents cannot afford such a luxury? "Yeah, well, that's a problem," he admits.

I say his position is inconsistent with the rights of parents as put forth in the ACLU's own handbook, which states parents have the right to determine their minor child's religious training and education and the right to determine his overall style of life. The various rulings handed down have negated these rights.

"Well," he ponders, "that's a hard question."

Coxe asks me if a child should be denied exposure to education because it conflicts with a parent's religious belief, and then he rails against the famous landmark Amish Case, where the Supreme Court in 1972 ruled that the Amish children did not have to attend school beyond a certain age because it was against their parents' religious beliefs. I remind him that he has told me earlier he is against compulsory education—period. "Yeah, but I object to compulsory education because of what it does to the child—not because of what it does to the parents. I don't regard children as the chattels of their parents," he says.

He finds it very hard, he says, "to buy the proposition that parents of a 6-year-old or an 8-year-old should have the power to insulate the child from any influences except the parents' influences."

Coxe says he thinks public schools are oppressive, too compulsory, and he does not like the values they are teaching. "But I also don't like the values that a lot of parents teach. And I object—I am very troubled by the idea of—I am troubled by the idea that parents should be able to tell a school anything about this because they disapprove of it. How about that child's interest in that subject? Maybe the child *wants* to know something about contraception. How about the child's rights?

"I think you're raising some very difficult questions," he says. "But I don't think the answer is to give parents a veto power over whatever they may object to that's being taught in public schools."

Coxe claims I want government in the public's lives. I say I want it out of our lives. I begin to realize that we are both accusing the other of the same thing: government intervention. We are looking at it in two different ways.

This, I decide, is probably one of the major differences between the conservative and the liberal. Coxe sees government as being out of the picture by eliminating certain laws. I see the liberal as wanting the government in when it suits his purposes. The liberal will think nothing of taking money from the government to support his positions—such as abortion and the teachings of the public schools. The liberal refuses to see the tie-in. By limiting the power of the states to make laws, I see federal intervention where Coxe sees neutrality.

In the end it is a frivolous argument. If we have no government intervention, why have government at all? The real bane of the concerned parent is that it now knows government is compiling programs, strategies and laws that are ruining the lives of its youth and ultimately the family. It is no longer a positive, but a negative government.

What Coxe has told me, he assures me at the conclusion of our long discussion, would be a "good idea of what you'd hear from any ACLU place."

Browsing through *The Rights of Young People*, which is subtitled, *The Basic ACLU Guide to a Young Person's Rights*, I found it extremely interesting to read the following statements, taken from the preamble of the United Nations Declaration of the Rights of the Child:

Abortion sprang to mind on the following:

Principle 4.: The child shall enjoy the benefits of social security. He shall be entitled to grow and develop in health; to this end, special care and protection shall be provided both to him and his mother, including adequate pre-natal and post-natal care.

Principle 6.: The child, for the full and harmonious development of his personality, needs love and understanding. He shall, wherever possible, grow up in the care and under the responsibility of his parents, and in any case, in an atmosphere of affection and of moral and material security; a child of tender years shall not, save in exceptional circumstances, be separated from his mother . . .

Principle 7.: The best interests of the child shall be the guiding principle of those responsible for his education and guidance; that responsibility lies in the first place with his parents."

And Cox called the conservative a hypocrite.

I am angry that I did not read this before I interviewed Coxe. I wonder if Coxe has read it. I wonder what such incongruous statements like these are doing in an ACLU handbook.

41.

William Bentley Ball in Balance

Because the Amish Case had seemed like such a thorn in the side of Spencer Coxe of the ACLU, I decided to take some of the same questions asked Coxe, and some of his replies, to William Bentley Ball, the famous constitutional attorney who had successfully represented the Amish parents.

Ball has a reputation that stands without equal in constitutionality that affects parents and the guiding of their children's education. He has worked closely and successfully to keep government from rough-riding over private, religious schools.

Referring to Coxe's assessment that the courts did not set the trends for the young but followed a trend already set by the young, Ball said, "Youth today is not doing its own thing; it's doing what clever adults, ideological elitists as well as people in commerce want them to do. These are the true and dominant source of the real child abuse in our country today. The courts would be wrong if they capitulated to the desires of youth, but they're far more greatly wrong in following the trends on youths from essentially antichild sources."

How does one square the conflicts of the minor child's rights as they are emerging today with the legal rights of parenting? Attorney Ball says much of this is taking shape today, because there are two categories of "bad parents."

In the first category, he said, are the cases on record of children who have been harmed personally, physically, mentally and morally by a parent. "Society, the public, should not be thought of as the first in line to help, but the last, the ultimate, an extreme recourse, because the state is inherently unfit to act as a parent. The state's failures, and indeed abuses of children when it tries to do so, are often extremely evident," he said. Before a child is turned over to the state, Ball feels relatives, the church or its agencies, or other private sources should first be exhausted.

Coming down hard on the other type of "bad parents," Ball gives this description of them: "The growth of selfishness in our society in a pervasive materialism, the abandoning of religion and the decline of self-reliance on the part of individuals—these things have set the stage for '1984,'" he says, making reference to George Orwell's fictional novel, in which well over a hundred of the ominous predictions made by Orwell in a mythical country that sounds much like America have come to pass. "The state in which human liberty will be extinguished, as parents forsake the work of faithfulness, the drudgery, the sacrifice, the giving of love which are needed for the rearing of children. They are also," he said of this new breed of narcissistic parent, "forsaking the child and, in many cases, asking that state laws and state power take over. I'm not speaking here merely of custody—state custody of a child—but I'm speaking of the forming of our laws in such a way that the child is no longer responsible to the parents."

Referring again to the minor consent laws that have been enacted, rendering the parents inactive in many areas of their children's lives, Ball differs from those who claim society is putting an old head on young shoulders. "What they're doing is keeping children as children in the sense of making them far less independent, far more dependent on the state. The children aren't being matured by according them the sorts of freedoms that some groups are advocating for children. The child cannot mature if he is accorded the freedoms which these groups desire the child to have.

"The way a child matures is the way a plant matures—through good nurturing, through the care of others. The reason we have a growing irresponsible youth group in our country—the reason for the great mediocrity of mind, the lack of quality among so many young people today—is the fact that they are being given liberties which they ought to be denied and are being left to be victimized by the ideological and commercial interests to which I have referred . . . these often coming together as a single force in the media."

In general, Ball continued, a great deal of the minor consent laws in the form of statutes and especially in court decisions "have been extremely destructive of the parent-child relationship and therefore to the child itself."

Does he think these court rulings have simply prohibited

government agencies from siding with the parents against the children, thereby making the government "neutral"?

"No, I don't agree at all. Not remotely," said Ball with strong conviction. "I'm first of all concerned at the view that government agencies should be playing any major role in respect to family life. But the contention expressed here, that the government, by virtue of recent court rulings, is now being rendered 'neutral' misses the point completely. First, the government should be largely out of those relationships. When it is involved in them, it must give first priority to the rights of parents, if these rights are being disputed."

As for Spencer Coxe's contention that the Court's ruling on abortion for minors merely prevents the parents from using the power of the state to enforce their will upon the child—which Coxe called a "proper trend"—Ball says, "This is a totally false contention. First of all, it says that a parent may have no say in restraining the child from becoming involved in acts of violence. And there's no violence more extreme than the intentional destruction of a human life.

"Secondly, the contention is extremely erroneous when it says, or implies, that the action of the courts is preventing the parent from using the power of the state to enforce the parent's will upon the child as some sort of vindication of child rights. What you have instead is the power of the state, through the court, being injected into the family relationship and destroying a fundamental, personal liberty—that of the parent in respect to his child and indeed [in the case of abortion] to the parents' grandchild."

On the issue of busing, Attorney Ball said that without reference to a particular statute or program, it is his conclusion "that here again personal liberties of parents have been greatly injured by court decisions which have ignored their rights in this matter and have sacrificed their interests in favor of social programs whose value to this date must be called completely speculative."

The eroding of parents' traditional rights governing their minor children, said Ball, destroys the family. "I believe that the ideological push behind this trend is very consciously aimed at the destruction of the family. You must understand," he continued, "that families are what some people have called mediating structures in our society. Traditionally, the family in America and in Christian society was a locus—a place where children were taken care of, where old people were taken care of, where there was mutual sustenance, where there was teaching. It's out of the families that the nation emerged. What the antifamily people will have is simply digit-type people who will be part of the state."

When I mention that the ACLU is on the side of the child's desire for knowledge, even if it should conflict with what the parent wants the child to learn in school, Ball calls this stand "ridiculous."

"Suppose that—just suppose for example that a school were to teach [that] genocide is a good thing. Would ACLU say that if a parent didn't want his child to hear that racial extermination is a good thing the parent should have no right to object and no right to keep his child from learning what a 'good' thing genocide is? Of course not.

"Then we come to the question of who is to judge what's good in learning. What the ACLU statement doesn't address itself to is who is providing the learning in question. Who's going to judge whether it's good or bad? Under the reasoning of ACLU, if the state says that something must be learned in one of its institutions, and if a parent then says, I don't want the child to learn that—or I don't want the child to learn that now—nevertheless the will of the state must prevail, or a judgment of a collectivity, like a school board, or a state board of education, or even a majority in the community. I had thought," he said in obvious mock bafflement, "ACLU was not that greatly in love with the state or with government agencies or with majorities.

"The question here is who is going to say what the child should learn," said Ball. "Between saying the state will determine it, or saying the parent will determine it, I pick the parent every day; not only because I stand for parental rights, but because I believe in individual liberty.

"The child doesn't know what the child's interests are!" he said emphatically. "Suppose the state tries to take a neutral role, say, in any kind of controversial matter. Suppose it says: Jews teach this. Presbyterians teach that. Lutherans teach something else. Now, we'll be neutral and you, the child, pick whichever one you wish. We're not pushing one of them. If there's anything the child can't do," said Ball, "it is to choose in these extremely value-related areas."

Giving his opinion on the Supreme Court's ruling that religious observances are no longer permitted in public schools, Ball said, "Well, the Supreme Court's opinions have gone far beyond that. What the court has essentially said is that the public school may not in ANY SENSE be used as a vehicle for the sponsorship or promotion of religion—religion broadly.

"It is my view that the public schools cannot have it both ways. They cannot prefer nonreligion over religion. They cannot prefer secular humanism to Christianity. However, it's also true that there is no way that the public schools can play a neutral role, because life is right there before the schoolteacher in the classroom—the lives of children with all their interests, with all of their emotional drives."

Teachers, he said, have to respond to these elements. "And when that occurs, we are going to be teaching values. The heart of the Supreme Court's decision on religion in the public schools, if it is to mean anything, must mean that there cannot be advanced, even by inference or indirectly, any particular set of values.

"As the structure is today," he said, warming to the subject, "religious liberty is *plainly* denied in the public schools' setting." The best solution, he said, "is that children be permitted economically to attend schools of their parents' choice," which, he said, would rid the system of the "discriminatory use of tax funds in order that the values of the state be promoted and individual realization of the values held by individuals be discouraged."

Addressing himself to those who have changed the face of our youth, he said, "The first culprit is the parents—faithless, worthless parents growing greatly in this country. Secondly, elitists who have secular humanist solutions to social problems. Thirdly, and very, *very* importantly, gigantic commercial interests." This, he said, is found in every aspect of everyday life, involving clothing, the recording industry, television, and what he calls "virtually the whole entertainment industry."

"I think some recent decisions of the Supreme Court are extremely destructive of parental rights, while there are other decisions, strange as it may seem, that protect parental rights," said Ball. Such was the case successfully pleaded by Ball in the state of Wisconsin versus Yoder. There the state had brought criminal prosecutions against Amish parents for their refusal to send their children to high school. Their religion precludes the concept of higher education beyond the age of adult baptism.

As to the rampant indulgences of the public schools in sex education, Bell made these observations: "I've always believed that programs of sex education, which are extremely offensive to particular parents, should be voided by law courts. A proper test ought to go all the way to the Supreme Court, and the basis of any such lawsuit would be, of course, the individual liberties of parents; their rights with respect to their children; the right of familial privacy; the right of the child against invasion by the state of his child sensitivities, his relationship to his family, his right to be let alone by the state.

"Any such lawsuit would involve the use of the power and prestige of the state to thrust its values upon children and families. I think there's a very complete constitutional basis for a properly set up lawsuit."

When I tell Ball that Coxe said no one has ever protested sex education in the twenty-six years he has been with the ACLU, he replies, "I would not think, to begin with, that ACLU would be the place that a parent would want to go in order to protest sex education, because all too many ACLU spokesmen have indicated that they just love the power of the state in dominating the sensibilities and liberties of individuals in the sex-education setting. I'm astounded that he's unaware of the major problems parents are concerned with involving this issue. This is incredible. I mean, it is not to be believed."

Listed as a "deceptive phrase" by Ball is the time-worn argument that you cannot legislate morality. "We have the right to have laws that protect our liberties and the liberties of our children, and if these laws coincide, as they should, with moral principles, they're good laws; but you have not legislated morality.

"There are many, many legislative programs today which are said to be founded upon important moral principles. The program of foreign aid is said to be a moral imperative for the United States—to aid underdeveloped countries, for example. We've often heard programs such as that defended in purely moral terms. We're told it's the duty of the United States to help those less fortunate neighbors," he said.

"We have been told this in terms of aid to refugees, aid to Israel and [in] many other areas." Murder, punishable by law, most would agree, has a moral foundation, he says. "The phrase, you can't legislate morality, is employed as a debater's trick to oppose moral views that a particular person or group doesn't like."

In June 1978, William Bentley Ball scored yet another victory for parents in a case in Kentucky that involved integrated religious schools. Once again the parents of students in a religious school setting were being threatened with criminal prosecution, as Ball puts it, "for the great crime of having their children enrolled in these very wholesome, good-quality, religious schools."

In 1977 the state was pressing charges against the parents because the schools were not accredited. To meet state regulations, said Ball, and to be accredited, would mean the schools had to comply with what he calls a "vast range of state regulations which are not only in many instances badly worded and totally vague, but which directly interfere with the rights of private people to conduct education," and therefore interfere with the religious liberties of these schools.

When the parents balked, the state then arranged, said Ball, "to institute wholesale criminal prosecutions of the parents throughout Kentucky." At this point Ball's expertise in constitutionality was called upon by the parents of Kentucky. He filed suit seeking a temporary restraining order against all the state agencies, and the parents were granted a temporary injunction.

By June of 1978, an extensive trial was underway. "There the state did its best to see the destruction of these parental rights realized through court decree," said Ball. They were unsuccessful. In fact, the state had stirred up a beehive by exposing what, exactly, public education was all about and how poorly it was really serving the people. A swarm of state witnesses took the stand saying that the public schools are the model for all education. Ball's side examined the question: How good is the model?

"And there," he said, "is where we found that poor performance, bad learning on the part of public school pupils, immorality in the public schools and violence in the public schools do not add up to a good model to which schools should conform. The public schools are gorged with public funds," said Ball, taking up, in many states, 50 percent of the entire state budget.

"And yet it's notably turning out people who can't even read or write well; but the Fundamentalist school children *do* read and write well. In addition to that," he pointed out, "they are inculcated in Christian teaching. They're going to produce a population that is very, very badly needed in our country today."

The Fundamentalist Christian school is a movement that Ball sees as surging ahead at a rapid pace. "I think it's true too that some parents are feeling that they can do a better job at home than by having a child thrust into a school where he might, on the one hand, not learn and, on the other hand, might be exposed to immorality," he said.

At the conclusion of the Kentucky trial, Circuit Court Judge Henry Meggs declared, said Ball, "that the state's intrusion was totally unconstitutional and a violation of the religious liberties of the parent, the pastors and the churches involved.

"The crux of the matter," he said, "is the power of the state to license a religious ministry, because these schools are completely integral parts of the religious mission of the churches which maintain them. The state's plea has been that it must fasten all of its regulations upon these schools in order to assure that the children are getting an education.

"It's not the business of the state to require any such assurance from the private schools to start with. But in any event, we have felt that the proof is in the pudding," said Ball.

"These Fundamentalist Christian schools are performing way ahead of the public schools." This proven, indisputable fact, he said, may account for the excitement and the desire of the state to appeal the case and take it all the way to the Supreme Court, as they publicly announced.

If so, they will have a formidable antagonist in the person of William Bentley Ball—champion constitutional protector of parental and religious rights.

42.

Parents Go the Last Mile

At age 50, Donald J. Newman and his wife of thirty-one years, Dot, have pretty much raised their four children. It is a time, then, for many parents to begin to think of their own future and to save some money for the years that will follow retirement. For the Newmans those goals will have to be shelved for another five years, at least.

Newman's dilemma is one that is just beginning to surface in our country. It is a threat to every parent in the country who is under the age of 55 and has a child (no matter what his age) on welfare.

Teen-age pregnancies alone are currently costing American taxpayers about $8.3 billion a year in welfare and related outlays, according to a new study by the Stanford Research Institute. The government has decided to do something about the welfare outlay, and the parent is the target. Newman is such a parent.

Newman works for the government at Fort Dix, N.J., where he is chief engineer at the steam power plant that generates the steam for the block-long complex of the Walson Army Hospital. His take-home pay, he says, is roughly $14,000.

Newman suffers with a hiatal hernia, diverticulosis, duodenal ulcers and back problems (he was hit by a locomotive in 1956).

His wife Dot has had cobalt treatments for a tumor on her pituitary gland that is lodged behind the nose and above the roof of her mouth. It is inoperable. She requires medication to keep the pain in check. She also suffers from headaches, had a cancer operation ten years ago that terminated a five-month pregnancy, and has seen her share of troubles. "Ya see, these things keep draggin' ya down. They getcha behind," said Newman. Newman's monthly bills, he said, exceed his monthly income by about $140.

Other than his car, which is a necessity, a junker sits on the front yard. Newman said he is trying to put it together so his wife can get around. The Newmans own their home. It sits directly off a major highway in the state of New Jersey. It started out as a garage apartment. "My wife and I built this addition out of second-hand lumber," he said. His wife helped him knock the old nails out of the used wood. "It still needs a lot of work," he said apologetically. The last time the house saw a new roof was in 1958. It needs one now, but the Newmans can't afford it.

They were managing, however difficult it was, until Newman received a letter from the county welfare board telling him he would have to pay part of his once married, now divorced, 26-year-old daughter's support. It knocked the pins out from under him.

Newman's attorney, Edward J. Mangold, said the old statute, recently reactivated, probably reaches back to the New Deal era. It was on the strength of this old statute that Newman was asked to pay to help support his daughter. Newman does not have the option of bringing his daughter and her children home to live with him. The law states the child has the freedom to live wherever he/she chooses, and the parents must support that choice and contribute financially to it.

Newman, a thin man who reminded me of Bing Crosby, both in physical appearance and in his easy-going manner of speaking, tells the tale of woe that brought this ill-timed burden to his doorstep.

It was, he says of his daughter's marriage, that of a young couple expecting "to start at the top." When their plans did not materialize, his daughter and her husband moved out of their home state to "strike it rich in Nevada."

The Newmans heard that their daughter's marriage, which by now had two small children involved, was not panning out. Eventually the Newmans' son-in-law dropped their daughter, her two children, and their possessions off at the Newmans' residence, traveling from Nevada by U-Haul. Here the daughter, Joan, and her children stayed for a short time. On leaving her parents' home, Joan applied for welfare. "We kept her here for a bit," said Newman, "but she wanted to get out on her own."

Eventually, he said, Joan and a companion and the two children moved into a big home. "I think they was paying two hundred fifty dollars a month—something like that. Tremendous overhead," said Newman, "because it was a gigantic house with twelve-foot ceilings, ya know."

Then Joan moved into another apartment with what her father

described as a "fella." Joan worked in a bar, and the relationship with the "fella" began to deteriorate. "And she picked up another guy and he moved in with her," said Newman, to another residence.

After being on welfare for a year, Newman received the notice from the county welfare board. Joan was getting $330 a month from welfare. Welfare said that Newman had to pay $77 a month of that total.

Newman went to court to plead his case. The judge ruled that Newman would have to contribute to the monthly welfare support of his daughter, as stated in the statute, until he reached the age of 55. He was also ordered to pay $778 in arrears. "I had to cash all the bonds that I owned for seven years to pay these rascals," said Newman. "Either you paid 'em or you went to jail."

Cashing the bonds depleted his life's savings, since he decided he might just as well pay the back taxes he had owed on his house at the same time. It also dashed Newman's plan to give his high school graduating son a little bit of money to "help him down the road," since Newman said he couldn't afford a college education for him. "So I let him down," he said with concern in his voice.

Never once did Newman use any profanity against anyone involved in his plight. And never once did he give the impression that he didn't want to take care of his daughter. His problem was that his expenditures were already outstripping his income, and this would only make it worse.

When I interviewed Newman, he apologized for his appearance. Wearing a light-blue work shirt, dungarees and ankle-high work boots, he had not changed from his work clothes.

Newman is a well-liked and highly thought of figure in the seashore community where he lives. As a service to the community, he is the engineer for the train that runs through picturesque Allaire State Park, putting in easily, he says, 1,500 hours of volunteer time in a year.

Newman is also Chairman of the Board of Trustees of the New Jersey Museum of Transportation, Inc. at Allaire. "Because I work the hardest, I'm the boss, ya know," he says good-naturedly. "In a volunteer organization, that's how it works. The top honcho is the guy who works the hardest."

When the time came for Newman to cash in his life's savings, word had spread in his hometown. When he went to the local bank to cash the bonds, one of the bank personnel suggested he make the payments to the welfare board in pennies. "No, I didn't want jail if I did that," he said. What he did though, was to pay the money in single dollar bills, deriving at least some pleasure, he said, in watching the counting of the money as he waited for his receipt.

His daughter, Joan, he says with compassion, really cannot work with two children. "And she's livin' with a bum that's takin' some of her support money to feed him too. She came over here yesterday [the 10th of the month]. She got paid the first of the month, and she didn't have thirty-five dollars to go up to get the food stamps. She's broke," he said.

Talking about the resurrection of this statute, in which only a handful of cases have been brought before the courts to date, Newman's attorney, Edward J. Mangold, said, "There are a large number of women, and particularly women with children, who are on the welfare roll." Even where employed husbands contribute, he says, there are not sufficient funds to refill the welfare coffers.

This statute, he says, can even extend beyond the 55-year age limit if the parents' natural or adopted child is under the age of 21 years, and to a daughter with minor children whose husband fails to properly maintain and support the children if the mother applies for welfare.

Of Newman, Mangold said, "I would think at best he lives in a situation that is below middle class."

Mangold said a philosophy has developed in this country that "government is a giant hand-out. And no one realizes the consequences when you open up the welfare roles and take on more and more people; it's gotta come from somewhere and the people are just finally beginning to realize that." He said he is very concerned over the whole system of welfare. There are, he said, generations of people growing up with the welfare gift theory. "They just don't know what work is all about, and never will.

"There is a moral standard if you will, or an ethical standard in this generation that we're seeing coming up," said Mangold, "that's different from the old generations.'" Mangold said he sees this difference among his own clients. Older clients who need help, he said, often refuse it. "They would not take that money because they felt it was charity and they were not going to stoop to charity. They'd rather starve to death."

Then, talking about today's children, and speaking also as a father, Mangold repeats what I have heard a thousand times, and like the weather, everybody complains about it, but nobody seems to do much about it. "We have given our children almost whatever they ask," he says. For those parents who have not given financially, he continued, many of today's children "found the other source, which is the welfare giveaway.

"I am a firm believer that if we're going to give a person a day's wage or some money, let him work for it. But I can't convince many other people," he said.

This statute, Mangold says, unfortunately taxes the individual for welfare funds and then, such as in the case with Mr. Newman, makes him pay again. It is not fair, he says. The availability of those of Mr. Newman's generation permits this law to work effectively. It comes down to those who are the decent, honest, hard-working, law-abiding parents. "Our system is structured that way," said Mangold. "Not only in welfare, but in income tax."

Mangold said Newman's case will be appealed to the Superior Court of Appeals in the state of New Jersey, but there will be more cases throughout the country.

Mangold made it clear that a parent of a teen-ager or an older child who goes on welfare could even be forced to sell an extra car, a boat, or even a summer home to satisfy the court's contribution to support his children on welfare.

Newman said he would be only too happy to help his daughter, if he were able. The law, he said, is unfair in not honoring the clause which states that payment is required based upon "sufficient ability." He feels that this is not the case with him. It is a fair law, he says, "if it's applied the way it's read." How many other parents, even if they are financially able, will agree it is "fair" once they are tapped to help support their welfare child is yet to be seen.

Newman says he would not have permitted his father to support him. "I never asked him for nothin'. I woulda starved first before I'd have my father keep me. Back in 1948 when I first got married, we lived home. I mean, we was poor as we possibly . . . my wife and I, we started off with nothin'. She was 16 years old and I was 19. This was a marriage that everybody said wouldn't work, ya know? Here we are goin' on thirty-one years now," he said with a satisfied grin.

Newman rejects flat out any notion of moving away to avoid the payments. "My family's been on this property here a hundred and fifty years," he said with pride. "A hundred and fifty years! I got roots here. My house—I built it to raise my family in. This is my home. I expect to stay here till I die, as my grandfather did, my father before me, and his father before him on the same piece of property.

"They got the father here where they can grab ahold of 'im," he said of the welfare board. "They know where I am because I own a house here and I've lived here fifty years, ya know, established in the community."

I ask him if his daughter, Joan, feels badly about the predicament she has inadvertently gotten him into. "Nope," he says. Has she thanked him? "Nope," he says again.

"As I understand it, she was taken into court to make him [her former husband] pay alimony, because she's got those children. And as I understand it, she's refused the alimony payments."

I ask him if that makes him angry. "What can I do about it?" he says with resignation.

"I was so sick I had to go on tranquilizers. I had to take sleepin' pills. I mean, this thing bothered me so bad I lost sleep. I would have either been a physical or mental wreck if I hadn't gotten some assistance from a doctor," he says.

And then, thinking about his volunteer work at Allaire State Park, he says, "If I didn't have somethin' like the railroad, to just forget what's goin' on, ya know, and I get involved in that—it takes the misery away, ya know?"

43.

What Do Parents Want for Their Children?

There is no question that there are more young married couples who are either hesitant about having a child or have definitely made up their minds not to have children. But babies are still being born, and those who have preteen-age children were recently polled for General Mills by Yankelovich, Skelly and White, to find out what they wanted for their children. The results were printed in a report called *Raising Children in a Changing Society.*

The groups fell mainly into two categories.

The first group, while placing little or no significance on marriage as an institution for themselves, with religion and patriotism getting the same treatment, did not want the same for their children. In what seems a contradiction, they said they wanted schools to teach their children moral values; they want their children's duty to take precedence over their pleasures; and they said they would instill patriotism and hard work in their children and tell them that sex without marriage is wrong.

Terry Herndon, executive director of the National Education Association, was, to say the least, exasperated with this group of parents. "These parents want the schools to produce kids with a different set of values from themselves?" she said with incredulity. "They want us to improve their children's values?"

Why not, Terry Herndon? For almost twenty years now the public schools *have* been teaching values counter to those of most parents and it has peppered society with children that are setting epidemic and pandemic records of destruction. Why not try it their way?

On the other side of the coin were the more traditional parents who made up 57 percent of those polled. Like the other group, they wanted their children to grow up with traditional values too . . . only they believe and practice these values themselves. They cited an additional aspect as being important for their children: religion.

If this survey is an indication of what these parents want, it differs not one whit from what parents in general have always wanted and expected from their public schools and society—only for almost two decades they have not been getting it.

It will be interesting to watch those parents in the first group operate against the bureacracy and their children, should they step out of line. I wonder how their children will fare when they try to con their "experienced" parents when it comes to free sex, drugs, and drinking. After all, many of these parents know all the ins and outs themselves. Apparently the parents from the first group feel it is too late for them to change, but they know, like every parent before them, that they want something better for their children.

If they are sincere; if they probe deeply into the schools and society; if they stand up for what they believe; if they take the torch from the parents who have carried it so valiantly for so long: how long will these parents, and the ME generation that will follow them into parenthood, sit still for that intruding old "relative" Uncle Sam interfering in the upbringing of their children?

These will be the generations who are used to getting their own way. Who will tell them that they have no control over their children if they say it will be otherwise? Maybe these kids, who have been through so much themselves, are the hope after all.

But if they fail to put their shoulders collectively to the wheel and fail to continue to fight to the finish the good fight that has already begun, absolutely nothing will happen.

Reverend Jesse Jackson is not as optimistic. "Some argue that we need to focus on 'institutional sin' and change the evil system. Agreed. But it is individuals within groups who make up the army that fights for structural change. And if the army is too drunk, too high or too weak to confront the sins of the system, who, then, will be the agents of change?"

44.

The Cause (in My Opinion)

Life with today's youth is so uncertain that parents live with only a day-to-day assurance that comes down to: "So far, so good."

Who built the fire that fanned our teen-agers into action, eventually scorching their lives and everyone else's they came in contact with?

The groundwork was being laid in the early '60s . . . the how, the why, the strategies . . . all being worked out.

The experiment: to control the population growth.
The focus: our children.
The place: the public schools

It would be futile to work with parents on this experiment. They loved children, were too religiously oriented, and had already established a strong sense of right and wrong. "Raise up a child in the way he should go and he will not depart . . ." The children were the answer.

The experiment could be justified legally since it was being done "for the sake of public interest."

By the mid-'60s the experiment was put afloat. The public schools were marked to be the precursors of the population-control experiment. The government supplied the funds to train the teachers and to set up model programs.

The teachers first had to be desensitized to areas that were formerly taboo before they could pass on their new-found attitudes to the students with ease. That would begin in the colleges. For the established teacher, there would be sensitivity-training sessions. Many would balk, some would leave the system, but most stayed and went into training.

I still remember the teacher who told me that the doctor who was training her was annoyed because she was unable to publicly say the word "f——." He told her to go home, run the vacuum cleaner, and repeat and repeat the word until she was comfortable saying it without the aide of the vacuum and without feeling embarrassment.

For the experiment to be a success, two barriers had to be torn down: parental involvement and religion, which encompassed moral standards.

The schools could safely say at the outset that religion was forbidden in the public schools. The Supreme Court had already ruled out prayers. In the ensuing years the last vestiges of religion would be swept out of the school doors. That hurdle was the easiest to clear. But parents were another thing. They refused to go away.

Those parents who scrutinized the new program from its inception accused the public schools of using their children in an experiment. Some school officials refused to give any credence to the charge, but others admitted it. Just what the experiment was, no one said.

So that the experiment would be made palatable to the proletariat, it was given high-sounding euphemisms. The movers and shakers of the experiment would sprinkle roses over the cesspool that eventually would be called sex education. The goal of the experiment was shielded by more high-sounding aims to justify its existence and make it appear desirable to unsuspecting parents.

In order that not one of the 40-some million schoolchildren who would pass through the school doors each year would miss participation in the experiment, the new program would be woven into every subject. It would eventually dilute the basics, bringing to us, other than in the areas of sexuality, a dysfunctional society of youth. Like docile sheep, the masses submitted their children blindly to this new experiment. It was to be the beginning of a derailment of parents from their destination to raise good children.

French philosopher Henri Bergson said: "No man knows he's in danger until someone tells him." Parents did tell other parents, educators and school boards, but few listened.

Concerned parents foresaw and talked of the ramifications of this new incursion into the schools. They warned of sexual promiscuity that would reach down to younger children the longer the programs continued, the malnutrition of the basics of education, a schism that would grow between parent and child, and the fall of morality and religion. They warned of a society to come whose children would crave more and more bizarre experiences. Again, few heeded their warnings. The propeople had counted on the trusting, the ignorant, the unconcerned and the spineless parents. Their calculations proved to be right on target.

How better to win over the children than by reward? Behaviorist B. F. Skinner had proven the method infallible. As a reward the experimenters would dangle before the youth a formerly forbidden fruit: indulgence in sex, as long as they were "responsible"—responsible becoming the euphemism of the experiment for "use a contraceptive." They could then do their own thing. And they did. Unless and until the children were sexually active, there would be no way to gauge the success of the experiment. So sexual experimentation was encouraged. It was called "choices."

They could have sex alone, by masturbating; or with another partner—male with female, male with male, female with female. The Gay Rights movement was a shot in the arm for the experiment. Homosexuality and homosexuals could respectively be taught and brought into the schools. Could we discriminate? The more homosexual relationships, the less babies to worry about. It would simply be another "choice."

But the epidemics associated with the insatiable appetites of our children continued to grow and multiply. They broke all records in sleeping around, getting pregnant, and being riddled with the mark of their sexual promiscuity: VD became pandemic. The spinoffs of the experiment were devastating.

The population groups screamed for more and more reinforcements, and Uncle Sam obliged. Laws were passed inking out parental involvement in the treatment of venereal disease, and the population groups' coffers were refilled.

The population agencies regrouped. New programs involving the young and population-control people were planned. The parents were again excised. In desperation to keep a lid on an experiment that was blowing up in their faces, Planned Parenthood went into the schools, blowing up condoms and encouraging the kids to feel the contraceptive foams—anything! Just use contraceptives! But the kids were ignoring their plea. They were deep into doing their own thing.

In the beginning I do not believe either the government or Planned Parenthood ever intended to get involved with abortion.

When these school programs first began in the mid-'60s, Planned Parenthood, in answer to the question: Is abortion birth control? said in print: "Definitely not. An abortion kills the life of a baby after it has begun. It is dangerous to your life and health. It may make you sterile so that when you want a child you cannot have it."

Our children continued to go wild with their new-found freedoms. Abortions were performed on minors whether it was legal or not. The experiment continued to sour.

The new morality was being sold with a noble sounding phrase: "Individual choice." The truth was that the masses of children were being coerced, their individualism mutilated. Like herded cattle they were sent to the marketplace of academia for the wholesale slaughter of their right to be different. And the government and the population people sank their fangs into their jugular veins, draining from them every last vestige of morals, conscience and religion—the very things that once made them individuals.

Teen-age pregnancies were mounting. Disciplinary problems were breaking out in homes, in schools, on the streets. Everything was running amok in the experiment. By 1976 the U.S. Supreme Court ruled that every minor child in America could get an abortion without parental knowledge or consent. If abortion was not made palatable and available to our youth, the population figures would explode. Parents had to be ruled out of the picture, and they were.

The population control agency coffers were replenished once again. While the government always presents a public image of staying at arm's length on abortion by stressing that federal money to Planned Parenthood cannot be used for abortion, it lies. Any minor who is on welfare and carries a Medicaid card can get a free abortion, and the government pays for it. The cry would be that the government was helping the poor and minorities—they were popular phrases and got a lot of votes. But the poor and minorities were allowing genocide to happen to them. How much longer before *any* minor child can get an abortion—free?

The billions of dollars that the government was pouring into the population clinics were used to treat our youth from the fallout of their promiscuity—VD—and to continue to push the experiment by giving them free contraceptives. It would be given a nice-sounding term: family planning. In states where it was not legal, teen-agers and other minors would still be given contraceptives. It seemed the population-control people had a special kind of immunity. The law didn't apply to them. As Patricia Burks of Planned Parenthood said to me, "no one has ever successfully sued a Family Planning Clinic."

The CIA in its mind-control/drug experiment was able to get rid of some of the people they had experimented on by "killing" them, or by putting them out of commission with drugs. But enough survived to tell the story. Now that drugs have become so widespread among our youth, how will the government solve this epidemic? Will they put our youth into a war to cancel out a failed drug experiment that grew out of control? Already the branches of our military know who the drug users are by testing the urine of our soldiers. With equal rights in the services being pushed for male and female alike it simplifies matters. A war, the drug users pushed up to the front lines, and poof! You get rid of an experiment that went bad.

How different would that be from having our children killing their babies in utero by abortion for the population control experiment that failed?

As national panic set in, it was the population people that were called to meet in Washington with government officials. It was they who were given more money for more experimental programs. But their experiment continued to go haywire. In the most recent congressional report on fertility and contraception that was issued by the House Select Committee on Population, it was pointed out that one out of every five 13- and 14-year-olds in the United States has had sexual intercourse, that more than one-half of all illegitimate births in the United States involved teen-age mothers, and that fewer than one-third of sexually active teen-agers regularly use contraception.

Throughout the traumas that followed the implementation of this experiment, parents were called on only to "communicate" with their children and to "cooperate" with the schools, while by degrees their parental rights were being stamped null and void. "We should be wary about any group that claims to be working for our welfare and yet overtly or covertly denies our participation in those decisions," said Robert W. Terry, author of *For Whites Only.*

Today the parent is little more than a nonperson. The once natural and pleasurable ties between parent and child have frayed and in many cases snapped. Parents today often live in hand-wringing misery when they look askance at the product of their consummated love. The harm done to the family in this experiment is beyond redress . . . child and parent alike bear the scars of it.

When Wilhelm von Humboldt said, "Whatever we wish to see introduced into a life of a nation must first be introduced into its schools," the experimenters obviously thought that was good advice.

If parents were initially guilty of anything, it was in their quest for a quality child that would surpass any our nation had ever seen. But as the final chapter is being written, parents are finding they have aided the experimenters, if only by their silence. You, I, we— all are guilty to some degree. Had this been done to us as children, our parents would have dismantled the schoolhouse brick by brick, or gone en masse to jail rather than buckle under.

Stubbornly, some children clung to the values and morals their parents had instilled in them. To unhinge them, more experimental programs were brought into the public schools to aid the experiment. They called them by such names as situation ethics and values clarification. This time parents were totally circumvented. The schools had learned their lesson with sex education. So subtle and secret was the weaving in of these programs that child and parent alike were unaware of their existence for the most part. It would be a long time before the average parent would stumble onto them. Most today are still unaware of their existence. But once parents found out, the alarm was sounded. The *Philadelphia Inquirer* carried one such article.

Christine Tonkinson of Villanova, Pa., told of shuttling her daughter to three different schools in a vain attempt to find a school that was not a participant in the new scheme of things. "I can't wait for her to get out of school. I have to detoxify her all the time," she said of the "values" teachings of the schools. She might just as well have said she had to deprogram her daughter—they are that damaging.

Another mother, Mrs. Parkie Hilles, who considers herself more liberal than some of the teachers, and whose husband is an attorney in the ACLU, has devoted herself full-time to fight "secular humanism" and values education in the schools. "The children [are taught that] they are autonomous. In school they have been systematically liberated from their parents and their churches and in many cases their original values," Mrs. Hilles said.

As the CIA had experimented with the mind, so would these programs. They were designed to change the values the children were clinging to. The report from the Comptroller General's Office called them "behavior modification," and admitted that it was a professional term. It was something that teachers can use, said the report, to bring about changes in students. And our children did change. They resembled no other group of their age in the history of our country.

By 1977 the statistics were on the pages of every newspaper: Half of the nation's population of teen-agers were having intercourse. Parents began to scream that they wanted the schools to teach morals. Over the labels of sex education/situation ethics/values clarification, they pasted a bigger label. It was lettered "morals education" to lull the parents back into complacency. Parents wanted morals? No problem. Change the labels.

By 1979 the statistics reflected that teen-age intercourse was soaring to new heights. By now almost two of every three female teen-agers were engaging in intercourse.

"We have morals," insisted one young boy to a reporter. "Most people have morals, but they are just lower or maybe different from our parents'." To say the least!

Women began moving in droves into the working world. It was an unexpected plus for the experiment. A busy mother is not a nosy mother. She would not scrutinize the schools.

Busing was another plus. Parents were not likely to come poking into schools that were miles from home. Divide and conquer.

And parents, in spite of the incontrovertible evidence of the damage done to their children, continued to fight each other over the merits of these new social programs. United we stand, divided we fall.

Private and religious schools began to open in every state. It would spell disaster. Criminal charges were lodged against these parents. If this trend would grow, it would surely spoil the experiment.

No one can fault the news media for not doing their job. In most cases, reporters wrote what was happening at school meetings on the subjects. They kept the nation informed as to the latest teen-age epidemics too. Newspapers printed the letters to the editor from the opposing parents. Columnists, UPI and AP did the best jobs. TV and radio did interviews and specials about these controversial areas. What was lacking in all branches of the media was deep and solid investigative reporting.

In a look back at the last decade, Clark DeLeon wrote in *Today* magazine, a Sunday supplement of the *Philadelphia Inquirer:* "And even if all else were forgiven, the irredeemable fault of the 1970s has been that no matter how vulgar, dirty, nauseating or simply *tasteless* things became—no one seemed to care much."

Whether the subject with our youth is violence, drugs, disrespect, vandalism, pregnancy, VD, sleeping around or titillating entertainment, all the experts say the children involved defy categorization—they come equally from good and bad homes, from the rich and from the poor sections of our country, and defy racial barriers. The one common denominator has been overlooked: the public schools, where every child by law is forced to attend. It is here that the equalizer is found. Every atrocity that has befallen our youth can be traced back to the time that the schools took on the role of "change agents" or "experimenters" or pushers of "social programs," whatever name you want to call it.

Before these programs, illegitimate births were manageable. They have quintupled since 1940. Arrests for juvenile delinquents have tripled since 1963. Professor Alexander Astin, a University of

California-Los Angeles professor who headed a study for the American Council on Education charting college freshman readiness, career intentions and social and political attitudes, said: "It seems clear secondary schools' grading standards have been declining since the late 1960s."

A recent Gallup poll said the results "were ominous for the future of organized religion." Today 50,000 to 80,000 young girls and women are made sterile by gonorrhea every year from their "choices." Before these programs, runaways were practically unheard of. Today, a quarter of a million kids run away from home. Drugs were unheard of; today their use is pandemic. Alcoholism is rampant among our youth—they are doing their own thing. The illiteracy among 17-year-olds graduating has risen 42 percent. Cohabitation, once not even thought of among the young, has more than doubled in the last eight years. The illegitimacy rate for teenagers has increased in the last fifteen years by 50 percent. Abortions, now permitted across the country, have the young, down to the age of 13, tripling the amount of abortions done on adults. Since all of these programs began, the suicide rate among the young has nearly tripled. Experts are bracing for yet another teen-age epidemic. Dr. William C. Swansom, a sociologist at Louisiana State University and a leading suicide expert, cited excessive freedom as a cause of the high suicide rate among our young.

Who will mourn them? The population experts who know that at least these kids can't produce any more babies?

The latest projections by the U.S. Census Bureau show but another backfiring of the population-control experiment. In twenty more years, the average age of the American will be 35. Eighty percent of the world's people will be substantially younger than Americans.

Who will refill the social security coffers? Who will pay the hospital costs of the elderly? Or will our youth have learned their school death lessons so well they will use euthanasia on their elderly parents? Should we have to engage in military confrontation by the year 2000 we will have the oldest army on the battlefield.

When a psychologist, Jerry Bergman at Bowling Green State University, wrote a magazine article exploring the possibilities of government licensing only "qualified" couples for parenthood (the determining factors being their IQ, earning capacity and emotional problems), most of the respondents to the article, said Bergman, were "teachers, psychologists and school administrators. They said it was about time we looked into something like this." It is only another indicator of how rabid our educators are, and how thoroughly they have been inculcated with the concept of population control at any cost.

Had our children prospered, had this experiment made them happy and productive, this book would never have been written. It was not the case. For many, the life of "choices" would prove too much. They would wind up on psychiatrists' couches, on drugs, drinking, thrown out of their parents' homes, in mental institutions, as suicides.

Why are our children striking back at their parents in so many ways? Are they perhaps wondering: How could the parent, who could make everything right when they were small and frightened, let everything go so wrong? Do they think their parents have betrayed them? If so, then what better way than to strike back in anger to vent their frustrations? They punish their parents, their teachers, and society.

Our children apparently don't like themselves, and they know that other people don't like them too. If I have overheard people making caustic remarks about our youth—rest assured they have too.

The message they are giving us is coming through loud and clear: Help us to turn around and be a part of society again ... give us a place in your world.

45.

The Cure

The government and the population experts must be forced, through legislation or a Supreme Court decision that does not equivocate, to pack their bags and get out of the business of experimenting with the children in the public schools. A court case is probably the most expedient, since it would take the burden of "special interest groups" away from the politician. If every parent in the country would contribute a dollar to a national parent group to hire an attorney with expertise in constitutional law, it could be finished with.

All federal, state and local funding must be cut off for the damaging population-control and behavior-changing experiments and their accompanying paraphernalia that exist in the public schools and colleges. While Senator Orrin Hatch's Amendment is a step in the right direction, it is only a Band-Aid for our deeply wounded and bleeding youth.

I can think of nothing more heinous than to prey on the minds of innocent, trusting and unsuspecting school children.

"Whatever we wish to see introduced into a society must first be introduced into its schools." This time, let us reintroduce a strong emphasis on basics and skills, discipline, true grading, and a civilized sense of what is right or wrong.

Those teachers who have been too "brainwashed" to go along with the changes and who persist in undermining religion, the child, the parent, the family, and morality, must be drummed out of the school system and be replaced. States must by law set new standards and qualifications for teachers.

It has been painfully obvious that schools can turn out neither serious scholars nor skilled craftsmen when the basics of learning are thinned by interspersing damaging experimental programming.

Yearly, taking an extremely conservative figure, the American taxpayer has been spending well over $40 billion dollars for destructive, emaciated education.

Parents must again assert themselves. "No" must mean no, and not "maybe," when parents are talking to their child, or to the institutions that have destroyed their child. As Father Mannion said, make a decision and then don't back down.

NO speakers should be permitted into our nation's schools. Let our children learn in peace. When these social experimental programs are scrapped, there will be no need for a parent to worry about point-counterpoint on any of the now controversial issues that engulf their children.

All federal funding and laws pertaining to services for minors must be scrapped in the areas of human sexuality, hot lines and runaway homes. Let the child once again turn to the family in his or her hour of need instead of to Uncle Sam. For the unfit parent, let the courts help the child. No one wants to see a child abused, either physically or psychologically.

Of the minor consent laws passed, favoring the child's autonomy, Concerned Parents, an organization of parents much involved with today's upside-down world, said it well: "Minor consent legislation in fact adjudicates all parents as unfit and irresponsible, without benefit of due process. Such legislation effectively makes all minors wards of the state, subject to ministrations of educators, counselors and others of questionable ability." Unquestionably, the courts must return to the parents their right to guide their children, even if it takes a Parental Consent Amendment to the Constitution to do it.

I would like to see legislation passed that would raise the drinking age across the country to 21 and legislation that would forbid a minor to drive a car on the highways until he was gainfully employed and could maintain the entire cost of owning and operating his own vehicle. It would save young lives and be a work incentive.

As for the entertainment media—they have proven that given an inch they will take your eyeballs. I would like guidelines of morality and decency laid down for them. The Seven Dirty Words Case is a good beginning. Censorship? A journalist suggesting restraints?

Every journalist who does not delude himself knows there is no such animal as total freedom of the press. The press also has rules and regulations. None—absolutely none—of the filthy words that come out of the schools from teachers, textbooks, movies, or slides being used in these programs have ever been spelled out in a decent newspaper. Neither have the Seven Dirty Words.

Every editorial writer knows the "slant" that is required by the owner/publisher of the newspaper for which he is writing. If he insists on not toeing the line on important issues—and political endorsements—he will be told to go out and buy his own newspaper. Then he can print the news and views the way he sees fit. A reporter cannot hide under the First Amendment all the time, and neither can the entertainment media.

For families where both parents are working, I urge them to look hard at the cost to the family of not having a parent at home when the child needs him. Ask yourselves in dollars and cents, and in the cost to the child and the family, if it is really worth it. If at all possible, someone should be home to find out what the children are doing, where they are going, whom they are with, and what they are being taught. Many are being neglected, and it shows in the fact that a national campaign is underway and laws are being passed to force parents to immunize their children. Does no one have the time to take them to the doctor for their shots? It could mean an epidemic of childhood diseases if it goes uncorrected.

Where are we headed if we do not insist on restoring family unity and parental control? Perhaps a Yes-No questionnaire compiled by the Washington-based Free Congress Research and Education Foundation, Inc., in 1979, the International Year of the Child gives an inkling:

> Should the federal government or the child's parents be ultimately responsible for a child's upbringing?
> Should children be eligible for minimum wage if they are asked to do household chores?
> Should the children gain the legal right to sue their parents for being forced to attend church?

We must stop giving our children so many "choices." What they need are solid direction and rules and regulations to live by.

In a program on teen-age suicides done by colorful TV Philadelphia talk show host Joel A. Spivak, Judi Goldstein, a teenager who had attempted suicide, said there was too much put on our youth today. She said it made life "hard, confusing and scary."

Dr. C.J. Frederick, a scientist at the National Institute of Mental Health, attributed the climbing suicide rate among the young to changing lifestyles, the breakdown of the family unit, the inability of our youth to deal with the greater independence that is offered them and the absence of early mother-child attachment.

Many, many apologists have stepped forward lately expressing distress or sorrow for the part they have played in the lives of our children.

States that lowered the drinking age are now looking strongly to legislation to raise it back up. It was, most said, a grave mistake.

The teachers who were the encouragers of the new permissiveness are now the victims of it. They are crying for stricter disciplinary measures in the schools. Until the experimenters and their philosophy are kicked out, disciplinary measures will continue to fail.

Dr. Benjamin Spock has apologized for the serious injury done to the parent and child when he urged the parents to leave the rearing of their children to the experts.

Dr. Robert Kistner, who helped in the research of the Pill, regrets that it added to sexual promiscuity and epidemics of social diseases.

Sociologist James S. Coleman, the busing for integration advocate who traveled around the country selling his thesis, now sees little value in it.

A lot of liberals have come forth to say things have gone too far, and they are crying for more conservative measures.

Apologies, apologies, apologies. Good to hear, albeit a little late. But there are no apologies from the government or the schools for the experiments they have subjected our children to.

For the juvenile offenders, there appears to be a highly successful solution on the rise. It is the much talked about program taking place at Rahway Prison, where the young offenders are talked to by the lifers, and they get to see just what prison life is all about, first-hand. Over a thousand juvenile offenders have gone through the program. Fewer than 10 percent have gotten into trouble since.

Could we do the same for our young marijuana users? Could they go to a hospital and watch an addict going through the "Jones" withdrawal? Could that do for them what the Rahway Prison program has done for juvenile offenders? It would be worth a try.

The billions of dollars that are being spent on experimenting with our children's sexuality and in changing their behavior, instead of going to Planned Parenthood and the schools, should be rechanneled into a massive campaign to raise the moral conscience of our youth, to elevate the parent and to stress the importance of the family once again. It could be done effectively with posters, TV and radio spots and movie theatre shorts. It has been done successfully in other areas. It can be done here too.

When the national speed limit was lowered to 55 mph on the nation's highways, almost everyone balked. They soon found out that fuel and lives were saved. In fact, in a recent survey done by the U.S. Transportation Department, more than half of all American drivers said they have grown to like the 55 mph speed limit.

The same type of campaigning that went into raising the conscience of the public to the ills of cigarette smoking can also be applied to the destructive paths our children have taken. Today hospitals, doctors' offices, and private businesses have "No Smoking" signs.

Ten years ago a smoker thought nothing of puffing smoke into a fellow diner's face. Now many will ask: Do you mind if I smoke?

Said one Harvard student of the public attitude toward the smoker: "People really look down on you. They're condescending. They preach to you."

We have to start looking down on cohabiting, sexual promiscuity, marijuana smoking, the undisciplined child, instead of throwing our hands up in disgust and saying we can't do anything about it. We have to campaign for it.

As we raised the public's consciousness about the danger signals of cancer, so can we raise our kids' consciousness of the dangers of their actions.

We have to, we must, and we can once again resurrect the moral conscience of our young.

In his political campaigning debut, the late President John F. Kennedy said, "We, in this country, must be willing to do battle for old ideas that have proved their value with the same enthusiasm that people do for new ideas and creeds."

We must apply that to our schools and return them once again to their original intent. But first and foremost, we must push the experimenters out and return parental rights to their rightful place.

The next time Uncle Sam points his finger and says, "I want you!" tell him he can't have your children anymore.

Index